JACKY LAW is a pharmaceutical journalist. For the past 25 years she has written about health issues. For seven years she worked as associate editor for *Scrip Magazine*, a monthly international pharmaceutical title. She left in 2004 to write *Big Pharma*.

Jacky Law acknowledges the enormous contribution of her editor, Dan Hind, and agent, Jessica Woollard, in making this book possible. Mention must also be made of those who offered valuable perspective in what are complex and often contentious areas. They include Professor Martin Bobrow, Dr Philip Brown, Professor Joe Collier, Dr Peter Fletcher, Dr John Griffin and Professor Eric Topol. Jacky would also like to thank everyone at the top pharmaceutical titles *Scrip Magazine* and *Scrip World Pharmaceutical News* (www.scripnews.com) with whom she worked for seven years. Last but not least, she sincerely thanks all her friends and family for encouraging and putting up with her.

Big Pharma

How the world's biggest drug companies control illness

JACKY LAW

CONSTABLE • LONDON

Constable & Robinson Ltd
3 The Lanchesters
162 Fulham Palace Road
London W6 9ER
www.constablerobinson.com

First published in the UK by Constable,
an imprint of Constable & Robinson Ltd, 2006

A copy of the British Library Cataloguing in
Publication Data is available from the British Library.

ISBN 1-84529-139-5

Printed and bound in the EU

1 3 5 7 9 10 8 6 4 2

Contents

Preface

When medicine is not an option ...

On 5 June 1981, the first official report of what is now a global pandemic appeared in the weekly newsletter of the US Federal Centers for Disease Control. The report stated that a rare parasitic lung infection had shown up in Los Angeles in five young men. Moreover, all the men had an inexplicably depressed immune function. This date is now known as the start of the worst plague in modern history, AIDS (acquired immune deficiency syndrome).

Before then, young men like Stewart Anderson had been diagnosed with what was known as Gay Syndrome, a mystery plague that mostly killed gay men. I interviewed Stewart in 1987, at around the time Princess Diana famously shook hands with an AIDS patient on national television. It may be hard for younger readers to appreciate the fear most people felt knowing a transmissible killer disease was at large. Official health advice, for example, included not having sex with Americans, so little was known about it. And ambulance men could be seen wearing full 'spacesuit' protection when dealing with patients suspected of carrying the mystery plague.

Stewart had been living with AIDS for some years and just moved into a brand new and unusually bright basement flat in Hammersmith. He was a skinny guy in his 20s with a toothy smile and a face covered in the purple blotches characteristic of Kaposi's sarcoma, a skin cancer common in AIDS patients. He said from the outset he wasn't sure I was going to be able to convey what he wanted to say. I said I would do my best.

It wasn't until I visited him at the old Chelsea and Westminster Hospital a week or two later that I began to appreciate what he might be trying to express and what became the germ of an idea for this book.

Nothing could have prepared me for the despair I felt in that ward of young men who should have been out starting lives, not visibly wasting away. The fear was palpable, and the many doctors, busily reading charts and talking among themselves, could do nothing to assuage it. They had nothing to offer.

Stewart, who had been booked in for a blood transfusion, was nowhere to be seen. I wanted to ask the doctors if they felt the course of the disease could be altered by anything patients might do, knowing as I did how hard Stewart was fighting to extend his life. But I knew the answer already, and the doctors seemed to have more than enough to do. The question I should have asked was addressed in a special *Newsweek* report on the twentieth anniversary of AIDS, in June 2001. Sharon Begley, the writer, talked about how AIDS had changed what it meant to be a patient. The despair I had felt in those wards did eventually find channels of expression. 'People with AIDS stormed scientific conferences, banded together in ways no other patients ever had,' she wrote. '[They] helped revolutionize the process of testing experimental drugs and they inspired others.'

Stewart was nowhere to be seen because he had discharged himself. His main battle was to be optimistic, and hospital didn't help. He was one of the world's longest surviving patients, despite his Kaposi's sarcoma having spread to his stomach and lungs. Just months before we met, he had developed the lung infection that had been the original diagnosis. It very nearly killed him. On the eve of 1987, he couldn't stand up for longer than three minutes. 'This kind of illness changes your attitude to life,' he said. 'Each breath is precious. I was determined to start the new year on my terms. There are things I still have to do. It is easy to give in and die.'

Stewart fought tenaciously for the right to make sense of his disease on his terms, and this was the message he wanted to convey. He went on to do a series of interviews, mine included, something very few people did at the time given the fear and prejudice surrounding the disease. He embarked on a strict macrobiotic diet and programme of cycling and swimming. He also founded, with seven others, the self-help group Body Positive.

Stewart was just trying to make sense of his life before it was gone. All he knew was that he wanted as little medical interference as possible and that there must be some upside to his situation, that his life should not pass by in vain. 'When you look in the mirror and see marks all over your body it is hard to feel good about yourself,' he said. 'But I have learned that the whole key to feeling in control is how you feel about yourself. You have got everything in your environment telling you that you are going to die and there is no cure. I couldn't go out because of people's reactions so I started getting to know me and realized it was the most important relationship I was ever going to have. This was a turning point because until then my nature had been to do anything to avoid facing me.'

His message is that however dire the prognosis, however eminent the specialist, the only thing that will help you is your own sense of what is happening to you. Stewart passed away on 12 October 1989. He insisted, shortly before he died that he had no regrets. 'If you can develop a sense of purpose about why something bad is happening to you, you can grow through it,' he said. 'People are scared to feel. But through suffering you can create purpose. I gained my self-respect through challenging AIDS. I now want to help others, to at least give them hope. I can honestly say I like myself for the first time in my life. I can't say that AIDS is the best thing that ever happened to me, but it has given my life meaning. Because suddenly it could be taken away.'

Stewart was able to use this dreadful disease for positive effect, but it has to be said he had no alternative. Medicine had nothing to offer him. He had nothing to lose by using the medical system on his terms. And although he missed out on his three score years and ten, he died peacefully and, I believe, content. Apart from anything else, he was tired of trying to win.

Today Stewart would be on the antiretrovirals, the class of drugs saving the lives of anyone with HIV (human immunodeficiency virus) in the West. Because medicines save lives, their value is infinite. But there are two things medicine cannot address. One is contained in the thousands of stories like Stewart's wherein people have transformed what it means to be a patient. This might be called the human factor, because patients started taking an active involvement in their treatment.

'There is no question that breast cancer activism started because of AIDS activism,' Fran Visco, president of the US National Breast Cancer Coalition, told Begley. AIDS changed the culture of medicine in many ways. The fact that younger doctors see patients, rather than the profession, as the centre of treatment decisions, stems from the efforts of people like Stewart who felt compelled to make some sense of their life before it was taken away.

The second thing medicine cannot address is the political factor that determines whether it is used by those who need it most. Everything else medicine can embrace; and as we live longer lives because of it, we have more reason that ever to understand the dynamics that drive its development.

Part 1

Not wanting to know

1

The cost of convenience

The fundamental problem with medicines may be quite straightforward. It may have nothing to do with the tens of billions of dollars single drugs such as cholesterol-reducing Lipitor earn year in year out. Or the corruptive forces such rewards inevitably set in motion. The fundamental problem with medicines could be as simple as not wanting to think about them that much.

Certainly, it is hard to find any healthcare more essentially disengaged than popping a pill. Medicines are designed to get into the body as seamlessly with 'normal life' as possible. Whether drugs are popped, injected, inhaled, chewed, or slapped on one's buttocks as a patch, passivity prevails. A good drug is one you don't even know you're taking, for the all-too-human reason that no one wants to dwell too long on their need for prescription drugs.

The world's top pharmaceutical companies are able to prosper precisely because they are so effective at blotting out every pain, every anguish, every doubt we have, or might have, about being able to eat properly, concentrate properly, have sex properly; indeed, live properly. So much of what we are designed to do naturally can now be improved by medicine. And because we all so much want to be better, the diagnostic criteria that provide access to fabulously large markets are extraordinarily elastic. In this way we become a more morbid society.

But in this growing preoccupation with providing unfailing good health, it is not so much clinical need being addressed, as the convenience factor, the production of drugs that can ease our passage through life with as little discomfort as possible. The convenience factor goes some way to explaining why our global pharma bill continues to rocket year on year, despite there being so little evidence that the spend is in any way worth it. More than in any other sector, pharma dollars are earned on the slimmest of marginal benefits. Because in no other sector are the existing markets so lucrative, the opportunities for expanding them so great and the competition so intense.

Consider the world's top players. Just ten drugs earned no less than $48.3 billion in 2003.[1] Each of these products on its own represents more income than most companies see in a lifetime. Leading the table was Pfizer's Lipitor which earned $10.3 billion, followed by another cholesterol-reducing drug, Merck's Zocor, which had sales of $6.1 billion. These statins, as they are called, are just two players in what was then a $26.1 billion class of drugs and had grown to $29.2 billion in the year to September 2004, according to global pharma data company, IMS Health.

These drugs have been shown to save lives by reducing cholesterol levels. To compete in such markets, companies need not only good candidate players (drugs), but also sufficient marketing spend. When Anglo-Swedish drugs company, AstraZeneca, launched its statin Crestor belatedly in late 2003, for example, its unprecedented promotional budget of a billion dollars was justified by then US president and now CEO, David Brennan, who told the *Financial Times*, 'What our campaign will cost will depend on the level of activity of our competitors but we will do what it takes to have an adequate share of voice of the market.'[2] The same instinct lies behind all other drugs, as indeed it must, because they are commercial products that must survive in a commercial world.

In third place was Lilly's latest antidepressant, Zyprexa, earning a $4.8 billion share in a $19 billion market. The next three drugs, one for ulcers, one for high blood pressure and one for anaemia and renal failure, each earned more than $4 billion. The bottom four were all in the $3 billion range, comprising another anti-ulcer drug, another heart drug, an asthma agent and another antidepressant, which came in tenth with a still respectable $3.4 billion.[3]

For some time the big pharma money has been directed mainly at effecting small but significant changes in products that serve the largest markets. For example, when Shire brought out Adderall XR, a slow-release form of its attention-deficit drug for youngsters, in October 2001, it soon became the company's biggest earner, taking a 15% share of the $3 billion-plus attention-deficit disorder (ADD) market by the following June.

Just eight months later, in February 2003, analysts at Banc of America Securities estimated that the drug had a 22.6% share of the US market. The original version, a composition of four amfetamine salts, had fallen to just 4.1%, despite the fact its price had plummeted as it was now open to generic competition.[4] Parents – who don't pay the full cost – moved in droves, in other words, from a much cheaper drug which required frequent dosing to one that spared their kids the embarrassment of having to medicate during the school day. Soon, the market was bursting with long-acting stimulants (speed to anyone buying it on the street), as Celltech's Metadate CD, Johnson & Johnson's Concerta XL, and Ritalin LA all came on board. By now, their original appeal had become less relevant than ever. Far from the users being ashamed about taking drugs, experiences of how they helped regulate attention span became a staple of playground gossip.

Similarly, one reason Prozac was so hugely successful in creating a $19 billion depression market in just ten years is that it had a much better side-effect profile than the earlier drugs and could also be taken just once a day. Dr J. Raymond Depaulo, professor of psychiatry at the Johns Hopkins University School of Medicine, says the selective serotonin reuptake inhibitors (SSRIs) had the advantage in that half the patients taking them could feel as though they were taking nothing more than a vitamin pill. This wasn't the case with their predecessors, the tricyclics.

> In general, when you're taking a tricyclic, although the side effects may be trivial and you may be thrilled to make the trade of a little dry mouth and a little constipation for not being depressed, you know you're taking it. But they're good drugs. They are equally efficacious, equally potent, against depression. Some of the managed care people [who pay the medicines bill in the US] want to say therefore that you should choose the cheapest drug, because it's true, none of the new drugs works better than Imipramine, the original antidepressant. But besides the side effect improvement, the other thing about Prozac that was nice was that one pill a day was the right dose. You didn't have to fiddle with the dosing. That made it simple to use.[5]

A good drug is one you can almost forget you're on, until, of course, you try to come off it. And indeed, the devastating so-called 'withdrawal syndrome' associated with some of the SSRI antidepressants, coupled with an increased suicide risk particularly among young people, again in only some of the drugs are why the pharmaceutical industry has been getting a bad press recently.

More money, fewer drugs

But it is the dynamics of the markets themselves that expose the public to greater than necessary risk. Intense pressure on companies to increase their share of the big markets has, over the years, developed a momentum of its own, compelling companies to merge if they want to survive. Such a competitive environment inevitably shifts the balance of power not only within the industry itself, but also within the regulatory framework in which pharma operates.

The regulatory bodies are staffed with people better qualified than the general public to say if drugs are safe and whether we are getting value for money. Nevertheless, at virtually every juncture, the shifts in power have tended to favour commercial interests, increasingly drowning out any notion of public good and leading to a widening public–private disparity in the ownership of science.

This is one reason why the global spend on pharmaceuticals has risen 25-fold numerically over almost as many years, from $20 billion in 1972 to more than $500 billion in 2004.[6] Although not adjusted for inflation, the increase in spend can in no way correlate with increases in health or well-being because these are measures that are almost impossible to quantify. Nor does it mean we are getting a lot more new drugs to justify the spend. Innovation, the traditional measure for society's deal with the pharma industry, seems to work in an inverse relationship with cost.

In 2004, the total number of new active substances approved had dwindled to a new low of just 23, down on the 31 recorded in 2003 and the 29 in 2002. Of those 23, says Ian Lloyd, managing editor of the global pharma research database, Pharmaprojects, only four can be described as significant therapeutic advances.

> In the 1990s, around 40 launches per year was considered reasonable and, if anything, that number was expected to increase as pharma R&D became more efficient. However, the opposite now seems to have occurred.[7]

This downward trend looks starker when contrasted against productivity in the post-war years, the so-called golden age of drug development, when hundreds of new and affordable drugs that made a serious difference were being delivered. In 1940, the medicines cabinet was virtually bare. By 1975, doctors had access to 24 new antibiotics, 15 new anti-cancers, 10 treatments for psychiatric disorders, 13 for rheumatological conditions, 18 for circulatory disorders, 11 for hormonal conditions, several synthetic steroids which seemed to work on everything they touched, and various other new drugs.[8]

Even as late as the 1960s, around 70 new chemical entities a year were being filed. Somewhere along the line between then and now we have arrived, blindfolded it seems, at the bizarre situation whereby the few drugs being registered that bring significant new therapeutic benefits are so expensive that not everyone who could benefit has access to them.

This does not refer only to the antiretrovirals for HIV that tens of millions in the majority world are dying for want of; that is a separate book. Healthcare services everywhere are struggling to buy the latest life-extending cancer drugs, for example, the costs of which (tens of thousands of dollars per patient a year) are generally seen as a test case as to how much markets can afford. Middle-income countries have faced mini-trade wars with the pharma industry's staunch supporter, the US government, as when South Korea protested that the $27,000 a year cost of Glivec for a rare skin cancer was too high.

The pharmaceutical industry has been able to amass such colossal power in a single human lifespan. The year my father was born, 1928, was also the year Alexander Fleming had his serendipitous insight into the nature of mould that went on to consign many infectious diseases to history. Since then, medicine's achievements have transformed people's lives.

Specifically, my father's life has been saved twice, both times by surgery supported by modern medicine. Nevertheless, for reasons that are largely cultural, he holds onto that rather old-fashioned view which says one should only take medicine when strictly necessary. He refuses to take a simple statin to lower his cholesterol, for example, despite what the pharmaceutical industry, and his doctor, would urge for a man of his age.

Such a mindset belongs to a time that no longer exists. The dominant tendency to medicate – above all other kinds of therapy, including doing nothing at all – stems from that golden era when drugs were coming out of the pipeline fast, furiously and from today's perspective, extremely cheaply.

When ignorance was bliss

It may be hard to appreciate now what it was like to have drugs that could do things for the first time. Fleming's discovery of penicillin was swiftly followed by the isolation and purification of insulin from the pancreas, which meant metabolic disorders such as diabetes could be treated for the first time. The steroids were introduced, widely seen as a wonder drug for a whole range of inflammatory disorders, including rheumatism, skin conditions and sepsis. And revolutionary new products for schizophrenia and depression allowed many patients to live in the community for the first time. Even lifestyle medicines, such as the contraceptive pill, which was introduced in the 1960s, were welcomed for their clear benefits to society.

It didn't seem to matter that no one knew how these medicines worked. The post-war therapeutic revolution occurred in the absence of the most basic understanding of disease processes. The important thing was that they brought tangible improvements to people's lives. It was only when the innovation drought became seriously prolonged that the extent of the problem at the core of the medicines business became clear.

In the past, chemists had been making replicas of chemical compounds in our bodies and investigating them for a therapeutic effect that could be developed as a medicine. 'The origins of virtually every class of drug discovered between the 1930s and the 1980s can be traced to some fortuitous, serendipitous or accidental observation,' says Dr James le Fanu in his book, *The Rise and Fall of Modern Medicine*.[9]

Indeed, it couldn't have happened any other way because, contrary to popular belief, serendipity was the only route chemists had open to them. They had virtually no knowledge of how our cells worked. 'In essence, the therapeutic revolution started with a "lead" – a chance observation that some chemical seemed to have some effect on a diseased state,' explains le Fanu. 'Then the research chemists played around with it, the fecundity of chemistry being such that it is possible to synthesize literally thousands of related compounds from a single lead.'[10]

The compounds were narrowed down, tested for safety and given to people with the disease in question. If one had a demonstrably beneficial effect, you had the basis of a new medicine. Although this description is hugely simplified, the discovery process shows how human observation was the only way of providing a hunch about a new treatment. It is a tried and tested method that still brings about impressive results. Viagra, for example, was discovered by observing the side effects of chemicals being tested in angina. The active ingredient, sildenafil citrate, increases bloodflow, whether it is to the heart (on which it was originally tested), the eye (Viagra has caused blindness by prompting an optic stroke), the lungs (Viagra is widely used to treat pulmonary arterial hypertension, PAH), or the penis (its main purpose in life).

The trouble with this approach was that chemists ran out of things to investigate. Meanwhile, a whole universe was opening up with the decoding of the human genome at the turn of the century, confirming that our general state of health might be defined more by the regular rhythms of complex interrelated networks of biochemical activity than any single defect. 'The heart of the problem,' said geneticist Philip Gell, emeritus professor at the University of Birmingham, 'lies in the fact that we are dealing not with a chain of causation but with a network that is a system like a spider's web in which every perturbation at any point of the web changes the tension of every fibre right back to its anchorage in the blackberry bush.'[11]

The truth is that the deeper the understanding of the genetic origins of disease, the harder it is to develop drugs that serve large markets. The fairytale began to take a distinctly dark turn as the magical process that had produced so many breakthrough drugs stopped working. Countries everywhere began paying more money for fewer drugs delivering smaller marginal benefits. Worse, no one had a clue what to do about it, other than to continue to pay up, because that was the deal.

The deal

The basic legal frameworks outlining how pharma operates had been worked out in the industry's heyday. They differ from country to country and will have been revised countless times to reflect the changing political climate. Essentially, however, the equation tries to balance society's need for safe and effective new drugs with the industry's need to prosper. For years, this equation boiled down to companies innovating, and governments paying for whatever they come up with.

So long as drugs have been shown to be safe and to do what is claimed of them, they are made available to doctors, the de facto brakes in the system; because why would they prescribe something if it wasn't strictly necessary? What is researched is left almost entirely to market forces, because at the level where these things get debated, people have tended to follow the rather simplistic circular argument, whereby higher prices equals more research, equals better drugs, equals higher prices, equals more research, and so on.

It took years before governments realized that doctors were fairly hopeless brakes in the system. In the 1990s, the goalposts were changed to ask also if drugs were any good, if they were better than what had gone before, and if they provided value for money. By then it was too late, however, because billion-dollar revenues develop a momentum of their own. Once they began flowing in at the start of the age of blockbuster medicine in the 1980s, they were hard to stop.

If the post-war years were a golden age of pharmaceutical innovation, the 1990s were a golden age of blockbuster medicine, of medicating the masses. Marketing became all-important and spends started to dwarf what went into R&D. In 1990, the top ten companies spent around 11% of sales on research (a figure which rose to 14% by the end of the decade). The rather imprecise category, marketing and administration, meanwhile, accounted for 36% of sales, a share that remained more or less constant throughout the decade.[12]

Doctors and patients came to be inundated with information about medicines, particularly those developed in the 1980s for conditions such as stomach acid, allergies, high cholesterol and depression. These were drugs that transformed the industry, delivering consistent blockbuster (billion-dollar) returns year after year.

The top ten drug companies enjoyed profits of around 25% of sales for most of the decade, far outstripping any other industrial sector and illustrating how marketing can work wonders to offset a drug's fixed research and development (R&D) costs. Because although drugs are expensive to develop to the standards required by law (how expensive is a moot point), the money is more quickly recouped the more readily people can be persuaded to believe in the magic of drugs. Then it is simply a question of setting the price at a level that makes it affordable.

Marketing teams worked hard, and soon pharma companies were delivering better returns than all other industry sectors. 'In 2001 the ten US drug companies in the Fortune 500 list ranked above all other US industries in average net return, whether as a percentage of sales (18.5%), of assets (16.3%), or of shareholder equity (33.2%),' says former editor of the *New England Journal of Medicine*, Dr Marcia Angell, in her book, *The Truth About the Drug Companies*. 'These are astonishing margins. For comparison, the median net return for all other industries in the Fortune 500 was only 3.3% of sales. Commercial banking, itself no slouch as an aggressive industry with many friends in high places, was a distant second, at 13.5% of sales ...[13]

'The most startling fact about 2002 is that the combined profits for the ten drug companies in the Fortune 500 ($35.9 billion) were more than the profits for all the other 490 listed businesses put together ($33.7 billion).'[14]

Blockbuster figures continue to rise. The figures for 2004 show more billion-dollar-plus brands than ever. 'Around 85 blockbusters are expected to account for 30% of global sales by year-end, up from 69 in 1993,' *Scrip Magazine* reported, adding that there was also an increase in the number of brands achieving sales of more than $2 billion – about 40 in 2004, up from 25 in 2003.[15]

When money gets scarce

Meanwhile, governments around the world were getting distinctly jittery because there seemed to be no limit to the demand for healthcare. In 1960, the UK NHS spent around US$84 per person per year on health, which can be expressed as 3.9% of the UK's wealth or gross domestic product (GDP). In 1980, that figure was $977 (5.6% of GDP), and by 2002, it had shot up to $2,160 (7.7%). Similar leaps are seen throughout the world. In the US, for example, the equivalent spending in 1960 was $114 per person (5% of GDP), $2,738 (8.7%) in 1980 and $5,267 (14.6%) in 2002. These figures are based on 1995 prices and have been calculated to show equal spending power, or 'purchasing power parity' in the language of economists.[16]

Purchasing power crisis is a better way of describing the predicament many countries now find themselves in. And this is despite warning signs that had been sounding for years about a business waging war over our ailments that can only result in overmedication. 'In today's prescription-drug marketplace a host of similar products compete for essentially the same population of patients,' said David Kessler in 1994, while heading up the US medicines regulator, the Food and Drug Administration (FDA).

Writing in the *New England Journal of Medicine*, he and a team of drug reviewers said that only a minority of the 127 new drugs approved between 1989 and 1993 offered any clinical advantage over existing therapies.

> Pharmaceutical companies are waging aggressive campaigns to change prescribers' habits and to distinguish their products from competing ones, even when the products are virtually indistinguishable.
>
> This is occurring in many therapeutic classes – antiulcer products, ACE-inhibitors, calcium-channel blockers, the SSRIs, and non-steroidal anti-inflammatory drugs, to name a few. Victory in these therapeutic-class wars can mean millions of dollars for a drug company. But for patients and providers it can mean misleading promotions, conflicts of interests, increased costs for healthcare, and ultimately, inappropriate prescribing.[17]

Top management of the FDA has changed many times since Kessler's day and such candid observations are certainly no feature of the decidedly pro-industry regime that has been ushered in under President George W. Bush. Current thinking sees no essential difference between the interests of the public and the interests of industry. Indeed, in the summer of 2004, the FDA's chief counsel, Dan Troy, came under fire for inviting drug companies to inform him of lawsuits against them so the FDA could help in their defence. 'We can't afford to get involved in every case – we have to pick our shots,' he said, advising them therefore to 'make it sound like a Hollywood pitch.'[18]

To suggest the interests of the industry and the regulator do significantly differ is to commit treason, because it implies either that the regulators are in some way lax in how they interpret laws designed to protect the public interest, or that this powerful and highly conservative industry is somehow duping them.

Wealth or health creation?

The evidence suggests that the picture is rather more complex and that, for largely pragmatic reasons, the problem has been that the regulators and the industry they are paid to regulate have been able to coexist rather too cosily for rather too long. In the case of the UK, there are historic reasons why commercial issues have become so entangled with public health; but, in fact, all countries are driven by political agendas that have always put far greater weight on the creation of wealth than health.

Indeed, one of the more pertinent observations of an all-party UK parliamentary inquiry into the industry's influence in 2004 was the fact that taxpayers sponsor the industry at the same time as being the major purchaser of its products. The MPs' final report said:

> The Department of Health has for too long optimistically assumed that the interests of health and of industry are one ... This may reflect the fact that the department sponsors the industry as well as looking after health. The result is that the industry has been left to its own devices for too long.[19]

The MPs went on to severely criticize the regulator for its lax oversight of the industry.

> The Medicines and Healthcare products Regulatory Agency (MHRA) has failed to adequately scrutinize licensing data and its post-marketing surveillance is inadequate. The MHRA chairman stated that trust was integral to effective regulation, but trust, while

> convenient, may mean that the regulatory process is not strict enough.[20]

Safety was only one of several concerns.

> The consequences of lax oversight are that the industry's influence has expanded and a number of practices have developed which act against the public interest ... The industry affects every level of healthcare provision, from the drugs that are initially discovered and developed through clinical trials, to the promotion of drugs to the prescriber and the patient groups, to the prescription of medicines and the compilation of clinical guidelines ... The most immediately worrying consequence of the problems described above is the unsafe use of drugs.[21]

But the MPs also acknowledged how companies boost sales by encouraging the belief that every problem requires medical treatment.

> While the pharmaceutical industry cannot be blamed for creating unhealthy reliance on, and over-use of, medicines, it has certainly exacerbated it. There has been a trend towards categorizing more and more individuals as 'abnormal' or in need of drug treatment.[22]

Even though the elected representatives of ordinary people, such as this UK health committee, can make recommendations to improve the deal the public gets from pharma, it cannot be assumed these will be followed through. Indeed, the strong response from the government to their report was that things were largely fine. Their complacency is more obvious when one considers that most of the recommendations they were being asked to implement concerned things most people probably imagined were happening anyway.

They reflected, for example, the MPs' concern that the aim of new drugs should be real therapeutic benefit for patients, prompting the question as to what exactly the aims had been previously. To this end, they wanted clinical trials to ask questions that are relevant to patients, more restraint in the marketing battles and much more research into the downside of drugs, particularly once they are on the market. Most crushingly of all, they wanted a wholesale review of the regulatory process.

Even if the report was to have some dampening effect on pharma's influence within the NHS, it could have only a minimal effect on the industry globally because the UK accounts for no more than 3% of its sales by value. Nevertheless, it is a strong indication of a new and general sense of unease among politicians and citizens as they gradually wake up to the fact they are not getting a particularly good deal for their drug spend.

These reasonable concerns of ordinary people must, however, be set against the combined might of companies that have enjoyed decades of escalating indulgence and are reluctant to slim down, despite the fact they are not producing drugs fast enough to compensate for the bumper profits they earned throughout the 1990s. Pharma was expected to lose global sales of around $28 billion between 2000 and 2005 as monopoly prices vanish on patent expiry.[23]

The human race can survive perfectly well without an endless supply of new drugs but the corporations that produce them can't. Naturally, they start doing what most people have long suspected and what Harvard Medical School professor Arnold Rehman articulates when he says their role has changed from 'developing the drugs that society really needs to trying to extract as much money as they possibly can from the healthcare system'.[24]

No new drugs

The problem no one can get away from is the lack of effective new drugs. The significance of this is more apparent if one considers pharma innovation as a basic global utility where, instead of water or gas or oil, ideas circulate through the pipelines. In times of drought, when these ideas, for any number of reasons, stop translating into useful drugs, companies can continue to thrive at the taxpayers' expense because very few questions are asked about what goes on in those pipelines.

The longer the drought, the greater the pressure for answers, however, and the greater pharma's need for money just to stay on an even keel. Managing this exquisite expectation-management corner has even persuaded the US government to send out trade representatives in an attempt to get the rest of the world to dismantle their price controls on drugs to move them nearer to US levels.

The most cursory comparison with other industries shows how audacious such a move is. No Hollywood boss, for example, would even consider trying to convince Europeans to increase the price of cinema tickets specifically so that Americans could pay less. But that is what is happening with drugs. The US movie business is not so dissimilar from pharma. It is under the same pressure to deliver 'sure-fire' global hits. And just as it designs and develops films and TV shows for US audiences that then go global, so the rest of the world tends to get drugs catering to the US market, which accounts for half the global drugs bill on its own.

The lower prices the rest of the world pays are to do with controls, but the reasons those controls are in place are not only to do with affordability, as the Americans would have us believe. They are consistent, of course, with what countries can afford to spend on health, in the same way the price of cinema tickets is generally in line with what people can afford to spend on entertainment.

But the bodies of law that try to balance the public interest with that of the pharmaceutical industry embrace other, broader, concerns, where pricing cannot be readily extracted from the mix. The laws in place in most countries to protect people from pharma's marketing zeal, for example, are intimately tied up with those to do with pricing, certainly to do with profits. In the UK, where a mechanism known as the Pharmaceutical Price Regulation Scheme has been in operation in some form since 1956, the central idea is to control profits, not prices (see Appendix). So, to ask for pricing controls to be dismantled is to open up the whole basis on which medicines are researched and produced.

And this shows quite clearly that while the rest of the world may pay lower prices for drugs, their input into the global innovation pipeline is also less. The research agenda is largely set by the US, because it is the country that generates the highest profits. The rest of the world gets US drugs much like it gets US movies and US fast food, in other words.

Pharma's desperation can be seen from the fact that companies have tried each of the Hollywood options: the sequels (me-too drugs); special effects (fancier methods of drug delivery); increased marketing spend (increased marketing spend). Above all, they have stuck to the tried and tested method of enlarging existing markets.

But each of these frantic attempts to plug a dire innovation gap has been rumbled: as scientists have argued publicly about safety studies, as patients have fought pricing and product liability suits, as US consumers have battled for cheap drug imports, and as citizens everywhere start to at least wonder what they are paying for and how the industry in its current form can survive. Even Sir Richard Sykes, former CEO of Glaxo Wellcome and now rector of Imperial College, London, wants change. He told the UK parliamentary inquiry, 'Today the industry has got a very bad name. That is very unfortunate for an industry that we should look up to and believe in, and that we should be supporting. I think there have to be some big changes.'[25]

The wall begins to crumble

But the real earthquake to hit the world of medicines regulation came in the summer of 2004, when first Professor Eric Topol, a cardiologist at the Cleveland Clinic, Ohio, spoke to the *New York Times*, and then, Dr David Graham, an FDA official, supported him by telling a US Senate hearing in October 2004 that his agency's approval of Vioxx had led to the 'single greatest drug safety catastrophe in the history of this country or the history of the world'.[26]

Graham, an associate director in the FDA's Center for Drug Evaluation and Research's Office of Drug Safety, had written a report, made public in August 2004, based on a study of Vioxx using patients' insurance records. It estimated 28,000 Americans had had heart attacks and strokes as a result of taking the drug while he was arguing with his FDA superiors about the risks. He maintained the equivalent in deaths of two to four jumbo jets dropping out of the sky every week, a figure that has been hotly disputed. 'I would argue that the FDA, as currently configured, is incapable of protecting America against another Vioxx,' he said. 'Simply put, FDA and its Center for Drug Evaluation and Research are broken.'[27]

Their claims were made more plausible on both sides of the Atlantic, when the safety profile of some of the SSRI antidepressants was rewritten to reflect both the problems coming off the drugs and the increased suicides in children. And further back was the European drugs scandal of 1993, which provided tangible proof that drugs regulation was corruptible.

This was when investigators uncovered a Machiavellian substructure to Italy's formal drug pricing and approval systems. Revelations from one of the main players in the intrigue, Professor Duilio Poggiolini, set off a chain reaction, which saw the resignation of a health minister, the suicide of a member of the drug pricing committee, and the dissolution of both the pricing and approvals committees.

Poggiolini had been head of both the Italian medicines directorate and the main European decision-making body for medicines, the CPMP (Committee for Proprietary and Medicinal Products). Holding the most influential position in European drugs regulation, he had been showered with valuable art and money in an attempt to displace science as the basis for regulatory decisions.

Subtler forms of influence are endemic. Just finding experts with absolutely no connection with a drug to sit on the regulatory panels that decide whether a drug should get a licence is not easy. What else can explain the final twist in the Vioxx saga when a 32-member FDA committee voted (17–15) to allow the drug back onto the market?

Even though the withdrawal of Vioxx had prompted the most serious reflection on regulatory procedures since Thalidomide, and even though everyone was at pains to restore public trust, the *New York Times* was able to prove little had changed. The newspaper's own investigation showed that ten members of that panel were linked to companies that made Cox-2 inhibitors. These ten voted 9–1 in favour of Vioxx's return. The Center for Science in the Public Interest said the inclusion of these ten members violated an act which prohibits scientists with direct conflicts of interest from serving on panels offering advice to federal regulatory agencies.[28] Predictable squabbles ensued over the details about who gets what for what, while everyone else was asking, Where have all the public scientists gone? Do they really no longer exist? Does everyone work for industry?

The patient voice

While all these conflicts have been raging outside most people's field of vision, the strongest hope for their resolution has been gradually building strength. That comes from patients themselves who, for largely pragmatic reasons, are now being helped by governments to find a voice. Crippled by healthcare's rising open-ended cost and being virtually powerless to do anything about it (within current legal frameworks), the UK government, for example, is trying to move with the democratic tide and encourage patients to play a bigger part in how their healthcare systems work. The government wants to inject some life into large monopolies that traditionally have had virtually no way of hearing, let alone responding to, the patient voice.

Healthcare policies centred around patients are based on an admission that the guiding principles that led to the setting up of the welfare state no longer apply. One of the chief architects of this kind of market socialism is health economist Dr Julian le Grand.

> When the welfare state was set up in the 1940s, it was unduly influenced by the common cause inspired by the Nazi threat in the Second World War. The [Labour] party had assumed doctors, hospital managers, school heads and teachers would be inspired by the same altruism and sense of duty to fight disease and ignorance. Patients and parents, meanwhile, were expected to be passive, grateful recipients

> of whatever they were given. The reality was that doctors and teachers were as likely to be lazy and patronizing as they were to be altruistic and dutiful, and that parents and patients were never going to be merely passive or grateful. Hence the need to put choice into the equation.[29]

Notions of patient choice are not limited to the current Labour government, nor to the UK, and how much choice is actually being offered is a moot point. Nevertheless, patient choice is now a central plank of government policy, starting with the absolute basics: which hospital (within a limited range) a patient gets to go to and the relatively new public health notion embodied in the White Paper, *Choosing Health: Making Healthy Choices Easier*. The idea of encouraging people to take more responsibility for their health is described as seminal by the *British Medical Journal*.[30] In the current health-obsessed climate, it can also be seen as a stroke of such apparent political genius, one can't help wondering why no one thought of it earlier.

The truth is, it was born out of necessity. People's choices have never been particularly central to healthcare planning in the past and the *BMJ* was not the only voice to be heard expressing scepticism as to how the well-meaning rhetoric was to be matched with sufficient action to get results: particularly as choice really is new in health, as new as democracy for the citizens of Eastern Europe. Ivan Illich, a Viennese philosopher, was particularly scathing about how citizens have allowed themselves to be treated in the name of health in his famous 1970s polemic, *Limits to Medicine*.

> They are turned into patients whom medicine tests and repairs, into administered citizens whose healthy behaviour a medical bureaucracy guides, and into guinea pigs on whom medical science constantly experiments. Health has ceased to be a native endowment each human being is presumed to possess until proven ill, and has become an ever-receding goal to which one is entitled by virtue of social justice.[31]

As people claim their own notions of what it is to be well, cracks inevitably start to appear in the foundations of healthcare systems that have been led more by the values of prestige and profit than anything that remotely promotes robust public health. Those cracks are expressed as a general distrust in what is on offer with the resources available. The NHS, like any healthcare system, works because there is some basis of trust that patients will do what doctors consider to be in their best interests. When that trust breaks down, for whatever reason, governments find they are not only paying mounting costs for drugs, but they are spending more than they should in other ways. A paper in the *Pharmaceutical Journal*, for example, says about half of all medicines prescribed in the UK are not taken.[32] If you believe the UK pharma industry association, the ABPI, the figure is much higher, at around 80%. If the numbers were translated into the field of education, it would mean using taxes to pay for everyone to be state-educated, while more than half the pupils either play truant or choose to be self-taught.

The authority of healthcare systems around the world cannot help but crumble in the face of much more confident and articulate customers. Unlike education, good health is not yet compulsory and people who choose to attach themselves to philosophies that lie outside the remit of conventional medicine are growing in number. Since some degree of choice has been introduced into the equation, as it had to be sooner or later, the questions facing society inevitably change, revolving around how far choice can be reasonably extended, what it can reasonably embrace, and how it can be reasonably restrained.

The patient as king

The idea of patients coming to believe, to a greater or lesser extent, that good health is an option is now fairly well-established. This conviction that health really is a commodity like any other, to be bought and sold, is one that rests easily with the vision of the future the pharma companies themselves hold. This is a vision that tends to marginalize the human aspect of doctoring – with all its homely wisdom, comfort and encouragement – and promote the technical, over which pharma has greater control. The intuitive powers of the doctor, honed over years of clinical practice, naturally wane as the art of healing gives way to the certainty of science, as exemplified in the various protocols they must follow in both diagnosis and treatment. Drugs offer such certainty. In this and many other ways, they are attractive options for people living busy lives and those responsible for public budgets.

Their only downside is that they require no change of habit, no understanding of how the condition arose, no reflection whatsoever. Convenience, as much as anything else, explains the dominant role pharma companies have come to play in our healthcare choices.

When pharma's vision comes to define the political rhetoric about choice in healthcare, the idea of greater patient choice assumes more of an edge. Moreover, the fact the NHS is doing everything possible to include the public, coupled with the Internet enabling a far more egalitarian distribution of medical knowledge than ever before, and doctors, for the first time in their history, being encouraged to put the patient's view of their illness at the centre of their treatment, bodes well for a stronger patient voice. Whether these conditions are sufficient for society to start engaging with the issues the pharma industry has monopolized for years remains to be seen.

These issues concern what it is to be healthy, the acceptable length of a lifespan, and how illness is treated. Essentially, they are to do with how we choose to live and how we choose to die. Brave voices such as Rachel Clark, who was diagnosed with a rare form of cancer at the age of only 25, urge people to get to grips with medicine sooner rather than later. In her moving book, *A Long Walk Home*, she wrote: 'Navigating your way through cancer and its treatment is rather like being dropped in a strange city, without a map or compass. There are no landmarks that you recognize and no familiar features. The city has no signs, no one speaks your language and your requests for help are incomprehensible: they are unable to help you.'[33]

And this was at the human end of the medicines business. Rachel was talking about her treatment at the hand of doctors and nurses in Australia and the UK who were doing their best to stop the spread of the alveolar rhabdomyosarcoma in her ethmoid sinus. They were on her side. Nevertheless, my heart went out to her when she confessed it took her two weeks just to pronounce the name of this illness that was to make her revise every dream she had ever cherished in her short life.

People's fears of what will become of them when they are ill are not factored into the medical process. How can they be? Doctors are extensively trained not to get emotionally involved with what is going on in the lives of their patients, and for good reasons. Their job is to help patients find the best treatment for their condition. Those treatments will have been expensively researched and extensively evaluated on the assumption that patients are largely passive vehicles in which medications can work their magic. The clinical trials by which their effect has been assessed cannot take into account the wealth of human feeling that usually accompanies being ill. That isn't how science works.

But the new science, the new knowledge that is proving so hard to translate into medicines that can serve the largest markets, confirms that the totality of a person's life fundamentally affects their performance. How we see the world or perceive pain, for example, does not rest on hard-wired systems at all but on intelligent networks working tirelessly for our benefit given the raw material provided.

Moreover, they readily adapt to new thoughts and new behaviour if those ideas make sense at a deep enough level. Indeed, this is how complementary medicine is increasingly thought to work, not by eliminating symptoms as conventional medicine might, but by somehow jolting networks back into a healthier rhythm. It works, in other words, because people intuitively trust what the practitioner says and does. The cause may be something as simple as a massage, but if that translates into that person getting a good night's sleep for the first time in weeks, and if that person has also been convinced to eat better food more regularly and in other ways to take better care of themself, then it is not altogether surprising that better health results. The scientific community, like everyone else, is bemused as to how it works, because the key rarely seems to rest with the practitioner, nor even with what they do, but with their ability to elicit trust, something that is as impossible to manufacture or measure as it is to market.

The fundamental problem

Trust has no place in science. Science creates the conditions for trust but on its own limited terms, which lie a universe away from where most ordinary people come from. This is why the fundamental problem with medicine concerns the all-too-human tendency not to want to focus too long on the things medicine addresses. Fears that something may be wrong are readily addressed by the pharma industry. With serious conditions, such as cancer, any steps forward are welcomed, but such gratitude must be set against the totality of industry's efforts to make us well. 'What has been described as the "medicalization" of society – the belief that every problem requires medical treatment – may also be attributed in part to the activities of the pharmaceutical industry,' said the final UK report into the pharma industry.[34]

The industry may be able to exploit our blind spots, but it doesn't create them. Company chiefs use our health-obsessed times as any industrialist would, to create the ideal environment for growth. Consider, for example, a classic manifestation of a modern malaise that has no name. For the purposes of this book, I have dubbed it Quest-for-Good-Health syndrome, a condition that has been observed to evoke two very different cascade reactions.

The extrovert response to excessive and alarmist health information results in people becoming terribly interested in all aspects of a disease, or imagined disease. The opposite reaction is to block all symptoms out in the belief that nothing like that could ever happen to them. One overworries, in other words; the other pays too little attention to their health risks – neither of which reactions suggests a particularly robust public health.

Japanese physician Hiro'omi Kono, concerned with the latter category, surveyed 50 of his patients with terminal gastric cancer and found that 70%, while aware of cancer-like symptoms, had chosen not to seek medical advice until it was too late. They were overconfident in their own good health, in other words.[35]

There is no legislation that can change how people respond to either their own sense of discomfort, or the increasing noise from pharma's marketing efforts exhorting them to do something about it. But as citizens, rather than patients or consumers who are naturally subject to such human frailties, they would surely want pharma's noise toned down to the minimum.

The machinations of a medicines business that enjoys infinite demand for its products, that incurs no penalties when it fails, that is obliged to work in the interests of shareholders, and is regulated by people who, for largely pragmatic reasons, have been convinced this is also the public's interest, require now more than ever a strong and autonomous patient voice to be heard.

It is not as though medicine has all the answers. Its post-war successes, built on the chance discovery of drugs, concealed the fact that no one understood the nature or causation of disease. 'And now, 50 years on, medicine still knows the cause of only a fraction of the diseases in the textbooks,' writes le Fanu.

He lists them as the bacterial and viral infections, those resulting from a defect in a single gene (like cystic fibrosis), tobacco and lung cancer, a handful of occupational diseases, and those primarily determined by ageing: arthritis, cataracts, the majority of cases of cancer and circulatory disorders. 'But everything else – all the neurological diseases such as multiple sclerosis, and all the rheumatological diseases like psoriasis, and all the gut disorders like Crohn's disease, and so on – their causes, quite simply, are not known.'[36]

Medicine has its limitations. The purpose of this book is not to celebrate its brilliant achievements but to consider how the medicines business works and how it might be directed towards delivering a better deal for the public who pay for it. Rebecca Solnit, author of *Hope In the Dark: The Untold History Of People Power*, uses the analogy of a theatre to point out how power works when it is no longer contested by the masses, and it works well for pharma's colossal influence over healthcare. 'The acts of the powerful and the official occupy centre stage,' she says. 'The traditional versions of history, the conventional sources of news encourage us to fix our gaze on that stage.' The result, she continues, is 'the too-common silence of those who settle for being audience and who pay the price of the drama.'[37]

As more people appreciate just how expensive this medical drama is and how it can never relieve our real angst about ageing, becoming sick and dying, so pressure naturally builds for change. And the process has already started as governments, healthcare purchasers and the public explore healthcare options that lie way beyond the pharmaceutical remit.

2

The company of giants

Pharma's presence may be hard to discern beyond the doctors and nurses who prescribe, and the pharmacists who dispense, its products. But its extraordinary wealth ensures its influence is felt where it matters and goes some way to explaining how companies have been able to buck the trends in the medicines business for so long. Having fewer new drugs, more questioning end-users and budgets that are stretched to the limit has made little difference to the inexorable rise in the drugs bill.

The extent of pharma's wealth can be gleaned by the sheer scale of its operations, not just geographically across the globe but by any standard economic term of reference – revenues, sales teams, profits, growth. In 2004, the top ten pharma companies had a combined income from prescription drugs of more than $205 billion.[1] If you can't think in billions, think of it as $205,000 million, just $10,000 million short of the gross domestic product (GDP) for Denmark, an affluent Scandinavian nation of 5.4 million people, that same year.

Pharma's growth has been dramatic. Consider, for example, that the 'blockbuster drug,' defined as having annual sales of more than a billion dollars, only emerged after 1984 when Glaxo's anti-ulcer, Zantac, was launched. This demonstrated not only that single products could enable companies to double or triple in size overnight, but also that reward need in no way equate with clinical benefit, nor with the research that has been invested in a product.

In the 1970s, before this class of drugs existed, people who produced too much stomach acid, took antacids which, as the name suggests, neutralize the problem. But a brilliant industry scientist by the name of James Black, who had already developed the beta-blockers, which block the effect of the stress hormone adrenaline on the heart, believed the same principle could be applied to stop acid being secreted in the stomach. It was surely an improvement to stop the production of acid rather than neutralize it once it was causing a problem.

Black's drug, cimetidine, which was sold by Smith Kline & French under the trade name of Tagamet, did just this. It pioneered the second generation of antihistamines. The first ones blocked allergic reactions, and these block the production of stomach acid. But his histamine (H_2) inhibitor did not bring in the billions of dollars that Glaxo's Zantac did, which worked in the same way but had a superior side-effect profile. This fact made Zantac quickly become not only market leader but also the world's number one drug, a position it held for years with far-reaching consequences for the industry.

Zantac was the first serious player in the war against stomach acid, a market that was able to flourish even as an agent that could eliminate the problem at source was becoming recognized among the medical community. The drug continued to sell around the world even when clinical guidelines had been introduced to insist doctors try a one-off course of this antibiotic-based agent first. If that didn't work and the problem persisted, then they should try the long-term maintenance approach.

One year before Zantac's launch, in 1983, Barry Marshall, a scientist working at the Royal Perth Hospital in Australia, had isolated the *Helicobacter pylori* bacterium that thrives in acidic stomachs and has since been shown to be the leading cause of stomach ulcers. News of this cheap and effective alternative was not enough to halt the rise of Zantac, however. An analyst at the state-funded US National Institutes of Health said at the time:

> A one-time antibiotic treatment regimen to eliminate *H. pylori*, as opposed to long-term maintenance with H_2 antagonist drugs, recurrence, and sometimes surgery as a last resort, is an obvious benefit both to patient and to the healthcare insurers. However [promoting this approach would lead to] the possible decline in sales.[2]

Actually, it wasn't even news. As far back as 1874, eight years before Robert Koch had discovered the bacterial agent that caused tuberculosis, another microbe hunter, the less well-known Arthur Boettcher, published a paper on a small, curved bug that was found repeatedly in stomach ulcers. Over the next half-century, several other scientists confirmed Boettcher's findings.

'By the late 1940s, peptic ulcers were being successfully treated with antibiotics in New York City hospitals,' says Paul W. Ewald in his book,

Plague Time. 'Then, around 1950, discussions of infectious causation of ulcers disappeared from the literature and from the treatment regimen. The medical texts from 1950 through to the early 1990s attributed peptic ulcers to gastric acidity, stress, smoking, alcohol consumption, and genetic disposition – everything but infection. Generally there was not even a reference to the possibility of infectious causation.'[3]

The kind of conferences that might explore, perhaps even confirm, the validity of antibiotic treatment for both duodenal and peptic ulcers didn't happen until after Zantac's patent had expired. There are various explanations as to why the medical community shied away from such a debate for 40 years. One is that the standards for identifying infectious causation for disease had been set in the 1880s when people were dealing with infections that killed whole populations. The standards had been set to find correlations between infection and disease quickly to minimize the casualties. The correlation between infection and ulcers is much fuzzier than that, say, in tuberculosis and it didn't pass the conventional tests.

'Applying one set of standards will allow early recognition of diseases that are easily recognized by the standards, and leave in the wake of that recognition those diseases that cannot be so identified,' says Ewald. 'Throughout most of the 20th century the experts maintained a stalwart grip on has-been standards that had largely outlived their usefulness.'[4] The result, he insists, is that thousands of people have suffered and died because antibiotic treatment of ulcers was generally recognized in 1995 instead of 1955. It was in 1995, as it happens, that Glaxo (which had become Glaxo Wellcome by that time) launched the first anti-ulcer drug to eradicate *H. pylori* specifically.

A second explanation is that the idea of infections causing a whole range of diseases that don't instantly kill is relatively new. It is known, for example, that infections cause 15–20% of human cancers and have been strongly implicated in conditions as diverse as heart disease, Parkinson's, Alzheimer's, atherosclerosis, as well as the coughs and colds more commonly associated with infection. Nevertheless, for reasons that remain unknown, it is often easier to accept lifestyle as a cause for ulcers or cancer, than infection. 'Thousands more probably suffered and died over a similar period because cervical cancer was treated as bad luck rather than a preventable sexually transmitted disease,' continues Ewald.[5]

Even when the patents on Zantac and the other H_2 antagonists expired, the next generation of drugs to control stomach acid, the proton-pump inhibitors, went on to enlarge the market further. So-called proton pumps are found on the cells that line the stomach and are used by these cells to produce stomach acid to help digestion. Two drugs that stop these pumps working were among the top ten best-selling drugs in 2003, mentioned in Chapter 1. One earned $4 billion and the other around $3 billion. The overall market for anti-ulcer drugs, according to IMS Health, was worth $25.1 billion in the year to September 2004.[6]

These new drugs are used in combination with an antibiotic to eliminate any *H. pylori* infection, because the reduced acid allows the ulcer to heal better. And their main focus has switched to treating other symptoms of acidity, such as heartburn or a reflux condition that sends excess acid back up the throat. Nevertheless, doctors acknowledge ulcers are being treated rather than eliminated and give several reasons people are persuaded to take a once-a-day pill for life. One is that the side effects of the antibiotic treatment are said to be unpleasant, and can involve sickness and diarrhoea. Another is that neither patients nor doctors count the cost. They probably don't know it; it certainly doesn't factor into the equation as it does for pharma.

The rise of the druggernaut

Zantac was the first real blockbuster the pharma industry had known. And it was an irresistible model. Markets got larger and larger. In 1990, when Glaxo's drug was still reigning supreme with annual sales of $2.4 billion, the next five biggest earners of that era pulled in sales of between $1.1 billion and $1.5 billion.[7] Just ten years later, however, when the idea of medicating huge swathes of the population had caught on, 36 drugs were earning no less than $76 billion a year between them. Each of the top 25 drugs of 2000 had higher sales than the number two drug just a decade earlier.[8]

One of Zantac's first tangible non-medical effects was to provide Glaxo with the funds to effect a hostile takeover of Wellcome to create Glaxo Wellcome in 1994. The newly formed British company immediately ousted US rival, Merck & Co., from its ten-year reign at the top of the pharma league table. It had annual sales of around $12 billion, half as much again as Glaxo alone and a third more than Merck & Co.'s $9 billion. Soon, however, both companies would be dwarfed as the importance of marketing muscle triggered a spate of mega-mergers that was to transform the industry around fewer players operating in ever-bigger markets.

The 1996 Swiss mega-merger between Ciba and Sandoz, to create the $60 billion druggernaut Novartis, the world's third largest pharma company, was then the largest deal in corporate history. Fervour in the financial press mounted. Company-courting calls were reported every bit as eagerly as the affairs of A-list celebrities in the tabloids. And none more so than those concerning a prospective marriage between Glaxo Wellcome and its rival, fellow UK pharma giant SmithKline Beecham.

Pharma speculation can be expensive where mergers are involved, however, providing yet another indicator of the far-reaching influence of our drug companies. When SmithKline Beecham was rumoured to be talking to American Home Products about a possible tie-up at the start of 1998, it was forced by UK stock exchange regulations to state its true intentions. Immediately, CEO Jan Leschly said the deal was off. Soon he announced a new object of desire, Glaxo Wellcome. Within days, however, he had changed his mind again and pulled out, wiping no less than £13 billion ($23.7 billion) off the combined share prices of the two companies.[9] The CEOs had no option but to sort out their management differences, and in January 2000, GlaxoSmithKline was formed, leaping back to the top of the pharma league table.

Dr Philip Brown, then publisher of pharma industry bible, *Scrip World Pharmaceutical News*, said shortly afterwards:

> This gigantic company of over 110,000 souls, capitalized at £110 billion (or £1 million for every employee) now sets forth to show us all what being gigantic really means. Just think of all that manpower and financial muscle being directed into new product discovery and development, all that power being delivered in global marketing, and all that energy for yet more mergers and acquisitions. The question is will it fly?[10]

No one had a clue, but that didn't stop the other major players also teaming up. In December 1998, Hoechst of Germany and Rhône-Poulenc of France announced the creation of Aventis. The same week, a deal was brokered between Elf Aquitaine and L'Oréal, majority owners of two French companies, Sanofi and Synthelabo. While everyone was still digesting the idea of a Sanofi-Synthelabo, an Anglo-Swedish company, AstraZeneca, with a market capitalization of $73 billion, was formed.

Pfizer, a rising star of 1998 on the back of Viagra, launched that year, took a different route to the top – via an aggressive acquisitions strategy.[11] This was illustrated when its high-earning Lipitor, marketed in a complicated arrangement with Warner-Lambert, was threatened. Rumour had it that American Home Products was merging with Warner-Lambert. Pfizer wasn't going to let its partner go without a fight. So it significantly trumped the offer with a hostile $70 billion bid at the end of 1999. This was $20 billion more than anything else on the table.

'Warner-Lambert reluctantly gave in to investor pressure and agreed to discuss merger terms with Pfizer,' said corporate pharmaceutical journalist Robin Davison in *Scrip Magazine* in February 2000.[12] Such was the fashion for mergers at the time, Davison added, that around half the world's top 25 pharma companies had been involved in either a merger or a substantial acquisition over the past two years. Since then, of course, Pfizer has acquired another major player in Pharmacia, and Sanofi-Synthelabo taken over Aventis to create a major French force in the global industry, Sanofi-Aventis.

All this corporate restructuring among the A-list players was mirrored every step of the way down the so-called value chain. A similar dynamic can be seen in the deals that took place in pharma's hinterland, at the level below pharma, where companies have also been taking their partners so they can dance along to pharma's new tune.

Throughout the 1990s and on into this century, everyone was buying up, scaling up or linking up in networks to provide the kind of integrated deals that got the business. The companies that conduct clinical trials were growing as fast, or going out of business. Companies offering consultancy services, sales and marketing services, discovery services, manufacturing services, packaging and transportation services, anything at all to do with the making and supply of medicines, did whatever it took to hold on to contracts with their increasingly powerful pharma masters.

In the course of just a few years, power has come to rest with companies that have become massively influential in how those classic human sufferings of old age, sickness and death are seen; and in how the scientific community sets its gaze in addressing those sufferings. The forces driving such consolidation are desperate, and the costs astronomical. 'Creating Glaxo Wellcome cost $14 billion; creating GlaxoSmithKline cost $76 billion,' says a managing director and senior analyst with Deutsche Bank Securities. And their value, she adds, is hotly disputed among shareholders. 'Three-quarters of all deals do not pay back their cost of capital, and stock prices have fallen. However, I think the real question is not whether they delivered, but rather: what would have happened to these companies if they hadn't made the deal?'[13]

Size matters

All the main pharma players are big. But some are bigger than others. The number one company, Pfizer, was worth $283.8 billion in April 2004. Based in New York, the firm had sales worth more than $40 billion in 2003, a 40% increase on 2002.[14] More than a billion prescriptions were written for its products in 2003; Lipitor, as we know, earned more than $9 billion single-handedly as the leading player in the global statin market. Equally impressive is how its sales have multiplied tenfold over as many years. In 1993, Pfizer was languishing in eleventh position in the pharma league tables with sales of just $4.5 billion.

To give some perspective to the top players, Pfizer's latest $40 billion sales figure was a third more than GlaxoSmithKline's $30 billion that year (2003), which in turn, was a third greater than the $22.5 billion earned by Merck, which came in at third place. The players then tapered down more gradually in size, with Novo Nordisk, a Danish company, coming in at number 20 with sales of just over $4 billion.[15]

These are sizeable incomes that carry much weight in the countries where the companies officially reside or do business. In the UK, for example, the industry invests around £3.3 billion ($6 billion) a year in R&D and accounts for 29,000 jobs, making it one of the largest employers of science graduates.[16] Since knowledge-economies can only grow by providing high-paying jobs for their best-educated citizens, the industry's employment record is its trump card.

Pharma employs top graduates throughout its business, in research, sales, marketing, manufacturing and management. Salaries are correspondingly high. Despite the high wage bill, pharma as a sector generates extraordinary profits for its shareholders. Takeda, a Japanese company, led the field with margins of 43.5% on its $7.5 billion sales in 2003.[17] In absolute terms, GlaxoSmithKline made the most that year with a trading profit not far short of $10 billion. Merck came a close second with profit margins of more than 40%. These kinds of sums are normal. Sometimes they take a dip, like Pfizer's did that year, not even making it into the top ten on this measure of success. But the bar is high: even tenth place in the profits league, taken by Abbott Laboratories, yielded a very respectable profit margin of 27.8% of sales that year.[18]

Since the early 1980s, pharma has consistently ranked as the most profitable industry in the world. In 2003, the tide turned and it dropped to third place in the 47 industries listed in the Fortune 500.[19] But it had built up so much free cash-flow by then that when GlaxoSmithKline was stung for a $5 billion tax demand by the US authorities in 2003/4, one analyst brushed it aside, saying, 'The company is just a cash-machine. A bill like this is just an ant on the back of an elephant.'[20]

The arguments that ensued over this particular tax demand revealed how global reach can increase and sustain extraordinary profitability. In the words of one columnist:

> In the wonderful world of pharmaceuticals, lateral thinking is prized as highly in tax planning as in the lab. The point about drugs is that once you have researched and developed them, they are cheap to make. The rule of thumb is that for every $100 of sales, only $5 should be spent on manufacturing. The trick is to make them in places with low tax regimes and retain as much of the profit there as possible. Puerto Rico is a current favourite and so is Ireland, where nine of the world's top ten have facilities. In other words, everybody does it.[21]

Indeed, the case for GlaxoSmithKline was partly that everyone had been doing what the US internal revenue service calls 'transfer pricing' (to artificially suppress the level of profits booked in the US market) for years and the company was therefore being unfairly discriminated against.

Pharma companies have global reach geographically, sumo-style staying power financially, and an influence so dominant in scientific research, with the line between public interest and commercial gain so blurred, that public safety is easily put at risk. Dr Eric Topol, chief of cardiovascular medicine at the Cleveland Clinic, Ohio, says pharma money now plays such an integral part in the entire licensing process that the public interest is only noticed when something goes wrong.

Topol was the first doctor to go public about the shortcomings of the Cox-2 inhibitor drugs for pain relief, Vioxx and Celebrex, in an article in the *New York Times* in October 2004. He has personal experience of how doctors are discouraged from speaking out in the public interest. 'The world very much wants new drugs and medical devices to succeed,' he says. 'Anyone who speaks out is cast as a heretic standing in the way of progress.'

The immediate effect of Topol's action in highlighting safety concerns about this hugely popular class of drug was to invite criticism from consultants. He was described as a 'luddite' in the *Wall Street Journal* and portrayed as having a financial incentive, which he did not. 'You are putting yourself at risk when you speak out in the public interest,' he says. 'The resources open to the industry are extraordinary and you find yourself in a very nasty and imperilled situation. It shouldn't be this way but it is.'[22]

The resources open to pharma can be roughly calculated from the broad breakdown of pharma's income for 2003 that was used in Marcia Angell's book, *The Truth About the Drug Companies*. In this, R&D took the smallest share (14%), followed by profits (17%) and, finally, marketing and administration took as much as the first two again (31%). Manufacturing and distribution largely account for the rest. Extrapolating these ratios over pharma's performance in 2004, when it earned $500 billion, means the industry spent roughly $70 billion on R&D, $155 billion on marketing and administration and took $90 billion in profit that year.

Influencing the doctors

Having $70 billion in research money to spend makes pharma the principal means of survival for thousands of smaller companies and university departments worldwide. The industry dominates the horizons of everyone in the business. As Topol says:

> The effect of the industry on the medical profession is subliminal. Their interests are totally aligned. The people doctors deal with from industry appear to be trustworthy. The trouble is that it is very easy to lose objectivity once interests have become so inseparable.[23]

Pharma, of course, has every reason to want the most hallowed consultants to be aligned with their particular therapy. Once the top consultants are on board, it's all plain sailing for a particular product, because medical authority is such that all prescribers naturally fall into line with what those above them do. The key is to get the best consultants on board. When pharma puts doctors in charge of the major trials, the doctors get paid a respectable amount and, perhaps better still, the chance to gain some real credibility in an important therapeutic area. There will be conferences to attend, papers to prepare, editors to deal with, and doctors who will listen to what they say.

The vast majority of the time, they can remain in control. It is only when safety concerns emerge and investigations are ordered that people can see how far from being in control the medical leaders really are. Sometimes they simply side step the uncomfortable issues. A cardiovascular journalist recalls one eminent doctor who was not on stage to announce the results of an important clinical trial he had led. When she asked him later why he had not announced the results himself, he said he hadn't been prepared to give them the company spin. He refused to articulate the message. He did not publicly state his opinion of the drug's clinical value; to do so would have been to break the rules of conduct. 'The industry has physicians in more of a choke-hold than they care to admit,' says Topol.

Influencing research

Pharma not only seeks to have the top doctors in its pay, it also largely determines what questions they should be asking in the search for new medicines. In the UK, the industry funds more healthcare-related research than every other source combined – six times as much as the Department of Health, five times as much as medical charities, and eight times as much as the Medical Research Council.[24]

Pharma exerts a similar dominance everywhere it operates. The young companies with the freshest ideas want research contracts with a Pfizer or a Merck or a GlaxoSmithKline, just as a young starlet longs to hook up with a Hollywood major – and for the same reasons: so their full potential can be given the opportunity to shine on the global stage.

These small companies work to pharma's rules, which largely set the standards for what is researched. The most important of these is that a drug, from the moment of conception, must have a market. It must have enough people in countries who will want it and can afford it, in other words, to make it worth developing. A close second is that it must be capable of delivering a profit within the 20-year stretch of time inventors are given exclusive rights – and therefore premium prices – to their inventions under patent laws.

Pharma's rules are identical to those governing any other commercial market except in one important respect, which is that its products are rarely paid for directly by the end-users. People pay indirectly, of course, through their taxes, but the costs to the individual are negligible. Besides, why would anyone want to question the global research endeavour, even if they were in a position to? One reason is that it can lead up an awful lot of expensive blind alleys when the intention is profit rather than robust health. And the costs of failed research are factored into the overall equation when pharma gets to negotiate prices of its drugs generally.

Case study: research into countering obesity

Pharma is free to go in any direction it chooses, and these directions do not necessarily bring commensurate medical benefits. The battle against obesity is a good example of market forces leading research in a direction that has not, as yet, proved a particularly good use of funds. It also doubles up in the telling as a starter lesson in pharmacology, showing how the cost of failure easily mounts up in a market where obsession is one of its guiding factors. And why we know so much about the life of fat cells with so little to show for it.

Market forces reflect what most concerns society. Since rich westerners want to be thin, money naturally flows into the battle against obesity. Even if this multi-billion-dollar effort results in no new treatments, the spend is justified on the grounds that it delivers new insight into the processes involved in making people feel full, controlling their digestion, translating food into energy, regulating fat stores, or any other way anyone can think of to stop us putting on so much weight – via a drug. It's a journey, industry says, not a question of getting to a destination. If people want new drugs, companies need a lot of money to be playing around with. 'Developing drugs is expensive,' says the *Economist*. 'If companies are to keep trying, they must expect to make enough profit to meet the cost of developing not only the drugs that work, but also the ones that do not.'[25]

What drug developers do is look for the biological mediators of these various processes. These are the things a company would try to affect when making a diet drug. In this purely pharmacological sense, our bodies can be seen as treasure chests of potential drug targets. The whole purpose of the pharmaceutical chemist is to tweak these biological mediators, which, in the case of obesity is to change in some basic way how food is translated first into energy, and then the excess into fat. The wonder of drugs is that they talk the same chemical language as our bodies, opening up or closing targets in the same way a key fits into a lock. By finding a molecule that can block or encourage the action of a particular target, you can adjust how the body responds in a useful way.

The trouble is that obesity research has so many avenues to go down, most of which interrelate to produce a picture of confounding complexity and a lot of expensive blind alleys. Over the past 20 years, literally hundreds of anti-obesity products have been evaluated by pharma companies and only four have made it on to the market. Of these, two have had serious side effects in causing heart-valve disease and were withdrawn in 1997. One, dexfenfluramine, branded Redux, was a drug that had been used safely to help people lose weight for years, restricted as it was to short-term use. But 'the US finally broke the mould,' pharmaceutical journalist Susan Hughes reported in 1996, 'licensing dexfenfluramine for long-term treatment.'[26]

This was to prove a fatal and expensive decision. By May 2004, the effects of the litigation that ensued had cost Wyeth, the company responsible, $16.6 billion in damages, with one investment bank, Prudential Securities, saying another $7.5 billion might be needed to fully settle the case.[27] Back in the early days, however, experts such as Dr Philip James, director of the Rowett Institute in Aberdeen, UK, and chairman of the WHO task force on obesity, were cited by Hughes as having said the present restriction to short-term treatment was 'completely illogical' and urging doctors to use what was to prove a highly dangerous drug when taken for any length of uninterrupted time.

'There is enormous prejudice in the medical community against the use of drugs,' he said. 'Doctors assume that an individual is personally responsible for his/her obesity and all that is required is to reduce food intake, but there are strong physiological mechanisms which do not allow this to happen. During dieting, the brain sends messages to return food intake to previous levels. Drugs can help reprogramme the brain not to do this but they must be taken long-term – as soon as they are stopped, appetite returns to normal.'[28]

Another obestity drug that has made it to market is Abbott's Meridia, an appetite suppressant. This is said to have had 34 deaths associated with it and been suspended in Italy,[29] and calls for its withdrawal can be heard elsewhere.[30] Because it can increase blood pressure and heart rate, it is in any case thought unsuitable for a range of problems people who are overweight often have, such as being at high risk of heart failure and stroke.

Many more drugs are in development, but expectations are frequently dashed. New York company, Regeneron Pharmaceuticals, recently lost more than half its value when it announced a large-scale trial of its lead product, Axokine, had failed to live up to expectations. Axokine is a modified form of a natural protein which signals the brain's 'satiety centre' to cut down on the food intake. Some analysts thought it would be the next obesity drug to reach the market, but the weight loss achieved in 2,000 severely obese people was less than the company had hoped and, in an unexpected complication, many developed antibodies against the protein.[31]

Which leaves Xenical, a drug that blocks fat entering the digestive system, passing it out through stools instead. This is hardly an impressive result from so much research. But it is precisely the unpredictable nature of research that is used to justify the high cost of medicine. Market forces, pharma argues, are perfectly capable of sorting out what is researched and therefore the kind of treatments people receive. Besides, research is hardly wasted and indeed, fat cells are being revealed as dynamic, complex and influential entities that, according to Rob Stein in the *Washington Post*, affect a staggering array of crucial bodily functions.[32]

'Like guardians of a strategic petroleum reserve,' he writes, 'fat coordinates how, when and where the body's energy supply is stored and how and when it is mobilized. Fat also emits signals that can unleash, or damp down, the immune system. Fat influences when blood clots and when blood vessels constrict. Fat even tells the body when it can reproduce, and when it must await more favorable conditions. And perhaps most insidiously, fat cells most likely beget new fat cells, perpetuating their existence and magnifying their effects.'[33]

There seems no limit to the influence of fat. Even if mortals can control its creep on their waistlines, they are defeated in the bigger war defined by Gokhan S. Hotamisligil, a professor of genetics and metabolism at the Harvard School of Public Health, when he says, 'Many people think your brain controls your fat. We promote the idea that your fat controls your brain.'[34]

This much broader and more illuminating picture of fat allows even more new approaches. One is a new gut-hormone replacement therapy, being developed by Merck as a nasal spray. It seems there is a peptide that signals the brain to stop feeling hungry after a meal. It sounds fantastic: one sniff and appetite goes and eating stops. Moreover, it is a natural substance, something the body produces anyway, and therefore is less likely to cause safety problems.

The medicines business deploys enormous ingenuity and spends vast sums developing products like this, while remaining essentially incurious about the psychology of overeating in a culture where anxiety about body image is rampant. The ingenious thing from a drug developer's point of view is to find out how to increase the body's sensitivity to this hormone, not to work out why it no longer responds to its signals. In one study of 12 obese and 12 lean volunteers, the results seemed good; people who had been injected with the hormone ate a third fewer calories than those who hadn't at an all-you-can-eat buffet two hours later. Larger studies are being done but sceptics point out that, as with Axokine, the body may stage its own defence.[35] In the longer term, the effects of this one peptide may well be compensated for by the general network environment in which it operates, in other words.

It may be that commerce really does reflect what people want, but generally there is no way of knowing, since the obese are grateful for anything they're given and no one else thinks about it that much. But pharma's studies only reveal what is asked of them to get a drug approved and then to get it sold. Most drugs have various effects and indeed, the unexpected can form the basis for an entirely new drug, as was precisely the case when the active ingredient in Viagra was being tested in heart patients. Enough of the trialists were so reluctant to stop taking it that further questions were asked.

But generally, the trials are designed with questions that home in on the results a would-be drug is expected to elicit. The relatively new European drugs conglomerate, Sanofi-Aventis, for example, is developing an obesity drug known generically as rimonabant that exploits knowledge of the 'munchies', a side effect of the recreational drug, cannabis. The modus operandi is to stunt activity of the canniboid receptors, thus reducing appetite. Such receptors are found throughout the body, including in the fat cells, and so far, the trial results have been encouraging.

'Data available so far have shown that the product is effective,' said pharmaceutical journalist Ailis Kane in January 2004. 'Almost 40% of patients who received the drug, plus a mildly calorie-reduced diet, experienced a weight loss of up to 20kg, compared with 12.4% on placebo.'[36]

But while everyone was getting excited about these figures, coupled with the drug's apparently good effect on the heart, there were also concerns about the psychological effects of the drug. People do not use cannabis to get the 'munchies'; they do so for the effects on their mind. Nevertheless, no psychometric testing of the drug had then been done. It was simply being called for.

Answers to questions that remain unanswered by tests on rimonabant may come from another source, however. A drug to treat multiple sclerosis and post-operative pain is also in the pipeline and this works in precisely the opposite way, by stimulating a similar set of receptors that rimonabant stunts ('prescription dope', in other words). Data on this drug refers to the same canniboid receptors as rimonabant but the questions asked were very different. Street sellers of cannabis would probably ask their customers another set of questions again, selling as they do the effects of the drug on the mind rather than on appetite or pain awareness.

A further avenue of questioning for anti-obesity research is the idea of a vaccine which can lead to lower appetites, thereby apparently making it easier to follow weight-reducing diets. The idea of therapeutic vaccines for chronic conditions such as obesity and drug addiction is relatively new and involves predisposing the immune system to deal better with conditions that have taken hold rather than the more traditional idea of vaccines, which is to provide protection against conditions we have not yet acquired.

Again, one doesn't have to go far to find well-reasoned scepticism. Dr Bruce Dan, an expert in infectious diseases and a former editor of the *Journal of the American Medical Association*, cautions against the very concept. 'If you are going to try to protect yourself against the cold it is better to buy a fur coat than to change your genetic system to grow hair,' he says. 'When you change your immune reaction, you may be changing it for good.'[37]

Dan introduces the idea that the enormous profit to be earned from anti-obesity agents obscures the fact that maintaining a healthy body weight is arguably not best served by taking drugs. Some say it also obscures the fact it is rather unlikely that our biological mechanisms governing weight have become dysfunctional so suddenly and on such a global scale. The obesity epidemic is relatively new, no more than a generation old at most. Obesity expert, Dr Andrew Prentice of the International Nutrition Group at the London School of Hygiene and Tropical Medicine, suggests the roots lie not in eating too much but in eating food that is too rich. His theory, reported in the *New Scientist*, suggests that the richness of modern food may be to blame. 'The high energy densities of many fast foods challenge human appetite-control systems with conditions for which they were never designed,' he says.[38]

He is saying that such foods trick the body, but how this translates into vastly increased fat stores is anyone's guess. Nevertheless the theory has some credibility given that the average energy density of a burger is about 1,200 kilojoules per 100 grams of food, and the typical energy density of the British diet is around 650kJ/100g. Moreover, Prentice continues, our bodies probably evolved to cope with an energy density of just 450kJ/100g. A constant onslaught of food so dense in energy that the body's self-regulating mechanisms fail to kick in makes some intuitive sense, and is backed by small volunteer studies which show that when people are selected at random and allowed to eat to their heart's content, those fed food with a low-energy density lost weight, and those on high-energy food put on as much as 65 grams of extra fat a day.

Such questions, and millions of others, do not fall within the remit of commercial medicine and are not investigated because our healthcare agenda, following very much the medicines agenda, is not set up that way. The idea is to find drugs that will help us lose weight, not eradicate the root problem. Prentice acknowledges the 'astonishing' progress that has been made in this respect but warns the work will always have its Achilles heel.

'Eating is so essential to our survival that there may be multiple redundancy in the system,' he says. 'If you could block one of these pathways and people stopped eating then in evolutionary terms that would have been a very vulnerable system.'[39] What he is saying is what research is proving: if you block the influence of one thing, something else pops up to compensate.

For too many people, this is not a problem. Where obesity is a source of constant anguish, not eating has become what is essential to survival and any help they can get in that respect is welcomed. Campaigners such as the influential author, Susie Orbach, however, point to much deeper issues driving what she says is a full-scale 'obesity panic', of which our colossal research spend into finding a pharmacological cure is just a symptom.

'Recognizing now that we are as a culture deeply confused about eating and dieting is essential,' she says. 'For many people, food is far from pleasure or a fuel. It is something to be watchful, wary and afraid of. People of so-called normal weight don't turn up in the statistics. They aren't interesting or dramatic.'[40]

They are when they buck the trend, however. And the success of the documentary *Super Size Me* may be because it hit on that gap between the scientific research agenda as presently defined and the public's concerns about the deeper problem. It concerns a young man called Morgan Spurlock who ate nothing but McDonald's for a month while taking the same amount of exercise as the average American. This was folk-science as entertainment that exuberantly ignored the methods of medical research. The process by which science is peer-reviewed by other scientists was non-existent. As for proper controls to eliminate bias, it was unashamedly a one-man show. And the results were as accessible to the general public as regular studies are obscure.

Yet it has arguably done more to highlight the importance of good nutritious food, and therefore more to help show people how to achieve a healthy body weight than all the research to date on anti-obesity drugs.

All the scientists in the world, funded by all the money in the world, cannot perform miracles. They cannot address what food means in people's emotional lives. Nor the fact that obesity exposes class society where the poor are fat and the rich are aspirant, controlled and thin.

Nor even, as Orbach points out, that 'fat is also an economic and psychological issue requiring innovative initiatives.'[41]

All these well-intentioned scientists can do is respond to their line managers, who in turn respond to theirs, and so on. They are all working to pharma rules. The result is the drugs we are offered in the surgery, which are generally taken with very few questions asked about what they cost or where the money goes. If they should be, the answer is partly in obesity research.

3

A question of trust

Pharma's dominance over the global research community is perhaps inevitable given its $70 billion a year spend to find new products. In terms of influencing prescribers and the general public, companies have even more to spend. The rough figure for marketing and administration, according to Marcia Angell's slicing up of pharma's overall spend, is $155 billion a year.

The actual amounts are notional, however, because pharma closely guards the details of its spends, and the line between research and marketing is flexible to say the least. Clinical trials to monitor the safety of drugs already on the market, for example, are usually paid for out of R&D funds but are widely recognized to double up as marketing vehicles because they also introduce drugs to doctors as early as possible in their limited lifespan.

The fact one is dealing with products that are differentiated only by research means the two functions are necessarily connected. To some extent, the research *is* the marketing. When a drug is launched into a crowded market, clinical trials will have been conducted in preparation. Such trials will have been designed with marketing purposes in mind because the important point is to have strong clinical support for a product. Post-marketing studies, conducted after launch, go on to strengthen the marketing platform, on which all subsequent salvos in the fight for a share of the 'noise' are based.

The first thing a drug company must do is build a clinical case, which means designing trials, both pre- and post-approval, to show its product in the best possible light. Dr Richard Smith, when editor of the *British Medical Journal*, highlighted some of pharma's most popular tricks:[1]

- Avoid testing it against another drug because it might compare badly.

- Test it against a small group of rivals, to show it is as good.
- Compare it with too low or too high a dose of another treatment – so the latter is less effective or has side effects.
- Report your trial's results only at the point when it comes out well. Publish the helpful 6-month results but bury the weak 12-month results.
- Conduct your trial across a number of countries, publishing each result separately to suggest that a huge number of trials back your drug.
- Keep republishing positive trials; the others can be buried in an obscure journal.
- Let journals know that you will buy £1million-worth of reprints if they review your product favourably.

And that is only the start of the process. Once you've got the clinical data you want, the idea is to spread the word. *Lancet* editor Dr Richard Horton describes such missions as information-laundering operations. Here's how it works.

> A pharmaceutical company will sponsor a scientific meeting. Speakers will be invited to talk about a product, and they will be paid a hefty fee (several thousand pounds) for doing so. They are chosen for their known views about a particular drug or because they have a reputation for being adaptable in attitude towards the needs of the company paying their fee.
>
> The meeting takes place and the speaker delivers a talk. A pharmaceutical communications company will record this lecture and convert it into an article for publication, usually as part of a collection of papers emanating from the symposium. This collection will be offered to a medical publisher for an amount that can run into hundreds of thousands of pounds.
>
> The publisher will then seek a reputable journal to publish the papers based on the symposium, commonly as a supplement to the main journal.[2]

The important point is that there is very little peer review in a whole raft of journals that pose as science journals. The process whereby other scientists knowledgeable in the field ensure the science is as impervious to bias or distortion as possible, in other words, hardly exists. 'The process of publication has been reduced to marketing dressed up as legitimate science,' says Horton. 'Pharmaceutical companies have found a way to circumvent the protective norms of peer review. In all too many cases, they are able to seed the research literature with weak science that they can then use to promote their products to physicians.'[3]

'We are being hoodwinked by the drug companies,' Smith says. 'The articles come in with doctors' names on them and we often find some of them have little or no idea about what they have written. When we find out, we reject the paper, but it is very difficult. In a sense, we have brought it on ourselves by insisting that any involvement by a drug company should be made explicit. They have just found ways to get round this and go undercover.'[4]

Evidence abounds of such practices. Estimates suggest that almost half of all articles published in journals are by ghostwriters. 'It's cleverness, not wickedness,' Smith adds. 'Nobody's doing anything illegal here – but it's not good science. It puts the pharmaceutical industry's interests ahead of the community's as a whole.'[5]

That science filters down the knowledge chain, being interpreted at every juncture by people with no reason to question pharma's findings. Drug company money effectively pays the wages of everyone writing for healthcare professionals because it buys the ads that make their publications, online and hard copy, viable. The reporting of clinical trials and scientific conferences is coloured at every turn by the general understanding that it is not a good idea to bite the hand that feeds you. Anything too untoward about these powerful patrons gets scant coverage (unless, of course, it is a major scandal such as Vioxx) because that isn't how the system works.

The part played by journalists is central to pharma's marketing teams. As with the doctors, no one is asked to act unethically as such; just to accept fees that are considerably larger than anything else they are likely to be offered. A good science journalist who also knows the industry can expect to earn thousands of pounds, dollars or Euros per project rather than hundreds. The projects vary and are generally seen as perks that bring journalists' salaries more into line with others in the business sector. It is easy money and generally sought after. The job is simplified because journalists are given the information, the angle the story is to be written from, and, if it is for the general public, the case studies and doctors to interview. Often the times to meet and the transport so to do are arranged. The journalist simply strings it all together.

Pharma companies, working through third parties, have been able to influence, if not control, every salient aspect of the healthcare agenda for years, whether it is how drugs are researched or how those results are made known. More recently, it has infiltrated ideas about how illness is perceived in the first place.

Pushing out the boundaries

If it is easy for doctors to be misled (however marginally), it doesn't take much for patterns of disease to follow a direction that leads inexorably to more and more medicine. 'Virtually every variable in a condition lies on a bell-shaped distribution curve,' says Kay-Tee Khaw, professor of clinical gerontology at the University of Cambridge. 'Prevalence of illness in any community reflects the population norms and deciding at what point someone is ill is often arbitrary,' she adds.[6]

Metabolic syndrome, for example, is a relative newcomer to the human anthology of disease. It covers a cluster of common metabolic disorders, such as obesity, abnormal lipid levels and high blood pressure. It is now said to be approaching epidemic levels with no less than 115 million sufferers. Such a syndrome wasn't even recognized before 1988, and each component part is an example of 'disease' being a much more fluid concept than one might have supposed.

The point at which a person is diagnosed as ill can go both up and down on a scale, depending on what is being measured. Cardiovascular disease, for example, is worth hundreds of billions of dollars a year if all the various treatments for high blood pressure, high cholesterol, and every other manifestation of the stress we pile on our hearts are factored in.

According to Marcia Angell, high blood pressure (hypertension) was defined for many years as BP above 140/90. An expert panel then introduced something called prehypertension in 2003, which is between 120/80 and 140/90.[7] 'Overnight, people with blood pressures in this range found they had a medical condition,' she said.[8]

It is the statin sector that illustrates best how the defining markers of disease are fought over to bring in higher sales for particular companies. The statins have been shown in several large-scale studies to prevent heart attacks and save lives. They do this largely by reducing levels of bad LDL cholesterol; the question is, by how much?

Angell points out that the cut-off for high cholesterol has been lowered gradually over the years. 'Once it was reserved for blood cholesterol levels over 280 mm per deciliter,' she says.[9] Then it was lowered to 240. Now most doctors try to knock cholesterol down to below 100.

Companies with aggressive products, like market leader Lipitor, naturally push the idea of 'the lower the better' and would like national LDL treatment targets to be set as low as possible. But others, such as Bristol-Myers Squibb, which markets one of the least potent statins, Pravachol, insist patients glean little incremental benefit by reducing their LDL levels too much.

Doctors, and their patients, are naturally interested if lower really is better. But pharma companies are usually reluctant to pit their drugs against competitors in head-to-head studies, unless they have reason to believe the results would favour their product. The authorities, amazingly, don't insist on such exercises or conduct them at the public's expense, despite the fact that it would save a lot of money in the long run and provide better information about which statin to take, if any at all. But the controversy regarding how low LDL targets should be has deep roots.

Pravachol was among the pioneering studies that helped demonstrate the life-saving capabilities of the statins in the first place. And although its potency is relatively low, this was not then thought to be a problem, for two reasons. One is that most doctors can still vividly recall the withdrawal of Bayer's statin, Baycol, in 2001 because of its potentially fatal muscle-wasting side effect. The second is that doctors are cautious by nature. Baycol was a potent product, and Christopher Cannon, a heart researcher at Brigham and Women's Hospital in Boston, says his research shows doctors typically prescribe statins at doses lower than those used in trials.[10]

Besides, they know that everything in the body has some function. If lower really were better, it would follow that none was better still. Can this really be the case? In an attempt to increase market share and throw some light on the problem, Pfizer sponsored a trial of Lipitor versus Pravachol using a novel technique for measuring the accumulation of disease in the artery walls. Researchers found, not surprisingly, an astonishingly good result for Pfizer. The 251 patients who had been randomly assigned to Lipitor not only had much lower LDL, but also the progression of disease in their arteries was essentially halted. Pravachol patients had higher LDL readings and their disease also continued to progress. 'We are excited that we found a regimen, albeit an intense one, that would stop [heart] disease in its tracks,' said Steven Nissen, medical director of the Cleveland Clinic's cardiovascular coordinating centre, and the principal investigator of the study.[11]

The patients, who were treated for 18 months, all had LDL levels ranging from 125 to 210 before they were treated. At the end of the study, those on Lipitor had levels that averaged out at 79, while those on

Pravachol averaged 110, above the US guideline targets of 100. But the really new perspective came from the before-and-after ultrasound images, from which researchers calculated the effects of the drugs from the volumes of plaque in the examined vessels. These findings show the plaque increased by 2.7% in the Pravachol patients and actually fell by 0.4% in those taking Lipitor. Bristol-Myers Squibb was naturally quick to point out that the images didn't actually prove anything; but to most people, Lipitor won convincingly.

According to the *Wall Street Journal*, Pfizer said it intended to talk to the regulators about whether the findings are sufficient to change its product label so it can add the effect to its marketing programme.[12] If validated in further studies, they could lead experts to lower national LDL for high-risk patients to below the current recommended level of 100.

Then came the PROVE-IT study, the results of which were announced in March 2004. This pitted an 80mg daily dose of Pfizer's Lipitor against a 40mg daily dose of Bristol-Myers Squibb's Pravachol in 4,000 patients who had been hospitalized for either acute heart attacks or unstable angina. This was funded by BMS in an attempt to show that lower was not necessarily better. The BMS drug was designed to reduce LDL cholesterol to 100, which according to US guidelines, is the target level for such patients. In contrast, the high-dose Lipitor was designed to reduce levels to 70, substantially lower than the guidelines. The investigators followed patients for up to 2 years, and noted significant clinical events including overall mortality, heart attacks, unstable angina, the need for revascularization, and stroke incidence. And it did what the trial name suggested, proving among the vast majority of cardiologists that lower really is better.

Exactly a year later, in March 2005, the results of the Treating to New Targets (TNT) study were presented to a 2005 meeting of the American College of Cardiology. This compared an 80mg dose with a 10mg dose of Lipitor in patients with milder heart disease and showed, again, that the more aggressive approach results in better clinical outcomes.

'The aggregate data from PROVE-IT and now TNT greatly help convict even so-called normal LDL cholesterol levels as deleterious and worthy of treatment in secondary prevention,' said Dr Carl Vaughan of University College, Cork, at the meeting. 'The concept of "lower is better" has been strengthened this morning with a call to treat to new targets with LDL cholesterol goals of less than 80.'[13]

In this way, the boundaries of diseases change. In disease areas such as obesity, blood pressure, bone density, depression, pain, the yardsticks are similarly flexible. While not entirely arbitrary, because they must reflect cultural and clinical norms, they are certainly open to commercial influence. In this way, patients become more readily subject to being told they are ill and will need to take a pill for life. Already we have seen the recommended levels of bad cholesterol reduced to ensure more patients take a statin to lower their level. And although the patents that allow monopoly pricing on the statins will run out, a new class of drugs for raising levels of good (H-for-healthy) HDL cholesterol is now being prepared for launch.

Several experts are optimistic the strategy will provide a meaningful next step in therapy. 'The HDL area is very hot right now,' says Nissen of the Cleveland Clinic. 'We're hoping the treatment effect will be similar to the statins. If we could add another reduction [in risk of a heart attack], this would be a spectacular achievement ... The whole area of lipoproteins is inordinately complex, but it is the same with other drugs. What we are counting on is that the beneficial effects outweigh the negative things.'[14]

The drug pushers

Doctors are our main line of defence against an industry that would make us well. London GP Dr Iona Heath, professor of clinical pharmacology Dr David Henry, and journalist Ray Moynihan articulate the mechanics of what they call corporate-backed disease-mongering, which they go on to define as 'widening the boundaries of treatable illness to expand markets for those who sell and deliver treatments'.[15]

Commercially, there is no case to answer, as that is precisely what your shareholders would expect you to do. But the easy alliance that can be struck between doctors, drug companies and patients to achieve this is not necessarily healthy because the central players, the pharma companies, are compelled to constantly expand their markets. They do this by raising public awareness about underdiagnosed and undertreated problems. The methods vary from country to country, but the template remains the same. Companies collaborate with healthcare professionals and concerned patients to establish a consensus in favour of increased medication.

These alliances tend to promote a view of their particular condition as widespread, serious and treatable. Alternative approaches –

> emphasizing the self-limiting or relatively benign natural history of a problem, or the importance of personal coping strategies – are played down or ignored. As the late medical writer Lynn Payer observed, disease mongers 'gnaw away at our self-confidence'.[16]

Pharma cannot help but gnaw away at our sense of wellness because companies are specifically in business to make us better. Increasingly we allow them to set yardsticks that suggest our collective wellness is less than it might be. They will fund patient alliances and work flat out to help us fit in with society, cushion a painful death, even to live a little longer. But their intention, at the end of the day, is to make money. This differs from the intention of the patient (which is to get better) and of the doctor (to help their patients get better). Pharma's natural inclination to put profit before public health has had far deeper consequences for healthcare than simply marginalizing the alternatives.

The real casualty has been the trust patients should be able to enjoy in their doctors. As pharma's marketing spends have accelerated, money has entered the surgery in ways that simply were not possible before. Pharma can therefore be considered a false friend to doctors if its marketing zeal is in any way able to influence the trust patients can have in them. When they are seriously ill a good relationship of trust with a doctor can be priceless.

Doctors are saying loud and clear, through their journals, that many people are using drugs inappropriately. Say Heath, Henry and Moynihan:

> In many cases, the formula is the same. Groups and/or campaigns are orchestrated, funded, and facilitated by corporate interests, often via their PR and marketing infrastructure.
>
> A key strategy of the alliances is to target the news media with stories designed to create fears about the condition or disease and draw attention to the latest treatment. Company-sponsored advisory boards supply the 'independent experts' for these stories, consumer groups provide the 'victims', and PR companies provide media outlets with the positive spin about the latest 'breakthrough' medications.[17]

The scale of pharma means that healthcare priorities are established on the assumption that the interests of the drug companies and the desires of patients are identical. There is considerable overlap, as we have seen, but in important respects, they come into conflict.

The result, say the team, is inappropriate prescribing:

> [This] carries the dangers of unnecessary labelling, poor treatment decisions, iatrogenic illness, economic waste, as well as the opportunity costs that result when resources are diverted away from treating or preventing more serious disease. At a deeper level, it may help to feed unhealthy obsessions with health, obscure or mystify sociological or political explanations for health problems, and focus undue attention on pharmacological, individualized, or privatized solutions. More tangibly and immediately, the costs of new drugs targeted at essentially healthy people are threatening the viability of publicly funded universal health insurance systems.[18]

But, as doctors also know, it is one thing to understand a problem and quite another to be in a position to do anything about it. It is a lot easier to go with the strong current of pharma's marketing operations – as well as the cultural tide – and prescribe indiscriminately.

'Inappropriate prescription of medicines by GPs is of particular concern,' the MPs said in the UK inquiry into the pharma industry, adding that this was partly due to their poor education which 'has meant that too few non-specialists are able to make objective assessments of the merits of drugs and too many seem not to recognise how little is known about the properties of a drug at the time of licensing, particularly about its adverse consequences.'[19]

A far more obvious cause is an observation made further in the report. 'The Department of Health spends around £4.5 million each year on providing independent medicines information to prescribers,' the MPs said. 'In contrast, the [UK industry association] the ABPI told us that around 14% of the industry's expenditure is on promotion and marketing. Spend on information from the Department of Health therefore represents about 0.3% of the approximately £1.65 billion a year that the pharmaceutical industry spends on marketing and promotional efforts.'[20]

A major part of the problem is the pressure companies are under to get drugs out as fast as possible to maximize earnings from their limited lifespan. Competition has intensified hugely over the years, as the length of time a first-in-class drug has exclusivity in the marketplace has fallen. According to US industry association, PhRMA, the first beta-blocker, ICI's Inderal, had nine years of uncontested market presence in the 1960s and 1970s. Lilly, in contrast, had only three years to get Prozac established in the 1980s before other similar drugs moved in. And in the late 1990s, the first Cox-2 inhibitors, Vioxx and Celebrex, were launched within months of each other.

Sales forces, already colossal by any other industry's standards, had to rev up somewhat to meet these challenges. When GlaxoSmithKline launched its asthmatic drug, Advair, in the US in 2001, it was able to pull all its sales forces together to visit 70,000 doctors within the first week.[21]

Companies in the US were now spending around $16 billion a year visiting doctors, a practice more commonly known as detailing, because reps get to run through how the details of how a new drug works and why it is better than anything that went before it.[22] Sales reps aren't cheap; each will cost a pharma company or the organizations they contract out to anything between $160,000 and $200,000 a year once cars and the latest in communications have been factored in.

James Brewer, head of sales force strategy at Lilly, said in 2003 that there were 88,000 reps in the US calling on the same 950,000 doctors. This compares with 55,000 in 1995, a time when there were also more drugs for them to sell. 'Of these, we recognize around 160,000 as being of top value to the industry. The average sales call is only two minutes so the complexity of our business revolves around deriving the most value from these two minutes.'[23]

Rising amounts of money honing in on those two minutes naturally led to new ways of selling drugs. Companies had huge capacities in sales and marketing from the repeated mergers they had been through. With fewer drugs to sell, the in-house sales armies gave way to hired hands who were cheaper because they could be brought in as and when they were necessary, as at a major launch, for example. These hired hands did little else but think of new ways to get the big selling contracts with pharma.

Sales companies became more intimately involved in how diseases are managed. Innovex, for example, one of the top three sales companies in the US, implements and manages nurse adviser programmes for the UK's NHS in an effort to build up business in Europe. It typically targets patients with chronic conditions who are on repeat prescriptions and therefore not often seen by their doctor. If these people can be helped to take their medication on a more regular basis, sales go up. Here compliance with what the doctor says makes good business sense. Deeper questions about the appropriateness of particular treatments are left unconsidered.

Similarly, Innovex's parent company Quintiles, has a European subsidiary that works with Dutch company, Diagnosis for Health, to help increase patient compliance in Germany. 'We try to offer real support to patients and doctors at the point of delivery in areas such as osteoporosis, where everyone benefits,' said Hywel Evans, president of Quintiles Europe.[24]

The largest contract sales companies now pay pharma to sell their drugs for them in return for a cut of the sales revenues. In a deal to sell Lilly's antidepressant, Cymbalta, for example, Quintiles agreed to provide more than 500 sales reps to sell the drug in the US for five years. It also paid Lilly $110 million. In return, Quintiles gets an undisclosed cut of US sales for everything neurological the drug is found to be good at treating for five years and, at a lower percentage, for a further three.[25] Lilly can't lose. The selling company was willing to bet $110 million on getting Cymbalta more widely prescribed.

Doctors usually insist they are impervious to all this selling. Perhaps they are right. Natalie Mizik at Columbia University, New York, and Robert Jacobson at the University of Washington, Seattle, tried to measure how doctors behave under normal sales pressure. They analysed data on visits that had been made to nearly 75,000 family and hospital doctors and on the prescriptions they wrote for three drugs over a two-year period. What we don't know is which drugs they were, an important factor since competition is much more marked with some drugs than others. Nevertheless, the value of those two minutes in face-to-face contact with the doctor is underlined.

To persuade doctors to write one extra prescription for a drug, the researchers showed sales reps had to make 0.6, 3.1 and 6.5 extra visits respectively. This may not be a brilliant ratio, but it shows, once again, how the dimensions of the medicines business make the most marginal of benefits worth chasing. Marketing executives may reason, for example, that even though it takes 6.5 visits for each new prescription, that will be followed by around three refills, each providing upwards of $50 profit, says fellow-researcher, Puneet Manchanda from the University of Chicago. The sales rep may also have promoted two or three other drugs in that same visit. And for these three drugs in the study, each visit increased their market share with the doctor by 6–11%. 'If I were a marketing executive, I would be ecstatic,' says Manchanda.[26]

Doctors, as one might expect, have reacted by being more protective of their time. Younger ones, keen not to be seen too close to the source of distrust, are even campaigning against doctors accepting any gifts. But their more established colleagues are in a tight spot because, like everyone else, they like to maximize their earnings. Dr Neal Moser, a pulmonary and critical care physician with a 13-doctor group practice in

Edgewood, Kentucky, for example, has made it known he sees nothing wrong in accepting $50 for listening to a short sales pitch from a drug rep in his office. This is the deal offered by Time-Concepts LLC, one of several companies that have moved in to ease the strain on that two-minute window.

The company receives $105 from a drug company each time it gets a rep in the office: $50 goes to the doctor, $50 it keeps, and $5 goes to a charity the doctor gets to select. Moser says the plan lets him control when and how he talks to sales reps and that the fee barely covers the cost of this time.[27] The trouble is, it goes against the rules of professional associations across the world. The American Medical Association (AMA), like its British counterpart, the BMA, prevents doctors accepting cash payments on the grounds that it is likely to distort their best medical judgement. Gifts are fine, if they cost under $100 and help in some professional capacity.

Such companies are upfront about their business and they are allowed to carry on. So, money enters the surgery. Dr Frank Riddick, chairman of the AMA's council on ethical and judicial affairs, sounds almost quaint when he says, 'If the purpose of the contact is to educate the physician, then there is no need to pay the physician.'[28]

However much everyone (including doctors) may agree with him, it takes no account of the fact that doctors are keen to be paid by pharma companies who, in turn, are usually more than willing to pay whatever it takes to get just two minutes of their undivided attention. Commercial realities usually win out.

Bring on the celebrities

There are also strict rules about what can and cannot be said about drugs to the general public, even in the US where the industry can communicate more openly with people than in Europe. But these rules, like those governing doctors' freedom to benefit financially from drug companies and those deciding the boundaries of disease, are flexible.

And the social and cultural norms they must reflect all seem to be going pharma's way. When the UK's health minister, Lord Warner, was asked by MPs in the 2004 House of Commons enquiry if he thought diseases were being created to sell more pills, he said social forces rather than clever marketing people were the main factor driving up the drugs bill. 'As a citizen and a father, sometimes we do wish to put labels on things which are part and parcel of the human condition,' he said. 'There is no one person [in government] saying that at all costs we have to have a pharmacological solution to this health problem. I would say that the arguments are the other way round, that people are being encouraged to take charge of their own health.'[29]

The use of celebrities to endorse drugs is a good example of how the rules are being stretched to embrace social norms, because it is a practice that is almost impossible to police. Where it has been policed, it has not been by the FDA. The fact that stars were being paid to discuss drugs on TV was exposed in the *New York Times*, prompting the US TV networks to draw up ethical guidelines to safeguard editorial integrity.

Millions of viewers had seen actress Kathleen Turner on CNN and ABC, for example, talking about her rheumatoid arthritis and recommending an information website. What they couldn't have known was the funding both she and the website took was from Immunex, the maker of the arthritis drug Enbrel. And when Lauren Bacall chatted about a friend who had gone blind from macular degeneration and been helped by Visudyne, she didn't think to mention that Novartis, the drug's manufacturer, had paid her a fee.

The extent of the fees is closely guarded information, but they are thought to be in the millions. The money spent has a global reach. When Pelé gave interviews in the UK encouraging men to discuss their sexual problems with their partners, his contract with Pfizer was in no way made explicit. 'Nor were readers of the sports pages told that the cricketer Shane Warne had been paid a reported £80,000 by the makers of Nicorette during his well-publicized attempt to stop smoking,' says journalist David Rowan. 'No wonder he was furious when a fan photographed him at a one-day match holding a cigarette.'[30]

Celebrity endorsement of drugs flourishes on both sides of the Atlantic, with the stars increasingly being marked out by the drugs they take. Kirk Douglas, Pierce Brosnan and Angela Bassett are all reported to take Bristol-Myers Squibb's statin, Pravachol. Wyeth has used singer Patti LaBelle to promote Prempro hormone replacement therapy and engaged musical comedy stars Debbie Reynolds and Rita Moreno to urge women to have bone-density tests. Former Republican presidential candidate Bob Dole as well as Pelé have both promoted Pfizer's Viagra.

The practice grows because it works. Skater Dorothy Hamill's appearance in TV and print ads for Vioxx had such an impact on Merck, that the company extended her contract with an extensive new set of commercials. 'Patients are said to be going to the doctors asking for "that drug Dorothy Hamill uses",' said pharmaceutical journalist Daniel B.

Moskowitz back in 2003, before the drug was withdrawn. Then, Merck was spending more than $150 million a year on its Vioxx ads, more than was spent advertising household names such as Pepsi-Cola or Budweiser, also just in the US.[31]

The success of celebrity endorsement does much to reveal the real power of an advertising budget and rules need be no obstacle. If anything they are a boost, says Barry Greenberg, chairman of LA-based Celebrity Connections, who is regularly asked to find big-name faces to fit drugs or ailments:

> Where you have restrictions on advertising, as in Britain, someone going on a chat show becomes a much more precious commodity for the pharmaceutical company. The message from the celebrity gets out there – 'I've got this terrible problem, go see your doctor to make sure you don't have it.'[32]

The problem with irritable bowels

As one can imagine, some categories are harder to fill than others. It is one thing to tell your adoring public that you take a statin as part of a glamorous early-morning routine. It is quite another admitting to the symptoms of either irritable bowel syndrome or urinary stress incontinence. Without celebrity endorsement, companies must fall back on their more traditional approach to medical education.

This is how drug companies describe the process of giving something like irritable bowel syndrome (IBS) the global makeover it has had in recent years. According to a leaked document from medical communications company, In Vivo, GlaxoSmithKline led a medical education programme in Australia as part of its marketing strategy for Lotronex, a drug designed to treat such a common dysfunction. 'IBS must be established in the minds of doctors as a significant and discrete disease state,' it said. Patients also 'need to be convinced that IBS is a common and recognized medical disorder.'[33]

The first step of the strategy was to set up an advisory board with one key opinion leader from each state of Australia. The job of this doctor would be to provide advice to the corporate sponsors on current opinion in gastroenterology and on 'opportunities for shaping it'. Further work included developing 'best practice guidelines' for diagnosing and managing IBS, and attending overseas meetings.

As it happens, Lotronex never made it onto the market. But the modus operandi is the same wherever a new drug is to be launched.

Once it is on the market, PR companies take over with briefs that vary depending on whether it is a first-in-class or one of many.

Their job is about building relationships with doctors and patients. Specifically, it is to change behaviour in favour of their client's drug. When PR firms are asked to account for their retainers, this change is one of the measures on which their performance is assessed. With doctors, it is to show extra prescriptions, and with patients, more people coming to the surgery for help. Good PR agents work their global media contacts to show real people, but preferably celebs, managing a certain set of 'normal' symptoms with drugs. The ethical concerns are easily put to one side, if only because the practices are so widespread and the issues so complex to assess.

Osteoporosis is a classic example of how corporations have changed the way populations think about disease, in this case about bone loss. According to Heath, Henry and Moynihan:

> Drug companies have sponsored meetings where the disease was being defined, funded studies of therapies, and developed extensive financial ties with leading researchers. They have funded patient groups, disease foundations, and advertising campaigns (on both drug and disease) targeted at doctors, and have sponsored osteoporosis media awards, offering lucrative prizes to journalists.[34]

It is no surprise drugs have such a dominant role in healthcare. Therapy, exercise, diet and, of course, their rival of old, the body's natural intelligence, are no match in a commercial environment where the rules can so easily adapt to accommodate the pharmacological route. This is despite the fact that conceiving osteoporosis, for example, as a disease is ethically complex.

Slowing bone loss does reduce the risk of fracture, just as lowering blood pressure reduces the chances of a heart attack. But for most healthy people, the risks of serious fractures are low to distant, and in absolute terms, you have to take the drugs for several years to show the slightest drop in risk. In one placebo-controlled trial in which the drug generically known as alendronate was taken by women for four years, there was a relative reduction in risk of 44% and an absolute fall of just 1.7%.[35] The relative drop was large because the risk was so low in the first place.

Consider this notion of relativity in real figures, where a group of 100 randomly selected people has, say, two who have something wrong with them. The idea behind medicines is to improve the lot of these two by treating the whole group, often for several years. If one of these two people recovers in some important respect, the effect of the drug can be said to improve the health of the population by 50% in that one thing that was being measured. The downside in terms of adverse effects (including the psychological toll of thinking something is wrong when it is actually normal) and the sheer expense of it all are given far less prominence.

Because patients who want drugs are ideal champions, they are used as spokespeople for their condition and given funding by pharma companies. The morbid alliance to expand awareness of a condition is now complete. A press release issued by Osteoporosis Australia, a medical foundation which receives pharma money, portrays this condition as a silent thief. 'If you're not vigilant, it can sneak up on you and snatch your quality of life and your long-term health,' it said.

Women are thus encouraged to have their bone densities checked out and, using controversial diagnostic criteria, are tested against people younger than themselves. 'Against a background of controversy over disease definition, poor predictive value of bone density measurement, and heavily advertised expensive therapies offering marginal benefits to menopausal women, corporate backed promotional activities are attempting to persuade millions of healthy women worldwide that they are sick.'[36]

It seems that no matter what rules are put in place to curb their marketing zeal, company influence is excessive and contrary to the public good. This was the view of a recent UK parliamentary committee investigation into the influence of the industry:

> A distortion in the balance between industry and public interests can be seen as inappropriate not by breaching any law but because the very excess might be a destabilizing influence and put patients at risk.[37]

It's official. Big pharma is bad for our health.

Crucially, it is only the scale that is bad. Years of refuge in healthcare systems led more by prestige and profit than anything that truly nurtures a robust sense of public health, has nurtured blind spots whereby people are unable to see the billions of dollars at stake in the promise of a treatment for irritable bowels or osteoporosis; they only hear the promise. It is not at all obvious how those billions are deployed building up a market for these treatments, or any other: we don't see the enormous effort that goes into bringing symptoms out of the closet, packaging them up, giving them a name, making them real and, finally, treatable. By this time, the effectiveness of the treatment hardly matters. We don't see how we pay for the most marginal of benefits.

We are largely blind, taking treatments on trust they are good, on trust it is money well spent, on trust any profits are put into further important medical research. If pushed, most of us are grateful there are things out there we can take because, in truth, it is hard staying healthy in today's attention-deficit society.

4

Old pills in new bottles

Pharma has various way of stretching out the mileage of its medicines. One is to make them available in more therapeutic markets. How it does this shows just how formidable a rival the body's natural intelligence is. So formidable, in fact, pharma companies have devised ways to get it to work on their behalf.

One of the most basic ground rules of the medicines business is that a drug must show some gain over an inert drug with no active ingredient to get a licence. All regulatory frameworks insist that once a would-be drug has been shown to be safe, it must be able to demonstrate its progress through the obstacle course of the body. It must be shown that it can be absorbed into the bloodstream, stay around long enough to have an effect, and be as clean as possible in the sense of only affecting the intended site. Each task in itself is a pharmacological feat that, as we know, can translate the slightest advantages into new billion-dollar revenue streams.

More streams become apparent when a drug moves into clinical trials. Here, it must be shown that the drug has a significantly positive effect on people who take it when compared to an identical group who do not, in at least two controlled studies. These large-scale Phase III trials often cost millions of dollars and must consist of at least two arms: one of people who are given the test drug, and a second group who act as a means of comparison. This second group is given a placebo, a sugar pill with no powers other than those evoked through the power of suggestion. Although the placebo effect is certainly not equivalent to natural intelligence, it shows what the mind and body are capable of in the absence of real drugs but with the expectation of benefit, as we shall see.

Potential participants are filtered through various entry criteria such as age, severity of disease, and so on. Finally, individuals are selected at random from the filtered groups of types, and the trial begins. It can be conducted in a single hospital or in a network of clinical centres around the world. It can last weeks, months or years. There can be a handful of people in each arm or there can be thousands. The most important thing is that no one, neither doctor nor patient, knows who is taking the drug and who is not. It must be double-blinded, in other words. The idea is to eliminate all possible sources of bias in showing whether or not a drug is any good.

The placebo, despite containing no active ingredient, often proves a surprisingly strong contender. Its performance in clinical trial after clinical trial shows patients inherently possess vast amounts of untapped healing power. They want to be well so much their bodies respond to the mere expectation that they will be. These hopes are easily exploited by pharma companies when they want to extend the reach of a drug, increasing the number of conditions the single drug is used to treat.

In this sense, it is important to understand that, at root, medicines are packaged science. The package, or label, plus what the doctor tells them, is all that most people get to hear about and respond to. Where the SSRI antidepressant drugs are concerned, the label can say almost whatever you want it to say. It could be for painful periods, for depression, to stop smoking, to become more engaged in the world, for panic attacks, irritable bowels, incontinence, shyness, for virtually anything that has some kind of anxiety at its root.

The active ingredient can be the same, but its effect will depend on what it is being tested for. If it has been shown in a trial to treat irritable bowels or help smoking cessation, and it has been approved by the regulators for that indication, then that is what it will say on the label and that is how patients respond.

The drugs work according to what the label says, what the doctor says, and what we believe. Our minds and bodies respond, in other words, to what the label says, to what we are told the drug will do. GlaxoSmithKline's Zyban for smoking cessation, for example, is a long-acting form of Wellbutrin for depression by another name. And Organon's antidepressant, Zispin, is also marketed for sleeping disorders, one of the top symptoms in diagnosing depression. Many lifestyle drugs are prescribed under a number of different names. Different studies are done to get different licensing data to get them known as different drugs so they can operate in different therapeutic markets.

The active ingredient, however, remains the same. As such, the various effects the drugs have can be put down to the response elicited from expectation. What makes a smoker more likely to kick their habit on Zyban than on the identical drug posing as an antidepressant is the fact that this is what the doctor says, what the label says, and what the data from clinical studies corroborate.

Such drugs are a triumph of branding. A single compound provides the basis for various therapies. Packages of symptoms that might otherwise be interpreted as fairly normal in the kind of fast, attention-deficit world we live in, become new ways by which we can express an angst that seems to have no limits and which no amount of research seems able to resolve.

Although few new drugs are being produced, the drugs bill steadily soars because morbid messages are being constructed around a broad generic conviction people have that there must be something wrong with them. With little resistance from regulators, payers and patients, drug treatments for depression and associated mental health problems are free to proliferate, becoming ever more differentiated even as the underlying chemistry remains the same.

And it is not only drug companies who benefit from this general understanding that we could all be a lot healthier. Most natural forms of healing are thought to work largely because they evoke a placebo response through the trust patients have in the treatment, the practitioner, or both.

Pharma stands accused, however, of actively trying to get people to internalize morbid messages that suggest they are ill. 'The way to sell drugs is to sell psychiatric sickness. If you are Paxil and you are the only manufacturer who has the drug for social anxiety disorder, it's in your interest to broaden the category as far as possible and make the borders as fuzzy as possible,' said US bioethicist Carl Elliott.[1] Barry Brand, Paxil's product director, told the journal *Advertising Age* that the company GlaxoSmithKline had been largely successful in this respect. 'Every marketer's dream is to find an unidentified or unknown market and develop it. That's what we were able to do with social anxiety disorder.'[2]

Cultural aspects of disease

As people age and as more research dollars are poured into the mysterious workings of our mind, a rapidly growing range of conditions is being developed that, ostensibly at least, can be dealt with pharmacologically. But these conditions, John Horgan says in his book, *The Undiscovered Mind*, do little more than reflect the culture we live in.

> Diagnosing mental illness is difficult; what appears to be depression to one psychiatrist might be diagnosed by another as schizophrenia, manic depression, or just ordinary grief. Therapists disagree, to put it mildly, over how a given disorder should be defined and even over what should be considered a disorder.[3]

These differences prompted the American Psychiatric Association (APA) to publish the first volume of its bible, the *Diagnostic and Statistical Manual of Mental Disorders* (commonly known as the DSM), in 1952. But although it was generated by teams of psychiatrists whose judgements are supposed to reflect the consensus of the profession, Horgan says the process highlights rather than eliminates the subjective nature of psychiatric diagnosis.

The number of official disorders surged from 106 in the third volume, DSM-III, when published in 1980, to more than 300 in the fourth, DSM-IV, in 1994. The new categories include attention-deficit disorder (ADD), antisocial personality disorder (impulsivity or failure to plan ahead), dissociative fugue (an overwhelming urge to travel away from home or one's customary place of work) and many other things most of us will have experienced at some time or other. Moreover, the fourth edition makes no mention of hysteria or neurosis, those two staples of Freudian psychology, nor of homosexuality, which had been listed as a pathology until gay activists took action to have it deleted.

The process of getting a new condition recognized by inclusion in the DSM also has no formal safeguards to prevent researchers with drug company ties from being involved with decisions that benefit their sponsors. 'The committee that recommended the generalized anxiety disorder (GAD) entry in 1980, for example, was headed by Robert L. Spitzer of the New York state psychiatric institute, which has been a leading recipient of industry grants to research drug treatments for anxiety disorders,' journalist Brendan I. Koerner alleged in a national newspaper.[4]

Lax controls coupled with huge potential financial gain from lifestyle diseases led US attorney Richard Scruggs to take on Swiss drug company Novartis a few years ago for allegedly inventing the condition ADD. This was a serious charge, alleging the manufacturer of the then top-selling ADD drug, Ritalin, had conspired with the APA to package up common behavioural traits – such as being unable to concentrate for long on everyday tasks – and define them as a single disorder with an official entry in the DSM. The conspiracy was compounded, Scruggs maintained, when the California advocacy group, Children and Adults with Attention-Deficit Disorder (CHADD), was lured in with a $748,000 donation to help publicize the condition.

Scruggs had already earned his law firm $1 billion in 1998 for forcing the tobacco industry to accept responsibility for the ill effects of smoking and believed he could do the same with pharma. Under California's business and professional code, profits can be forfeited and fines ordered if companies are found to have misled the public. This is what had brought down the tobacco giants.

ADD and its close cousin, attention-deficit hyperactivity disorder (ADHD) are conditions for which amfetamines had been found to work (it is thought) by speeding up children's nervous systems to the point where their natural calming-down mechanisms kick in. But the sharp rise in the number of children (mainly boys) with ADD – a sevenfold increase over the 1990s and now the fastest growing mental condition in adults – had convinced him of a perverse dynamic that both treats and perpetuates the illness at the same time. At a conservative estimate, 15% of all US school children (usually boys) now take amfetamine (speed) on a regular basis. The comparative figure in the UK is around 5–10%, although many feel the condition is seriously under-diagnosed. Moreover, although new non-amfetamine-based ADD drugs have since been produced, a significant minority of children are on mind-altering drugs with the goodwill of every authority figure they could know: their parents, teachers, social workers and doctors.

Medicating so many children has been the subject of intense debate in the media for years – not as to whether the condition actually exists because that is clear, but how it is so many kids can have trouble engaging with the world. The courts found there was no single cause. If Scruggs had won he would have had access to a slice of the profits in a soaring billion-dollar ADD market. But there was no case to answer. All Novartis had done, said the judge, was produce a drug doctors prescribe, parents and teachers want, and children apparently need. Aside from shareholders in Novartis and other pharma players maybe no one felt relief more keenly than parents whose children are on ADD medication. In an attention-deficit world, in which concentration and any real engagement with the world are the casualties, it can be helpful to have something to take, although most parents would be the first to admit that drugs are hardly ideal.

The dynamic that Scruggs identified may well exist but, as the judge ruled, it didn't *cause* the condition of ADD. That same dynamic is evident in many of the anxiety-based conditions that are being treated with the SSRIs, where even the regulators disagree about the value of the treatments. When, in March 2005, Forest Laboratories received a second refusal from the FDA to extend the use of its SSRI Lexapro beyond its original indication, GAD, into social anxiety and panic disorder, it can't have been much comfort to know that in Europe, the same drug (this time licensed to Lundbeck) could be marketed for panic and social disorders but not GAD. These decisions are taken, it must be presumed, on the same data. Yet the US and Europe managed somehow to arrive at diametrically opposed conclusions.[5]

While GAD, like ADD, can make life hell for sufferers and those around them, there is ample evidence that the ready availability of treatment can raise the numbers of people who suffer from it. When the FDA approved Paxil (Seroxat in the UK) as the first treatment for it on 16 April 2001, very little was known about GAD. According to a 1989 study, as few as 1.2% of the US population merited the diagnosis in any given year.

Koerner points out how, at around the same time as GlaxoSmithKline launched the first treatment for GAD, local news reports around the US were saying as many as 10 million Americans were suffering from an unrecognized disease. 'Viewers were urged to watch for the symptoms: restlessness, fatigue, irritability, muscle tension, nausea, diarrhoea, sweating, and others,' he said, describing a classic case study of the template mentioned in the previous chapter.

> On April 16 – the date of Paxil's approval – a patient group called Freedom from Fear released a telephone survey which revealed that 'people with GAD spend nearly 40 hours per week, or a "full-time job", worrying'. The survey mentioned neither GlaxoSmithKline nor Paxil, but the press contact listed was an account executive at Cohn & Wolfe, the drugmaker's PR firm.[6]

Meanwhile, as apparent evidence mounted from several studies conducted by pharma into their SSRIs, doctors started prescribing them for things beyond their licensing indications. Horton, of the *Lancet*, told the UK House of Commons committee, how so-called off-label use is driven.

> Companies have been very clever at seeding the literature with ghost-written editorials and review papers that promote off-label use of these drugs. You can dress up in an academic argument about 'would this drug X be quite useful for this condition; why?' and have an interesting debate about that. What it does in the mind of the prescriber is to think: 'Hah, this patient with this condition, perhaps I will try it.' It's an off-label use and that is how you had 2.5 million scrips a couple of years ago for SSRIs in the under-18s [in the UK] with no licensed indication for it.[7]

And Dr Jay Pomerantz of Harvard University adds:

> If what we are seeing is a pattern of widespread antidepressant prescribing for subsyndromal, amorphous, patient complaints, it suggests antidepressants have become the modern-day sugar pill, or placebo ... [if this is the case], taxpayers are paying the pharmaceutical industry a mighty high price for fool's gold.[8]

The problems people face are real enough and drugs certainly help, because otherwise, why would they be taken? Because the cause of the stress is inevitably sidelined, it is hard to escape from the cycle of paying drug companies to make inherently unhappy lifestyles more bearable. Those lifestyles continue to make us unwell, drug companies continue to make money, and so it goes on.

Weakening the opposition

The placebo effect is directly related to trust. Good doctors, who have the complete confidence of their patients, exert a placebo effect in how they listen and their general ability to convince patients they are being taken seriously. If patients believe a medicine will work, so the placebo effect of that drug is enhanced. The US writer Norman Cousins, who famously recovered from an incurable disease himself and wrote the delightful book, *Anatomy of an Illness as Perceived by the Patient* as a result, cites an experiment into the role of doctors. 'Patients with bleeding ulcers were divided into two groups,' he says.

> Members of the first group were informed by the doctor that a new drug had just been developed that would undoubtedly produce relief. The second group was told by nurses that a new experimental drug would be administered, but that very little was known about its effects. 70% of the people in the first group received sufficient relief

> from their ulcers. Only 25% of the patients in the second group experienced similar benefit. Both groups had been given the identical 'drug' – a placebo.[9]

But even if you trust your doctor profoundly, belief is fairly useless against killer bugs and viruses that wreak their havoc regardless. Nonetheless, the effects are broad. Cousins also cites the late Dr Henry K. Beecher, an anaesthesiologist at Harvard, who analysed the results of 15 studies involving 1,082 patients. He discovered that across the broad spectrum of these tests, more than a third (35%) of the patients consistently experienced 'satisfactory relief' when placebos were used instead of regular medication. The medical problems included severe post-operative wound pain, seasickness, headaches, coughs and anxiety. Other biological processes known to be affected by placebos include rheumatoid and degenerative arthritis, blood-cell count, respiratory rates, vasomotor function, peptic ulcers, hay fever, hypertension and spontaneous remission of warts.[10]

How the placebo works is the subject of endless discussion. American medical writer Berton Rouché wrote an article for *New Yorker* magazine in 1960 in which he said the placebo derives its power from the 'infinite capacity of the human mind for self-deception'.[11] Others believe the placebo is powerful not because it tricks the mind of the patient, but because, as Cousins himself says, it translates the will to live into a physical reality. 'The fact that a placebo will have no physiological effect if the patient knows it is a placebo only confirms something about the capacity of the human body to transform hope into tangible and essential biochemical change.'[12]

However it is explained, the placebo effect is a real headache for drug developers. And it is so effective in some conditions that companies go to some lengths to bar from clinical trials people who respond well, providing another example of how trial results can be skewed in favour of sickness.

Consider the dilemma facing pharma. In clinical trials for depression, people taking Prozac improved on average by 8.3 percentage points on a standard scale that quantifies the severity of the disease. Those on the placebo arm, however, also did well, improving by 7.34 points. People on Paxil/Seroxat improved by 9.88 points, and the placebo arm by 6.67 points. The scores for Zoloft were 9.96 (placebo, 7.93); Effexor, 11.54 (placebo, 8.38); Celexa, 9.69 (placebo, 7.71).[13]

The poor show is replicated in study after study. A couple of years ago, for example, a $6 million study found the herbal remedy St John's Wort was less effective than a placebo, apparently as a vindication of conventional medicine. While the herb had managed to help only 24% of cases of moderate to severe depression, the placebo scored 32%. It later emerged that Zoloft was also part of the trial and had helped 25%.[14]

The clinical difference is not that impressive – and it is getting worse. 'Somewhere between 30% and 50% of patients in depression trials get better when given fake pills,' says Leila Abboud in the *Wall Street Journal*, 'and that number has increased and become more volatile over time, making it more difficult to prove that a drug works. In comparison, only about half of patients taking antidepressants find their symptoms relieved by 50% or better.'[15]

Timothy Walsh, a psychiatrist at Columbia University, confirms that a higher percentage of depressed patients get better on placebos than 20 years ago.[16] Moreover, he suggests this is largely down to rising expectations from the public about what drugs can do, providing yet another illustration of the exquisite expectation-management corner pharma has driven itself into.

The answer has been to attack the placebo. Pfizer's Dr Earl Giller, executive director of central nervous system (CNS) drug development, told journalist Ailis Kane that what we call the placebo effect may hide improvements that come naturally through the course of the disease. 'The placebo effect could be the waxing and waning of symptoms of depression.'[17]

Rather than learn what this strong placebo response is telling us, Dr Ken Borow, CEO and president of the clinical outsourcing company, Covalent, suggests companies should design criteria to exclude susceptible patients.[18] But these criteria are published and will have an effect on the eventual market success of the product.

Two companies, Lilly and Pfizer, have therefore stumped up $1 million (not a lot of money in the scheme of things) to fund scientists at the University of California, Los Angeles (UCLA), to investigate how people who respond most to placebos might be isolated.[19] That means finding stricter criteria that can be used across the board as the conditions of entry into a clinical trial for depression. The latest brain-imaging technology can help researchers see what happens when people take either a placebo or the active drug. Specifically, researchers are looking for signs that are shared by the placebo responders. Then they want to find markers that show these people are not quite so depressed and can therefore, so the thinking goes, be eliminated from the trials.

Psychiatrist Andrew Leuchter, vice-chairman of UCLA's Department of Psychiatry and Biobehavioural Sciences, who is leading one of the studies, believes that placebo responders, although they appear just as sad as other patients, actually have less severe symptoms. Tests related to sleep and mental agility, he says, may be able to pick them out.[20]

Pfizer is also working on another tack by exploring whether the placebo responders have different DNA in areas of the genome that are linked to depression. All this work to pick out the really depressed from the mildly depressed is all very well, except that it must also make the trial results less convincing. Kay Dickersin, a Brown University professor who teaches courses on clinical trials, says such practices 'allow bias to enter' and constitute a subtle manipulation of trial results.[21] Certainly, making the trials more restrictive would make the test subjects less representative of the depressed people who actually show up in doctors' surgeries seeking treatment.

Nevertheless, selective enrolment strategies are high up pharma's agenda for all sorts of reasons that are to do with convenience and efficiency for the companies and, by definition, have the effect of making medicines less applicable to the very people they are designed to treat.

From the companies' perspective, removing the placebo effect would make it easier and cheaper to make decisions about the potential profitability of a drug and whether it should go on to Phase III development.

Borow makes a convincing commercial case:

> It could allow you to get the same statistical information, but be able to do it with less patients and to have tighter data, so you can more comfortably make the conclusion of difference. And you can do it for less money, because you have a smaller study or set of studies.[22]

But all this effort to control the placebo effect also obscures what can be learned about how our own healing mechanisms are triggered. Even the meagre knowledge about the placebo effect that has emanated now it has profit potential is deeply disputed. Dr Helen Mayberg, professor of psychiatry and neurology at the University of Toronto, has also observed the placebo effect in brain scans but arrives at very different conclusions to Leuchter. Ailis, acknowledging their results cannot be directly compared, says, 'Nevertheless, the differing conclusions regarding drug and placebo responders – Leuchter showing different patterns and Mayberg showing similar ones – illustrate the complexity of the brain and our deficit in knowledge.'[23]

According to Cousins:

> The placebo is not so much a pill as a process. The process begins with the patient's confidence in the doctor and extends through to the full functioning of his own immunological and healing system. The process works not because of any magic in the tablet but because the human body is its own best apothecary and because the most successful prescriptions are those filled by the body itself.[24]

Two for the price of one

Pharmacological chemists can exploit the placebo effect by using it to treat a whole range of new disease areas, as we have seen, or as a boost to the performance of their regular drugs. But they can't use it in any other way, both because it is impossible to measure, and because their job is to make drugs, not to suggest that this endeavour – which is also their livelihood – may not be strictly necessary.

To keep revenues coming in, companies must either sell more aggressively or make their medicines more attractive in some way. The truth is that convenience is another word for novelty these days, and pharma has a lot more tricks up its sleeve to make its products more marketable.

One of the latest new ways has been to package up two medications, enabling patients to make a two-pronged attack on a condition with just one once-a-day pill. Pfizer's Caduet, a mixture of Lipitor and its second-bestselling drug, the blood-pressure medicine Norvasc, does just this.

The combinations usually come with new patents that protect them from copycats long after the individual ingredients have lost their legal protection. In the case of Caduet, the salient facts facing Pfizer were that the patent on Norvasc expires during 2007, whereupon the company can expect to lose most of the $4 billion-plus the drug brings in each year. Meanwhile, two of Lipitor's chief rivals, Zocor and Pravachol, will become available either as generics or over-the-counter (either way, their prices will drop significantly) long before the patent on Lipitor is due to expire in 2011. Caduet's patent looks strong right through to 2018 and will be helpful in maintaining Lipitor's wide appeal in the face of all this cheap competition.

The gold standard in this new marketing strategy is GlaxoSmithKline's Advair, an inhaler that administers two asthma drugs, Flovent and Serevent, in a single dose, a ploy that brought in sales of an estimated $2 billion in 2003, less than three years after the combination was introduced. Other examples include Lilly's Zyprexa and Prozac to produce Symbyax for depression, and Novartis's Lotensin and Norvasc to create the new hypertensive, Lotrel.

Scott Hensley, a *Wall Street Journal* writer, has claimed:

> With their laboratories sputtering, almost every major drug company is mixing current or faded blockbusters to help fill the product gap. The strategy aims to blunt generic competition, create a new buzz for mature brands and enhance the chances that patients will stick with their prescription.[25]

With minimal risks and much less mandatory clinical testing compared with developing a new drug from scratch, the financial case is sound. Combination drugs can also be useful in introducing patients to new brands via old loyalties. One currently in development, combining Lipitor with one of the first experimental drugs to raise good cholesterol, torcetrapib, shows more clearly how such a strategy benefits the manufacturer rather than either the patient or the public purse. Despite the fact that studies have shown that torcetrapib can raise levels of good cholesterol, Pfizer has said it will only be studied in combination with Lipitor. Curiously, the FDA has not objected.

If the agency is presented only with data on the combination, doctors have pointed out, no one will know how torcetrapib works on its own. They will be unable to prescribe the new agent with any other statin, or even with generic Lipitor, when it becomes available.

Dr Jerry Avron has addressed this in the *New England Journal of Medicine*:

> Normally, antitrust laws would prohibit a manufacturer from offering a drug only when 'bundled' with another one of its products. It appears that Pfizer will avoid such antitrust prohibitions by having the FDA do its bundling for it. The FDA's acceptance of the proposed trial designs in effect acknowledges that since the new drug is Pfizer's intellectual property, the company's research plans are subject only to its own corporate prerogative.[26]

The price of innovation

All industries thrive on novelty; the differences with pharma are that, first, the degree of novelty can be well disguised, and second, its value bears little relationship to price. There are no stipulations in the licensing of a drug about the degree of innovation. And the rules by which science comes to be owned are by no means clear-cut. Patent decisions are often worth billions of dollars and are endlessly fought over, not by the public as such, but by the forces of competition.

Patents involve complex science and complex legislation, and are ultimately governed by politicians who, most of all, want to please everyone. Most countries operate a system whereby, in return for revealing all about the invention in question, society grants the inventor a monopoly on its use for a limited period, usually around 20 years. The idea is to protect intellectual property in the same way that copyright laws protect the creative works of artists. The trouble is that the world of knowledge is much harder to follow and infinitely more lucrative to represent than whether or not the structure of a few sentences or chords has been lifted.

The stipulation is that inventions must be novel, useful and not obvious. From a public health point of view, there are problems from the start. The first thing to grasp about the medicines business is not how patents maintain high prices but that they determine what is researched in the first place. Old, natural and obvious things, such as safe drugs that have been around for years, broccoli, walking sticks, or vitamins, for example, don't get patented and there is therefore little incentive to deepen our understanding of their benefits, except in the dwindling public health sector.

Moreover, most patent laws do not insist that inventions be significant advances in any way, only that they are novel, useful and not obvious. In a sense, they are tangible stamps of approval to give what is essentially an idea some currency in the marketplace. As rights change hands, they no longer reflect where the work was done. Much of the knowledge underlying the antiretrovirals that stem the damage from HIV was discovered in publicly funded universities, for example, as is the case for several other important drugs. That knowledge will have been patented, made public, and sold to big pharma for development. Those patents then get integrated into the more complex and hard-to-infringe packages that underpin most drugs today.

Patents are aggressively protected by pharma companies for the simple reason that they are their livelihood. The decision of 39 of the world's most powerful companies to enter into a dispute with the South African government in 2001 over the intellectual property rights to their drugs is a good example. At the time an estimated 5 million South Africans were living with HIV or AIDS, and the pharma industry objected to a clause in the country's Medicines Act which allowed the government to override commercial patents where there was sufficient public interest.

Prices to Africa were already a tenth of what Americans paid. The issue became not one of price but a frame within which everyone could see the enormous discrepancies in health and wealth between the developed and developing worlds. The international outcry that resulted forced the industry to withdraw having won no concessions whatsoever from the South African government. Instead, companies were forced to recoil in shame and regroup.

There are, as it happens, provisions in international law for governments to override patents where there is compelling public need for cheap drugs, as no one doubts is the case with HIV/AIDS. What big pharma objects to is more of its patented products becoming vulnerable to this kind of copycatting. It doesn't want people using its products on the cheap for illnesses that are not pandemics.

And one can see its point. Pharma companies, like those in other global industries, already practise differential pricing, whereby prices are tailored to what people can afford. But while the production company that made *Friends*, for example, will have sold the series more cheaply in Angola, say, than to Channel 4 in the UK, the pirating potential is limited because most people in the rich US market will have seen or taped it anyway.

The danger is always present with drugs that generics, with a little expert packaging, will be smuggled back into the affluent US, European and Japanese markets, making tidy sums for their operators. Pharma companies already spend significant sums policing their supply chains and are intent, for good reasons, on remaining in control of how their drugs get from A to B.

If poorer countries override commercial patents and produce generic versions of more commonly used drugs, industry argues, the danger of the drugs falling into the hands of unscrupulous traders increases. It is hardly surprising, therefore, that industry, backed by western governments, does everything possible to strengthen international patent laws and thwart pressure for change that would empower poorer countries to override the ownership rules and get the latest drugs.

The good thing from the public's point of view is that ownership rules always come to an end. As for pharma, this awareness informs their whole persepctive: which is why most patents are granted on new methods of drug delivery, formulation, or anything else that enables companies to extend the period during which they can charge monopoly prices, without doctors or the public realizing the product is not necessarily better than what went before at a fraction of the price.

Two drugs: same chemistry

One method, modelled by AstraZeneca, was the subject of a court case that alleged the company had engaged in a fraudulent and unlawful campaign to switch people from Prilosec (Losec in the UK) for ulcers, the world's largest-selling drug in 2000, to Nexium for ulcers, the follow-on drug.

The primary patent on Prilosec was originally scheduled to expire in October 2001. With sales of around $6 billion a year, there was a clear incentive to keep out the competition for as long as possible. Dr Marcia Angell, in *The Truth About the Drug Companies*, explains how cheap generics were prevented from entering the market until the end of 2002 by AstraZeneca filing a string of additional patents.

One centred around the idea of combining Prilosec with antibiotics, which means that any doctor trying to eradicate ulcers in this way using a generic version of Prilosec would have infringed the patent. Since antibiotics can kill the *Helicobacter* bug, which causes most ulcers and therefore eliminates the need for anti-ulcer medication in the first place, this was an audacious move. The company even patented a substance made in the body after Prilosec is swallowed, claiming infringement (by association) if a patient swallowed a generic. Three companies were prevented from entering the market because a court found they had infringed a patent on the drug's coating.[27]

When these tactics had run their course, the company came up with Nexium, which has been found to be pretty much identical to Prilosec and about ten times more expensive. The legal case maintains the company had a plan to deceive consumers and recoup the revenues that would be lost when the patent on Prilosec expired.

What the company had done was create a molecule that was, in effect, half of Prilosec, a cunning ruse that has been applied to several other drugs to extend their patent. This is done through the chemistry of organic molecules, whereby they can often be represented twice, as mirror images of each other, like a right and left hand. Each version is known as an isomer. Nexium is no more than one of Prilosec's isomers and would have remained that way but for a stroke of genius in the 1990s which developed a way of separating the two sides. The 2001 Nobel Prize for Chemistry was shared by K. Barry Sharpless of the Scripps

Research Institute, Ryoji Noyori of Nagoya University and William S. Knowles of Monsanto Company for that pioneering work.

Isomers could now be patented as a new chemical entity and submitted for approval as a different drug. According to Goozner in *The $800 Million Pill*:

> Recognizing the inadequacy of their solution, Astra scientists launched a desperate search for some way to differentiate Nexium and Prilosec. They authorized four wildly expensive studies comparing the two drugs against erosive esophagitis ... It wasn't a foolproof strategy, however, since a worse outcome would have to be reported on the label ... The company won its bet, but by the thinnest of margins. Astra discovered the more slowly metabolizing Nexium healed 90% of patients after eight weeks compared to 87% for Prilosec. Two of the studies did not show Nexium to be a better drug and were never released to the public.[28]

Angell was more detailed:

> Instead of comparing likely equivalent doses, the company used higher doses of Nexium. It compared 20 milligrams and 40 milligrams of Nexium with 20 milligrams of Prilosec. With the dice loaded in that way, Nexium looked like an improvement – but still only marginally so and in just two of the four trials. In fact, the only surprise is that at the high doses chosen for comparison, Nexium didn't do better than it did. The logical conclusion might have been simply to double the standard dose of Prilosec, allow generic competition, and forget about Nexium – but that would not have been of help to AstraZeneca, only to people with heartburn who object to paying $4 a pill (which in itself might produce heartburn). Tom Scully, the former head of the Centers for Medicare & Medicaid Services, told a group of doctors, 'You should be embarrassed if you prescribe Nexium.'[29]

George Sachs, a Scottish physician who co-developed the proton pump with Astra scientists, told Goozner, 'Both isomers in the end would appear to be equally active at the pump. Once they are activated, they are no longer isomers anyway. They are the identical molecule.'[30]

According to the suit, AstraZeneca launched a massive advertising campaign to persuade consumers that Nexium was a new and improved drug. The budget for that campaign was estimated by industry research group Wood Mackenzie at $257 million in 2003, more than for any other drug on the market at the time. Since Nexium costs up to ten times more than Prilosec, and was neither new nor much improved, the plaintiffs argued such a large spend was excessive.

The price of convenience

Dressing drugs up in new data so that they can serve new markets, doubling them up with established products to get them recognition, and extending patent life are all fairly common practices. Companies have one other major tool to boost their incomes without actually producing genuinely new drugs, and that is to change how drugs are delivered into the body and what they do when they get there. Such practices have flourished in recent years. In 1996, the drug delivery sector was worth around £22 billion ($40 billion) and growing at around 20% a year. By 2005, products incorporating drug delivery systems were thought to account for around a fifth of the total US pharma market of $300 billion.[31]

The name of the game in medicine, as we know, is to compete with what we are designed to do naturally. A good delivery system helps. It can make the medicine easier to take and also more effective clinically. Even something as low-tech as dissolving a medicine under the tongue beats the bog-standard oral method for anyone who has difficulty swallowing or keeping food down. Such sublingual technologies, in many forms, have been incorporated into more than 80 products, generating a billion-dollar market since their advent in the 1980s. Such formulations are in development in virtually every therapeutic class.[32]

And that is at the seriously low-tech end of the business, along with patches and basic controlled-release mechanisms that have been around for decades. Science moves swiftly when guided by the promise of billion-dollar revenues, riding on the tiniest of tweaks in any of the broad issues that concern chemists – how fast drugs work, how long their effect lasts, what else they affect when in the body, and how they can be designed for minimum intrusion on daily life.

Within a relatively short space of time, the routes a drug could take into the body had become immensely more attractive to delivery scientists. The skin, for example, is now viewed as an entry point to the entire body – a delivery route with huge earning potential compared with when oils and lotions for local dermatological conditions were simply rubbed on. Patches, for example, were devised which proved brilliantly effective at delivering drugs into the bloodstream at a consistent rate, opening up markets for things like hormones or nicotine replacement therapy and giving old pain drugs a new lease of life. But the skin has two major problems where medicines are concerned. It will only let through drugs with a low molecular weight, and then often too slowly and in small doses, if the skin is not to become disfigured.

Technologies to overcome these obstacles give some idea of the ingenuity being deployed to getting more drugs into the body via one route rather than another. One of these latest transdermal approaches enables drugs to be literally charged through the skin, for example. Called iontophoresis, it uses a small battery to establish a voltage difference across the skin, through which charged molecules are driven. Already used to deliver local anaesthetics to children, it is both non-invasive and usually faster acting than either a lotion or a standard patch. Moreover, it opens up another route, and thus a larger market, for drugs that would not normally cross the skin at all.

Similar progress has been seen in all the major routes, whether it is via the lungs, the eye, the digestive tract, wall of the mouth or the nose. In 2003, there were 99 different inhalable technologies, 209 that provided a modified-release mechanism, 134 that changed the composition of a drug so it could be taken orally, 76 different injectables, 167 transdermals, another 64 that guided the drug through the nasal mucosa, and 345 others, categorized by Pharmaprojects as miscellaneous.[33]

Drugs need efficient transport systems just as people do. And just as train companies actively want people to use the train, so those who have invested heavily in a particular delivery technology want as many drugs as possible to use that route. Not surprisingly, the market churns out, if not new drugs exactly, then a lot of value-added versions at massive cost. Drug delivery enables pharma companies to create entirely new products, using established active ingredients, for around $50 million instead of the $1.7 billion industry sources say it now costs to develop a new active substance from scratch.

Moreover, because some novel thing or process has been patented while creating the delivery-enhanced product (the exercise wouldn't take place otherwise), the drug delivery technology can extend the periods in which a premium price can be charged for a drug. In 2003, there were more than 30 product approvals for drugs incorporating a new delivery technology, far more than there were for new active substances, and around 70 deals between pharma and its specialist delivery sector.

According to the consultancy, PharmaVentures, drug delivery made up one in seven of all pharma deals in 2004.[34]

The success of the drug delivery sector not only demonstrates the sheer effort that goes into improving pharma's products, but also provides a glimpse of how the medicines business works. Numerous drug delivery firms must compete for business with just a handful of powerful large pharma companies. While the delivery market overall is indeed growing fast, for every successful drug delivery company there will be several that are not chosen by pharma and do not survive.

The delivery people must compete for business at a distinct disadvantage. In the battle to deliver a non-invasive form of insulin, for example, three drug delivery companies that had deals worth hundreds of millions of dollars, plus a share of royalties, were all severely jolted when their big pharma partners suddenly lost interest.

The desperate race to develop non-invasive insulin is another example of how market forces work to create products that, while valuable, have the same limit on development costs as society has over drug prices. The market for insulin products is predicted to be worth $20 billion in 2006. According to the International Diabetes Federation, nearly 200 million people around the world are already dependent on insulin. The World Health Organization believes this figure will reach 300 million by 2025.[35] The pharmaceutical database, Pharmaprojects, found 300 diabetes drugs in development in 2004, three times as many as eight years ago.[36]

Insulin is a protein that has traditionally been given by injection because other routes were not suitable. Oral insulin does not survive in the digestive system, for example, and insulin given transdermally would not provide diabetics with the capability to give themselves precisely measured doses. Drug delivery and pharma companies therefore have been trying to develop an alternative to injections, looking at, among other systems, a fine spray that delivers insulin to the blood stream through the lining on the inside of the mouth, various inhalers, and several pills that protect it from gastric juices.

The race for non-invasive insulin is as intense as the clamour for obesity cures and for the same reasons. People who chronically overeat create the conditions to become diabetic. Their bodies become less efficient and, in particular, resistant to insulin, which should take glucose (a kind of sugar) out of the bloodstream, directing it to other parts of the body. Instead, glucose accumulates in the blood leading to complications of the disease that include heart problems, blindness, ulcers and amputations.

As with obesity cures, the tens of billions of dollars in failed development costs are factored into a drug's 'average development cost' when the industry pleads its case for higher prices from healthcare systems.

The reward is that diabetics should get a better product from all this spend. Data on the first inhaled insulin product, Exubera (produced by a partnership between Pfizer of the US, Sanofi-Aventis of Europe and drug delivery company Nektar Therapeutics), was submitted in the US in March 2005. Whatever happens in the marketplace, however, doesn't detract from the fact that perfect insulin delivery is not an easy goal. Companies compete for benefits that become increasingly marginal. Most of the novel insulins in development are appealing because they act fast. But it is thought most patients will still need a conventional long-acting insulin injection in the morning. 'What is really needed is a non-invasive product that can provide both fast-acting and long-acting insulins,' says Nicole Yost.[37] The quest to match the ingenuity of the human body is great from the perspective of the science involved, but expensive from the perspective of the citizen who pays the bill, especially when one also factors in the marketing money that has to be spent promoting one non-invasive method over another, because the other routes are also promising.

Even from the science perspective, the public loses out because the dimensions of the market are such that it works in favour of the winner takes all; many projects fail because the development costs are so high and there are so few big pharma companies to take them on. Drug delivery people know the evidence shows that novel delivery expands drug sales time and again. In erectile dysfunction, for example, delivery skills have contributed to long-lasting 'weekender' versions and a stream of other improvements (sniffable, rub-on-able, inhalable, and so on) in the pipeline. When Viagra was first launched, the market figures stated confidently that as many as one in ten men couldn't get erect. Now, questionnaires, funded by the makers of all this largesse, put the figure at one in six, and rising.

But while delivery companies enable pharma's markets to expand in this way, they can't negotiate higher percentages from pharma. 'Stories abound of representatives of drug delivery firms turning up to deal-proposal meeting with a big pharma company, only to be met by a wall of 20 or 30 executives, scientists and lawyers,' says Yost.[38]

Naturally, other ways of doing business are sought. And, just as undervalued sales forces found new ways of selling drugs, so undervalued drug delivery companies are trying to do deals on a more equal footing, developing networks among themselves, for example. 'Increasingly, the terms that pharma is offering don't generate enough value for drug delivery companies,' says drug delivery publisher, Guy Furness. 'Delivery firms have, almost *en masse*, decided to move up a gear and, rather than developing technologies, begin developing their own products in-house.'[39]

Drug delivery companies are not the only ones trying to forge ways of doing business that suit their shareholders rather than pharma's. A new kind of player, known as specialty pharma, is emerging, for example. These companies might have originated from making generic drugs, selling delivery technologies, or from the research or selling routes. They realize there is work in areas that pharma avoids, which is to say anything that won't make billion-dollar revenues.

Furness describes how Jazz Pharmaceuticals, a US company formed in 2002, typifies this trend. The CEO Sam Saks had earned a personal fortune as head of a successful pioneering drug delivery company, Alza. He and other Jazz founders (mainly former Alza senior executives), using their experience, reputation, and their own money, were able to attract huge investment, sufficient to create a company with the serious capital required to play the drug development game, yet small and very agile, especially in comparison with cumbersome big pharma.

Specialty pharma companies are changing the structure of the medicines business. Pharma's hold over the industry has not been broken, but as these relatively new players gain strength in numbers, they collectively secure a larger slice of the pie for themselves, and big pharma's position is naturally threatened.

And while the giants have been merging away merrily at the top end of the spectrum to avoid addressing the real problems, a more dangerous threat has been emerging from companies that do what big pharma has traditionally done, research. The number of companies involved in research rose by around a third from May 1997 to January 2002. 'Many of these companies are start-ups or small niche firms with specialized technologies,' says Ian Lloyd, managing editor of global research database, Pharmaprojects. 'Thus the picture is of an industry which is consolidating at one end, while diversifying at the other.'[40]

The gap between the two ends may still be vast but it is not unbreachable. Small companies can, and do, grow into big companies, but rarely without the help of the ten or so giants at the very top. The tightening of rules to curb the influence of these giants would not mean fewer drugs. On the contrary, it should lead to a more level operating environment for the smaller companies, a more thriving market for scientists, a better deal for the payers and greater choice in the surgery for the public.

Part 2

When the good stay silent

5

The story of Vioxx

Vioxx was a new kind of painkiller, one of the Cox-2 inhibitors, that first hit the headlines in the late 1990s. They were a class of drug based on a scientific breakthrough that had enormous commercial potential. From the start it was a race between the two main contenders, Pfizer's Celebrex and Merck's Vioxx, to get to the market first. Both were supposedly better painkillers than their older, cheaper rivals, such as aspirin and ibubrofen, not because they were better at relieving pain but because of an improved side-effect profile. Indeed, the main selling point of the Cox-2 inhibitors had been what the science suggested, pain relief without exposing patients to the risk of intestinal bleeding. Unfortunately this wasn't all they delivered.

At the time the Cox-2s were being developed it was known that painkillers like aspirin and ibubrofen (non-steroidal anti-inflammatory drugs or NSAIDs) reduce inflammation and pain around arthritic joints by blocking the action of an enzyme that is abbreviated to 'Cox'. But because NSAIDs can also cause bleeding of the stomach lining, researchers reasoned that maybe by blocking the Cox enzyme, some other function to protect the stomach from excess acid was also being blocked. Maybe there were two versions of Cox. And they were right. By the late 1980s, public and private scientists had identified the Cox specific to swelling and they called it Cox-2. By blocking Cox-2, a drug should relieve pain like the NSAIDs but without the damaging effects on the stomach.

Merrill Goozner, in his 2004 book *The $800 Million Pill*, pinpointed the birth of Vioxx as 1994, two years after Peppi Prasit, a medicinal chemist from Merck's Montreal office, had seen a scientific poster at a small medical conference. 'The poster reported the latest research from a Japanese company that was trying to come up with a painkiller that targeted the newly discovered Cox-2 enzyme,' said Goozner. 'That summer, Prasit replicated the work in his own lab. His work excited Edward Scolnick, the director of Merck's research division, who authorized a major search for its own version of the molecule. By 1994, it had discovered Vioxx.'[1]

The first major problem with the Cox-2s was that the side-effect advantage over the NSAIDs couldn't actually be proven in trials. Indeed, the evidence at the time appeared to suggest the NSAIDs weren't that dangerous. A study in Scotland, for example, monitored more than 50,000 people over the age of 50 for 3 years and found 2% of NSAID users were hosptialized for gastrointestinal problems after using the drugs over a long period of time, compared with 1.4% who took no drugs at all.[2]

Nevertheless, articles starting flooding the medical literature about the major public health hazard posed by the traditional NSAIDs.[3]

> Relying on extrapolations from small group studies, one physician claimed NSAID use resulted in 41,000 hospitalizations and 3,300 deaths a year among the elderly. Another put the death rate at five times that level. Meanwhile, other articles reported the results from small clinical trials for Cox-2 inhibitors that hinted the new drugs might prevent the side effects.[4]

Before long, the popular press had picked up the story with headlines of stomach-friendly aspirins. And now the nocebo effect was kicking in with respect to regular aspirins and other NSAIDs. This is the opposite of the placebo effect and works to make drugs less effective if they are believed to cause harm. Arthur Barsky, a psychiatrist at Brigham and Women's hospital in Boston, for example, points to a study which found that patients warned about the gastrointestinal effects of taking aspirin were three times more likely to suffer from them.[5]

By the time Vioxx got its FDA approval, the *Washington Post* was claiming NSAIDs were responsible for 107,000 hospitalizations and the death of 165,000 people every year.[6] At the same time, the FDA-approved package insert for one popular prescription NSAID was only warning of one in every 100 people experiencing some stomach problems within 3–6 months, and 2–4 people in every 100 after one year. The vast discrepancies weren't picked up and the newly discovered epidemic of aspirin-related deaths went unchallenged.

Although the Cox-2 inhibitors cost around $3 for each tablet in the US and £1 ($1.80) to the NHS in the UK, compared with a few cents or pence for the older drugs in their respective markets, sales soared. The profit potential on drugs taken daily by tens of millions of people on a long-term basis soon adds up. With so few new drugs, it was important the Cox-2s did well.

Their efforts were impressive. Wall Street analysts considered the rollouts of Celebrex and Vioxx as the most successful drug launches in pharmaceutical history, helped in no small measure by the fact that prescription medicines can be promoted directly to the general public in the US, something the industry has long been calling for in Europe.

Merck spent $160 million advertising Vioxx directly to the American people in 2000, much more than was required to keep most other household names in the public eye. PepsiCo, in contrast, only spent $125 million advertising Pepsi that same year. The drug money was well spent. Sales of Vioxx rose to $1.5 billion, 3.6 times what it had earned in 1999,[7] and this can be taken as some indication of the enormous untapped demand for drugs that promise better quality pain relief – and therefore the reason why such promises should approximate to the truth. By the time Vioxx was withdrawn in September 2004 it was earning $2.5 billion a year and more than 100 million prescriptions had been filled in the US alone.

In an effort to provide proof that the Cox-2s were safer than the traditional NSAIDs and to have that officially recognized in the labelling of the drugs, the two companies launched a hugely expensive series of trials in 2000, pitting the Cox-2s against the older, cheaper rivals. Because so few people who take NSAIDs experience stomach problems, the trials had to recruit enormous numbers of people – more than 8,000 in each – to get statistically valid results. After nine months, the results weren't that impressive. The Vioxx study suggested that 41 patients needed to be treated for one year to prevent one such [stomach bleed] event. The Celebrex study, meanwhile, because it was so short, had 'no statistically significant difference between the groups'.[8]

Worse, much worse, as far as the Vioxx trial was concerned however, was news that no one had been looking for and which only became widely known when Vioxx was withdrawn and people started asking why it had not been taken off the market sooner. This was the VIGOR study that showed patients on Vioxx experienced a fivefold increase in cardiovascular events compared with those taking naproxen, the NSAID it was being compared to. Merck has always maintained that the beneficial, anti-thrombotic effects of naproxen were responsible for the results, and that the VIGOR study had used a 50mg dose, which is not recommended for long-term use.

Nevertheless, Dr Alistair Wood, a pharmacologist and professor of medicine at the Vanderbilt School of Medicine in Nashville, Tennessee, pointed out just how easy it would have been to clarify those first doubts about the drug. A study of just 2,500 people, he said, would have been enough to show a fourfold risk of major cardiac events. And this was a drug being taken by tens of millions. In an interview with National Public Radio, Wood said the story of Vioxx was an indictment of the whole industry because a much-needed confirmatory trial never took place after the first suggestion of a cardiovascular risk surfaced from the VIGOR study in 2000.[9]

Instead, according to Henry A. Waxman, a Californian Democrat who sits on the Government Reform Committee of the House of Representatives, the sales pitch just moved up a gear.

> What we learned [at a hearing to explore how Vioxx could have been taken by so many for so long] illuminated a hidden corner of the healthcare system: the practices that pharmaceutical manufacturers use to promote their products to physicians.[10]

On 7 February 2001, when the FDA was discussing the VIGOR study, its arthritis advisory committee voted unanimously that physicians should be made aware of VIGOR's cardiovascular results. According to Waxman,

> The next day, Merck sent a bulletin to its [Vioxx] sales force of more than 3,000. The bulletin ordered, 'do not initiate discussions on the FDA arthritis advisory committee ... or the results of the VIGOR study.' It advised that if a physician inquired about VIGOR, the sales representative should indicate that the study showed a gastrointestinal benefit and then say, 'I cannot discuss the study with you.'[11]

Merck also instructed its representatives to show those doctors who asked if Vioxx could cause heart attacks, a pamphlet called 'The cardiovascular card'. Waxman continues:

> This pamphlet, prepared by Merck's marketing department, indicated that [Vioxx] was associated with one-eighth the mortality from cardiovascular causes of that found with other anti-inflammatory drugs. The card did not include any data from the VIGOR study. Instead, it presented a pooled analysis of preapproval studies, in most of which low doses of [Vioxx] were used for a short time.

Waxman also casts his revelations against the backdrop of how much pharma spends misleading doctors in this way. 'The pharmaceutical industry spends more than $5.5 billion to promote drugs to doctors [in the US] each year – more than what all US medical schools spend to educate medical students.'

While family doctors remained largely in the dark, the VIGOR study was creating a stir higher up the cardiovascular chain of command. Getting those misgivings heard was a problem, however. In August 2001, Professor Eric J. Topol, who is in charge of cardiovascular medicine at the Cleveland Clinic, Ohio, published with two colleagues an article in the *Journal of the American Medical Association* (*JAMA*) that challenged the safety of both Vioxx and Celebrex.[12]

Rather than being picked up and taken seriously, the article prompted an industry backlash that helped prolong patients' exposure to the dangers of the drug for several years. 'When you do this kind of thing, you take on industry and put yourself at significant risk,' Topol told me in an interview. 'It shouldn't have to be this way but it is and you find yourself in a very vulnerable and exposed position. Companies have unlimited resources, including experts who will speak against you. Everything we said in the *JAMA* article was dismissed by consultants in the pay of the industry.'[13]

Undeterred, Topol spoke up again three years later, this time in the *New York Times* in an article entitled, 'Good riddance to a bad drug'. This was in October 2004, just days after the independent safety monitoring board of a three-year study of Vioxx in another condition called for the trial to be stopped early. This was the APPROVe trial that had been designed primarily to investigate whether Vioxx could prevent the recurrence of pre-malignant growths in the colon called adenomatous polyps. It was also the trial that broke the silence on Vioxx. The data showed the drug had been seen to double the risk of heart attacks and strokes, compared with placebo, after just 18 months. 'There were 15 heart attacks or strokes per 1,000 patients in the Vioxx arm compared with 7.5 in the placebo group, although the death rates were similar,' Ailis Kane wrote in *Scrip Magazine*.[14]

After the APPROVe trial had been stopped, and after the *New York Times* article, Dr David Graham, an FDA official, also went public with his fears. This was in October 2004 and the question quickly became how long had people known Vioxx wasn't as safe as everyone believed.

Topol was once again an outspoken critic, writing in the *New England Journal of Medicine*, for example, that had the 'many warning signs along the way been heeded, such a debacle could have been prevented' and criticizing the 'chance' nature by which the APPROVe study revealed the cardiovascular risk. He also pointed out:

> Merck was spending more than $100 million a year in direct-to-consumer advertising – another activity regulated by the FDA ... For the past few years, every month has seen more than 10 million prescriptions for rofecoxib (Vioxx) written in the US alone. At any point, the FDA could have stopped Merck from using direct-to-consumer advertising, especially given the background concern that the cardiovascular toxicity was real and was receiving considerable confirmation in multiple studies conducted by investigators who were independent of Merck.[15]

His words drew attacks on his professional reputation. In November 2004, unfounded rumours tried to suggest a financial motivation to what he was saying. A month later, he was described as a luddite in the *Wall Street Journal*. 'There is so much up tied up in new drugs doing well that you are seen as a heretic standing in the way of progress,' he said when asked why doctors don't speak up more often. 'The jeopardy factor is considerable. You are attacked from every possible angle, and in ways you don't know about.'[16] Even though everything Topol said has been entirely vindicated, he says he would think twice about speaking up again, not only for his own sake but also that of his family.

As such, he demonstrates the truth of the saying that suggests evil only prevails because the good do nothing. The Topols of this world are hardly recognized, let alone celebrated, for their efforts to protect the ordinary public from a significant risk factor for heart disease. He might say that as a cardiologist, that is precisely what he is paid to do. But doctors don't usually have to protect their patients from decisions made by the regulator. And Topol didn't have the job security from whistleblower legislation that FDA official, Graham, enjoyed.

> It is very easy for consultants to become part of the pharmaceutical machine [says Topol]. They are the vector towards higher visibility for the latest drugs and companies want to attract those with the most important academic reputations. Mostly the relationships are totally innocent. It is only when concerns about drugs occur, and controversies ensue, that the almost total alignment in interests can be seen.[17]

Once doctors had started talking in public, others followed and some had even longer memories. Dr Gurkipal Singh, adjunct clinical professor of medicine at Stanford University, said the dangers were clear in November, when, he said, Merck scientists 'were seriously discussing a potential [heart attack] risk of Vioxx'.[18]

Singh had reviewed email messages submitted to Congress that showed Merck scientists were discussing whether or not to include patients taking aspirin in their trials. One Merck scientist observed that if aspirin was forbidden, patients on Vioxx might have more heart attacks and that would kill the drug. Merck's failure to undertake a study of the cardiovascular outcomes was a marketing decision, Singh said.

John Davis, editor of the industry newsletter, *Scrip World Pharmaceutical News*, asked:

> Why did it take the results of a clinical trial for the cardiovascular risks to be finally laid bare? Patients are not likely to be satisfied with being told drug safety can be a long-term issue, with adverse reactions only emerging after prolonged use, or until sufficient data has been gathered in a subset of patients found to be at increased risk.[19]

Everyone seemed taken by surprise. Stopping an expensive trial early is a rare event. Regulatory agencies across the world acted promptly, with Italy and Denmark telling patients to stop treatment immediately, while Norway, the UK and Canada advised users to get advice from their doctors as soon as possible.

What had happened was that the findings of the VIGOR trial, along with other evidence, had been taken to an FDA advisory panel in February 2001. More than a year later, in April 2002, Vioxx's datasheet to doctors had been changed to reflect the drug's association with a seriously higher heart attack risk. 'How did that help?' asked Professor Wood of Vanderbilt, while pointing out that 2.5 million Americans were still taking the drug as of June 2004. 'That doesn't speak to the effectiveness of the warning,' he said.[20] The FDA had also sent a warning letter to Merck in September 2001 because its ads promoting Vioxx had failed to mention the increased risks associated with the drug. Nothing was mentioned about the size of the advertising budget or the guidance given to the sales forces.

Merck had no option but to admit defeat and withdraw the drug. Immediately, the company had a gaping $2.5 billion a year hole in its revenues and $26.8 billion wiped off its value. Merck CEO Raymond Gilmartin continued to insist to the end that 'it would have been possible to continue to market Vioxx with labelling that would incorporate the new data.'[21]

It was becoming abundantly clear that health risks that seem clear and objective are actually highly subjective, certainly in how they are communicated to doctors and the public. In most countries' regulatory infrastructures, a whole host of expert scientific advisory committees exist to advise a central body, which makes the final decision about a drug's safety profile. But it is not at all clear whose interests are being served by the experts who make these important decisions, despite whole rafts of rules to prevent the almost inevitable conflicts that arise between private and public interests.

Indeed, if companies are able to spend more money promoting a drug than Pepsi does on its leading soft drink, even after serious danger signs have been repeatedly pointed out, prima facie evidence seems quite clearly to suggest that all is not well in the present structure.

Why have rules in the first place?

Regulation of the medicines business was a response to serious public health disasters. The free-for-all in patent medicines in America and Europe only gradually succumbed to effective regulation and each time because the public could see for themselves why they needed protection. The Massengill Massacre in 1937, named after the company that caused it, is one of the first incidents in the US that showed how easily medicines could do harm, as well as good. It was a tragedy in which more than 100 people, mostly children, died after taking a safe drug that had been manufactured with what turned out to be a toxic solvent.

The public outcry that followed prompted a safety clause to be quickly added to the Federal Food, Drug and Cosmetic Act of 1938 that was then being debated. That clause resulted in the basic framework for getting a drug on to the market that persists to this day. It required all potential drugs to go through a series of safety trials to comply with the investigational new drug (IND) regulations. The company could then apply for a licence. If the regulator, the FDA, did nothing within 60 days, the drug could be marketed, this latter feature having profoundly changed over the years.

Back then, there was not even a specific requirement that a drug should actually work, no clause saying it should do what it purports to do. That would require trial by committees of professional experts and the kind of long-winded arguments about a drug's safety and efficacy we now see. Back then, pharma companies were still in a position to resist such calls on the grounds that such onerous regulation would go against the fundamental spirit of a free market.

Senator Estes Kefauver from Tennessee, however, continued to call for more thorough regulation of the medicines market until the late 1950s, when events in Europe gave him the public support he needed. This was when reports started appearing of babies being born in Europe with grotesque abnormalities. Pharma's cries for regulatory freedom were to fall on increasingly deaf ears as the American public started to appreciate those early safety requirements and to listen more closely to Kefauver and his supporters.

In October 1957, a new drug for pregnant women called thalidomide had gone on sale in Germany. It was sold as Contergan, a sleeping pill that also promised to relieve morning sickness. The drug was popular because it worked fast, left no hangover and was apparently safe. Between 1958 and 1960 thalidomide was launched in 46 countries under 51 different trade names, first hitting the UK in April 1958 as Distaval.

Curiously, the drug was not sold in France. Why French families were protected from the thalidomide tragedy is a mystery. In the US, Dr Frances Kelsey, a diligent medical officer at the FDA, had spotted danger signals associated with the drug when assessing its safety dossier. The IND rules had kicked in, in other words, providing a powerful platform for Kelsey to protect thousands of American families from a tragedy that went on to affect an estimated 10,000 babies worldwide, including 500 in England.[22]

But that wasn't how the regulatory and financial people saw it. As those first reports of the malformations started circulating in magazines and newspapers, Kelsey may well have been seen as a bumbling federal regulator unnecessarily delaying access to an important new medicine. As it happens, her concerns were not to do with the real damage caused by thalidomide but to do with peripheral neuropathy [nerve damage] and thyroid problems. But they were able to delay product approval long enough for people to see with their own eyes what the drug was doing.

They saw pictures of a previously unknown congenital malformation whereby babies were being born with arms and legs that seemed to belong more to a water creature than a human being and with a whole host of associated internal problems. Indeed, the condition was christened phocomelia because its limb manifestations were so similar to the flippers of a seal. 'Thalidomide is an excellent example of how regulators should not allow themselves to be hustled to approve drugs for marketing reasons or because patent term is eroded by delay,' says former UK medicines regulator, Dr John Griffin. 'Regulators should be not influenced by these commercial considerations.'[23]

The side effects of the drug were so dramatic that the link between them and the new drug soon became apparent. And Kelsey's standing was revised accordingly. The first cases were reported in Germany in 1959, and the drug was withdrawn from that market two years later, in November 1961. It was removed from the UK market a month later, in December 1961. Over the next ten months, it was banned in countries all over the world.

But any time delay was too long. Some people asked if pregnant women had been offered this drug while the manufacturer was steadfastly denying all evidence of a causal relationship between thalidomide and this dreadful new condition. Bill Inman, in this book, *Don't Tell the Patient*, says evidence suggesting thalidomide might damage the nerves in the limbs of adults was available to Chemie Grunenthal, the company that made it, as early as 1959. These were similar to Kelsey's concerns and, according to Griffin, had nothing to do with phocomelia.

> They have been accused of deliberately ignoring the [signs] because of the threat to the commercial success of the drug. At that time there was no reliable way to protect the public from ignorance, incompetence or fraud.[24]

As the facts emerged, the American people saw clearly how close they themselves had come to a public health disaster. Then as now, they were enthusiastic consumers of pharmaceutical medicine. Had a miracle cure for morning sickness been made commercially available, the toll on the unborn would have been far greater.

It didn't take long for the regulations to be tightened. In 1962, the Kefauver Act was passed without a single dissenting vote. Would-be drugs would now have to show not only that they were safe but, adding another burden, that they were effective as well. Meanwhile, in the UK, voluntary safety measures were set in place in 1963 before the 1968 Medicines Act became effective from 1971.

'The new law completely changed the way doctors and patients thought about drugs,' says Jerry Avron about the US in his book, *Powerful Medicines*. 'For the first time, the federal government, through the FDA, could require that a prescription medication had to be proven effective before it could be sold as a drug in the US.'[25] And the eight or nine years it took for the new medicines law to become effective in the UK can be taken as some indication of the impact it was to have on the European pharmaceutical industry.

The new infrastructure of rules covered not just the safety of a drug, but also how effective it was, the quality of its manufacture, and how to suspend, revoke or change its licence. The rules would also govern how research is conducted, how the results are made known, how drugs are labelled and promoted and, importantly, how these new rules might be enforced. The time scale was necessary because everyone needed time to adjust to a radically new way of doing things.

Since then, the rules governing the pharma business have been tweaked hundreds, perhaps thousands, of times on both sides of the Atlantic, each tweak leading to greater depth and complexity in the relationship between the regulator (read the public watchdog) and industry. Medicines, and their attendant rules, are divided, for example, into prescription-only products, pharmacy-only products and over-the-counter products in most countries. Prescription-only products are often further divided into useful and not-so-useful categories, each definition determining how they are promoted, reimbursed and priced.

Other whole swathes of rules surround how medicines are tested and how generic versions come on to the market once the patents on the originals have expired, with implications that translate into million, or billion, dollar revenues or losses for the companies concerned. For example, while researching this book, the European Commission had already been debating for a year a precise definition of 'a potential serious risk to public health', the reason being to limit the number of objections raised by member states to drugs that are approved under one of Europe's centralized procedures. Most countries also have prescribing rules, dispensing rules, ethical rules, so many rules in fact one wonders if any single person is capable of understanding them all.

We must therefore rely heavily on regulatory agencies like the UK's Medicines and Healthcare products Regulatory Agency (MHRA) and the FDA. They know how the industry works because they are charged with interpreting the laws enacted by democratically elected governments regarding medicines. Within that framework, they say how it works.

Where safety is concerned, they make recommendations as to a drug's use and run early-warning systems for unforeseen side effects in the longer term. Where quality is the issue, the regulators become inspectors to ensure manufacturing and distribution standards are met and to help ensure the supply chain for pharmaceuticals is free of counterfeits. Regarding marketing, regulatory staff are supposed to keep an eye on how drugs are promoted according to the rules of the country they operate in. The job of the regulator is to do everything possible to maintain a supply of safe and effective drugs, and to curb any unduly zealous promotion to either doctors or patients.

There are also things the regulators can't do by law. As these stand in the UK, they can't, for example, require companies to compare their drugs with ones that are already on the market, nor need the companies demonstrate medical need for products in any other way. The regulators are also not required to take price or value into consideration, an exercise that was only formally undertaken by the Department of Health in the late 1990s.

Over the years, mainly because of the rising workload emanating from increased regulation, most countries have initiated systems whereby industry pays the lion's share of the cost of carrying out this work. This is not unusual as most industries pay something towards the cost of being regulated, sometimes via a collective pool and sometimes directly for services rendered.

When Conservative MP David Amess questioned this practice at the UK parliamentary health committee looking into the influence of the pharma industry in 2004, the UK's chief regulator Professor Kent Woods confirmed it was common, even in a business as opaque and as important to public health as that concerning medicines. Woods, CEO of the MHRA, said his agency was 100% funded by industry, Sweden's agency was 95% funded and the FDA had 55% of its funds from commercial sources.[26]

In the UK, the idea of regulators being funded by the companies they regulate had arisen when the Evans-Cunliffe Report, commissioned by the Department of Health and Social Security (DHSS) in March 1987, was accepted. The brief had been to recommend ways of 'dealing expeditiously' with work arising from the Medicines Act.

Dr John Evans was a senior DHSS medical officer and Peter Cunliffe chairman of the pharmaceutical division of private chemicals company, ICI. This mini think-tank came up with a plan, supported by the Thatcher government of the day, to take responsibility for regulating the industry out of the hands of the DHSS, which also at this time split into its constituent parts, the Department of Health and the Department of Social Security.

The idea was to create a separate Medicines Control Agency, the forerunner to the MHRA, which was expected to be entirely self-funding with fees commensurate with the work performed for its client, the pharmaceutical industry. Similar mechanisms were set up in countries everywhere, because it made sound business sense to have drug companies pay their regulators. Moreover, regulatory bodies within the EU would compete with each other for the income that comes from licensing work, thus reducing the time it takes for a drug to get approved.

Even before the Vioxx withdrawal, many were extremely sceptical that this was the best way to protect public health. 'The criticism of the old Department of Health medicines department in the 1970s was that it didn't have any teeth,' says John Abraham, professor of sociology at Sussex University. 'Not only does it now not have any teeth, but it is not motivated to bite.'[27]

The logic, however, is clear when one understands how the business works; it also illustrates just how much power we have vested in our regulatory bodies. Since companies want their drug dossiers assessed in the shortest time frame possible, they should pay the staff to do the work. If the regulators demand so many studies, so much attention to burdensome detail, to get a licence, they must at least assess the evidence in a reasonable time, says the voice of industry. The regulators retort, meanwhile, that if you want it done fast, you pay. The key word for understanding the pharmaceutical industry is speed. Everything falls into place once one appreciates the imperative to get drugs to market as quickly as possible.

The regulators, more than anyone else, understand that urgency. They know a week's delay in the processing of an application for a drug licence can translate into millions of dollars of lost sales, because each lost week eats into the life of the patent on which a drug's profitability is based.

The ugly face of medicine

The aftermath of the Vioxx withdrawal was illuminating because it showed how the ugly face of medicine is notoriously hard for anyone, let alone Joe Public, to see. Medicines are produced in universities, conferences, ethics committees, corporate boardrooms, editorial offices, ministerial chambers and several other places that are rarely visited by ordinary people.

Science also has its own language, its own rules and etiquette, and resists informed inquiry by the public on anything other than its own terms. 'An austere disdain for media celebrity among scientists remains to this day,' writes Richard Horton. As an example, 'One only has to look at the way Susan Greenfield, who currently runs the Royal

Institution, has been criticized for what some see as her courting of journalists at the expense, so it is alleged, of her work as a scientist.'[28]

But if the great and the good are discouraged from talking to the media, lest it taint their earnest pursuit of truth, what hope do the rest of us have of ever knowing the true risks and benefits of medicines? Hospitals, surgeries and pharmacies are the only windows we have into this world, and then usually only when we are ill. People who don't follow the financial press may find it hard to appreciate just how aggressive the world of medicine is, how fiercely knowledge is contested to give a drug an edge, and how desperately hard it is to find a truly impartial assessment. A culture of scientific detachment, paternalism and professional mystique does little to help the public to a tolerably informed understanding about an industry that boasts more billion-dollar revenue streams than any other, has a more profound effect on the human condition than any other and, until very recently, had consistently earned more than any other.

But the reason the industry is also more misunderstood than any other is that the human struggle against disease must be portrayed in language people can understand. Whether about the alleged link between the MMR vaccine and autism, or the latest medical breakthrough or disaster, pharmaceutical stories are necessarily simplified because for people with no framework of basic scientific knowledge, ideas have nothing to associate with and are lost. People can only build on what makes sense to them. Indeed, it has been said the medicines business can never be transparent to the masses because it cannot escape this fundamental obstacle of widespread scientific illiteracy. We therefore have no option but to trust experts to ensure that what science delivers is the very best it has to offer.

But the UK parliamentary inquiry, which took evidence from a wide range of players in the medicines business, concluded that the basis for that trust was inadequate and the fault lay as much with the regulator, the MHRA, as with the industry, for colluding in the idea that their interests are the same. The MPs said in their final report:

> The interests of pharmaceutical companies and those of the public, patients and the NHS often overlap but they are not identical. For the industry, medical need must be combined with the likelihood of a reasonable return on investment. An effective regulatory regime to ensure that the industry works in the public interest is essential. Unfortunately, the present regulatory system is failing to provide this.[29]

Even if people are not in a position to judge the science, they can still make sense of how the industry operates. Vioxx gave the public a reason to know what goes on in the medicines business and to see how the regulators who are supposed to do the knowing on our behalf acted when the drug was being critically re-examined.

It didn't bode well that the FDA's scientific experts differed so profoundly among themselves that the US Government Accountability Group (GAG), a public interest group to protect whistle-blowers, got involved. Graham, the official who had said the drug had caused a death toll equivalent to two or three jumbo jets falling out of the sky every week, had approached GAG, appropriately enough, when he felt gagged. He had apparently tried to get the results from his study published in the medical journal, the *Lancet*.

These had showed that people taking high doses of Vioxx could triple their chances of a heart attack compared with those taking the rival drug Celebrex. Thwarted by the FDA's bureaucratic procedures on publication, Graham took his case directly to GAG. As it happens the group was already investigating the FDA about a separate matter after another of its experts, Andrew Mosholder, said his report warning of the risks of antidepressants in children had been suppressed.[30]

Dr Sandra Kweder, deputy director of the Office of New Drugs, dismissed Graham's charges, saying Merck's decision to voluntarily withdraw the drug was the result of the 'FDA's vigilance in requiring long-term outcome trials to address our concerns'.[31] Formal FDA complaints prompted GAG to make its own enquiries as to whose version of the truth was more acceptable, and it found in favour of Graham.

The spat did not look good for the FDA. 'Instead of acting as a public watchdog, the FDA was busy challenging its own expert,' said Senator Charles Grassley, who was just one of several US lawmakers looking at how the agency responded to safety issues in the wake of the Vioxx withdrawal.[32]

By the time Graham had got to the Senate hearing, he was going for broke. He may well have imagined his career had, at best, peaked. Whatever the reason and still speaking wildly out of turn, he went on to suggest another five big-selling drugs that could do with a few more safety checks. He alleged GlaxoSmithKline's asthma drug Serevent; AstraZeneca's statin, Crestor; Pfizer's latest Cox-2 inhibitor, Bextra; Roche's acne drug, Accutane; and Abbott Laboratories' slimming drug Meridia (Reductil in the UK), as all having had the same whitewash treatment to present their best side, rather than the warts-and-all version people need if they are to live in what can be considered a civilized society.

The stock market responded to Graham's remarks, with the share prices of all five companies concerned falling, some quite significantly. David Moskowitz, an analyst with Friedman, Billings, Ramsey & Co., told *Scrip* that as Graham was the FDA researcher who had questioned Vioxx's safety before it was recalled, 'a list of drugs he's also concerned about is going to be taken quite seriously.'[33] And his track record was impressive. Graham also pointed out how his research had led to the withdrawal of big drugs like Abbott's Omniflox, Pfizer's Rezulin, and Wyeth's slimming drugs Redux and Pondimin. It had taken the over-the-counter decongestant PPA off the US market, and it had contributed to the team effort that protected the public from the adverse effects of GlaxoSmithKline's Lotronex, Bayer's Baycol, and Johnson & Johnson's Propulsid.

Another indication that public trust in medicines regulation may be misplaced came when Graham returned to work, having just testified against his employers. According to the *British Medical Journal*, he received a standing ovation. Graham had not minced his words. He had said the American people were not adequately protected in the current regulatory set-up. He went on to cite five other worldwide drugs concerning which he said the public had reason to be concerned. Such a display of support came from scientists who would be acutely aware that to be with him was to be against those higher up the FDA chain of command.

What was the FDA to do? One of its first steps was to announce, in November 2004, the commissioning of an independent study by the Institute of Medicine to create a formal system for resolving internal scientific disputes. Not acknowledging anything was amiss, acting director of the Centre for Drug Evaluation and Research (CDER), Dr Steven Galson, told reporters such an idea had been in the pipeline for ages. The FDA had no 'culture of silence', he went on, but some kind of formal resolution process was required to resolve differing professional opinions (DPOs).[34]

People who cannot tell one DPO from another may have been under the impression the whole idea behind the scientific method was to rule out opinions so that what is fashionably called an evidence base for a medicine can be built. This is the public knowledge mountain, on which judgements as to the associated benefits and risks of a medicine can be made as reliably and as early as possible.

It slowly dawns, however, that the most important issue is not the creation of public knowledge so much as the weighing up of available evidence according to values most of us are not privy to. As Professor Iain Chalmers, editor of the James Lind Library, said in evidence to the UK parliamentary enquiry into the pharma industry in 2004, 'I have a long-standing interest in improving the quality of evidence about the effects of treatments in healthcare, an interest that was prompted initially by realising that I had been harming my patients by relying on "eminence-based" rather than "evidence-based" guidance.'[35]

But who is anyone to say whether the FDA failed in its duty over Vioxx? It selects the experts to do the appraisals of drugs. If those people believe the higher heart attack risks suggested by the VIGOR study could be explained on the grounds that the drug it was being compared with had a protective effect on the heart, then that is the case because they are the authority on such matters.

Nevertheless, to the surprise of many analysts and doctors, it has since been decided that the drug can be brought back. The reasoning is that since the downside of the drug has been found to apply to the entire Cox-2 class (including Vioxx's rival Celebrex) and since the entire class has some important benefits for people who cannot take the alternatives, they should all be allowed as a prescribing option, albeit with heavy warnings and no direct-to-consumer advertising.

But that is not the end of the story. Even though the withdrawal of Vioxx had prompted the most serious reflection on regulatory procedures since thalidomide and even though everyone was at pains to restore public trust, the *New York Times* was still able to demonstrate that little had changed, because 10 of the 32-member FDA committee charged with deciding the drug's future had ties with 3 of the companies that make Cox-2 inhibitors.

These 10 members voted 9-1 in favour of Vioxx's return in a vote that was decided by the narrowest of margins (17–15). The one voice of dissent in the decision on Celebrex came from the safety panel's sole member who was not a scientific expert and who clearly did not trust the warnings. He was someone representing the general public and with only common sense to guide him. According to *Scrip*, the thing that most concerned Arthur Levin of New York City was the FDA's ability to 'insist on and enforce conditions which will limit the distribution of these drugs to the appropriate population'.[36]

6

The SSRI story

The story of the SSRIs (selective serotonin reuptake inhibitors) takes place over a much longer time than the simple rise and fall of Vioxx, providing a different perspective on how the pharmaco-colossus works. More people have used these drugs than ever took Vioxx, Celebrex or any of the other Cox-2s. They have used them for longer periods of time, and for many more conditions.

Joe Collier, expert adviser to the 2004 UK parliamentary inquiry into pharma and professor of drug policy at St. George's Hospital, London, insists, for all these reasons, that the SSRI story has had a much more profound effect on the regulatory system than Vioxx. 'The lessons learned from the SSRIs are important because they reminded the authorities of how important it is to listen to patients,' he said.[1]

Perhaps for that reason, the SSRIs prompted much more public anger than Vioxx, with one popular newspaper, the *Daily Mail*, running a banner headline screaming of 'The happy pill betrayal', the day after new prescribing guidelines were announced. This wasn't the sense of shock that had been genuinely felt by many in the aftermath of Vioxx; more a self-righteous indignation, coupled with sheer relief that someone was finally acknowledging what patients had been saying for years, that there were serious problems associated with these drugs and they needed looking into. The new UK guidelines signalled a need for much greater caution about their use, particularly when dealing with those patients on the milder end of the depression scale. Collier calls the SSRI story a landmark, a new chapter opening in the regulation of medicines in the UK, because for the first time the powers-that-be had been forced to acknowledge that patients' experiences were not only true and valid, but that they painted an extremely worrying picture.

> The side effects of the SSRIs were all patient-oriented. They involved suicide ... and horrendous problems coming off. These things were not taken seriously for a very long time. That failure to understand the world out there, the one where patients have positions and interests that the data don't tally with, has been a very clear statement. What it has done is say it is no longer reasonable to ignore patient voices, no longer reasonable to say that it doesn't really matter what they've got or to fob it off. The reality is that doctors and regulators have a responsibility to proactively listen to what people are saying and what they are thinking.[2]

The SSRI story reveals a much broader picture of how the medicines business works than Vioxx because it ventures into how illness is perceived in the first place. The drugs provided a choice in the treatment of depression that people did not have before. Indeed, they provided choice in interpreting how people felt, because Prozac, the pioneer in its class, changed the face of depression. The $19 billion worldwide market it spearheaded was created in just a decade, a fact that was most certainly helped by the fact that the benefits were played up and, as is now known, the risks may have been overlooked. But commercial considerations in creating what became a cultural phenomenon were only part of the story. The reason they worked is that people were receptive to the drugs; they wanted to be happy. And why not?

Now, with some perspective, it is clear the drugs were always something of a massive social experiment, as all new drugs are to some extent. The thing about the SSRIs is that their promise resonated with the zeitgeist of a generation. Their story shows how successful drugs can transform notions of health, and especially mental health. As it unfolds, however, it reveals how the clinical benefits of the SSRIs were never any greater than the cheaper and safer drugs they superseded. And the talk of life-threatening dangers in a significant minority did not stop inappropriate prescribing that had been rampant for years. An analysis of the medical claims of 1,080 US patients in 1997 found that more than half (56%) of those taking an SSRI were taking them for conditions that had not been approved by the FDA.[3]

The meaning of happiness

The success of Prozac, the original SSRI, took even the company that made it, Eli Lilly, by surprise. The makers of this class of drug that now includes Seroxat, Cipramil, Lustral, Efexor, Dutonin, Faverin and others, seemed to have no difficulty persuading people that they could benefit from them.

> Not only are people with eating, sexual, and anxiety disorders, depressives, schizophrenics, and post-traumatic stress disorder patients candidates for Prozac ... [wrote psychiatrist Dr William S. Appleton in his guide to the new antidepressants back in 1997]. But also those who are subsyndromal: the timid, those with low energy and low self-esteem; those who are irritable, perfectionist, inflexible, or suffering from a general malaise or unhappiness; and those who are too aggressive or abusive. In short, anyone – sick or not – may benefit from the civilizing effects of Prozac ... Unfortunately, the nature of serotonin is about as clear as that of the id, and its effect on practice may be the same: everyone, no matter what the diagnosis, became a candidate for psychoanalysis or therapy, and now becomes one for Prozac.[4]

The profit potential from so many conditions became too tempting to ignore, and companies were soon coming up with new ways of tweaking brain chemistry. How they do this is not clear, aside from raising levels of neurotransmitters such as serotonin or noradrenalin in the brain. According to John Horgan's book, *The Undiscovered Mind*, even the originators of these models of mental illness acknowledge their weaknesses. 'Given the ubiquity of a neurotransmitter such as serotonin and the multiplicity of its functions, it is almost as meaningless to implicate it in depression as it is to implicate blood.'[5]

The drugs seemed to work. Around 70–80% of depressed patients were said to benefit, a figure which has since been revised to around 50%. In the real world, the only evidence that mattered came from the soaring sales. Over the 1990s, people started to feel very differently about the idea of a biological answer to depression. 'Within less than a decade, there was sufficient evidence to argue that mental illness could be explained by biochemical imbalances in the brain,' says Professor Elliot Valenstein, author of *Blaming the Brain: The Truth About Drugs and Mental Health*. 'Today, this theory is widely accepted as established.'[6]

Where this conviction came from is the kernel of the SSRI story, as it maps out a revolution in how the world's number one cause of disability, unipolar depression, is treated. Even before the two critical dangers – causing suicidal thoughts in a significant minority of patients and being far harder to come off than originally thought – were officially acknowledged, there was considerable public debate about so many people taking drugs to change how they perceive the world.

The good side was that it brought depression out of the closet; the bad, that it would come to be talked about almost exclusively as a condition to be got rid of, not to be understood in any social or personal context, or as something to be challenged, or in any other sense embraced for what it might reveal about one's life, and specifically, those tendencies that lead to a negative or anxious or depressed state of mind.

It is not as though the idea of changing brain chemistry is new. Anyone who has ever taken recreational drugs such as cannabis or alcohol knows that the whole idea is to change the chemical structure of their brain, sometimes with disastrous long-term effects. The crucial point is to get the chemistry right.

Even if drugs help, which they seem to for many, the thinking behind the SSRIs is conceptually flawed, Valenstein argues. Consider, first, the frequently cited analogy between SSRIs for depression and insulin for diabetics.

> Insulin corrects an identified deficiency; antidepressants are presumed to do the same. But this analogy is not valid. Depressed patients are commonly told they have a serotonin deficiency (or more generally, a biochemical problem), but no tests are performed to verify this statement. Moreover, unlike the case with insulin and diabetes, virtually nothing is known about the way a serotonin deficiency could cause depression.
>
> While *on average* [Valenstein's italics] depressed patients may have low levels of serotonin activity, about one half of these patients have normal levels of serotonin, and a few may even have levels that are unusually high. Other studies have found no significant relationship between serotonin activity and depression ... It is also not clear that antidepressants actually increase serotonin activity, except for a relatively brief period. Thus, there may be neither a deficiency in serotonin, nor a correction provided by the treatment. It typically takes several weeks before depressed patients begin to show clinical improvement, even though drugs such as Prozac or Effexor increase serotonin activity within hours. By the time clinical improvement occurs, serotonin activity is probably no longer elevated, because physiological mechanisms compensate for the initial effect of the drug treatment. For example, the number of receptors capable of responding to serotonin will decrease as weeks go by.
>
> Even if, for the sake of argument, it is assumed that low serotonin activity is found reliably in depressed patients, this would not prove

> that the low serotonin activity caused the depression. It might just as well be an effect of depression as its cause. Many depressed patients live in an almost constant state of stress. They may be agitated, pacing up and down, or almost immobilized. They may have insomnia or sleep excessively. Some depressed patients lose interest in food, while others indulge in binge eating. Because many studies in both animals and humans have demonstrated that the state of stress can produce biochemical, physiological, and even anatomical changes in the brain, any unusual feature found in the brains of depressed people should not be assumed to have caused the depression.[7]

If our brain chemistry can change how we think, as evidence from the SSRIs suggests, then how we think can also affect healthy brain chemistry, especially when one considers the vast potential of our mind. 'There are more cell meeting points in a human brain than there are stars in our galaxy,' Ian Robertson said in his book, *Mind Sculpture*.

> Everything which makes up 'you' – memories and hopes, pain and pleasure, morals and malevolence – is embroidered in a trembling web of 100 billion brain cells. On average, each cell is connected 1,000 times with other neurones, making a total of 100,000 billion connections.[8]

Moreover, as Milton wrote in *Paradise Lost*, 'The mind is its own place. Can make a Heaven of Hell, a Hell of Heaven.' The ability to reprogramme these connections so they bring about a more optimistic approach to life is well documented through strategies such as cognitive behavioural therapy (CBT). But unlike SSRIs, which are often paid via insurance premiums or general taxation and very convenient, changing the patterns of one's mind takes time, money and effort for the patient and many more headaches for those who must balance budgets. One reason the so-called talking cures such as CBT are not more generally offered is because they are notoriously hard to evaluate and therefore get through the various reimbursement hurdles. SSRIs are as good as it gets in the surgery because they suit everyone.

It is not entirely surprising therefore that people so readily colluded with pharma. People were easily convinced of the value of the SSRIs, particularly when everyone was raving about them and they were billed as non-addictive and therefore better than the benzodiazepine tranquillizers that preceded them. The horrendous problems coming off drugs such as Valium received such a bad press that UK doctors were finally issued with guidance not to prescribe them for more than 28 days, including a tapering-off period. They were supposed to deal with short-term events in people's lives. Nevertheless, in the year to March 2002, decades after their addiction potential was realized, 12.5 million prescriptions were still being written for the benzos in England alone.[9]

An estimated one million addicts remained locked in the twilight world induced by these drugs. Barry, an accountant in Lancashire, spent ten years addicted to various benzodiazepines and says, when he finally came off, 'I couldn't believe the colour of the sky and the flowers, and the noise was so loud.' But that wonder has since been replaced by anger as he asks questions that are as pertinent now as they were 40 years ago when the drugs were first launched. 'For me, the Government ministers are cowards. If they had gone through one-hundredth of what I've gone through then they would have done something about this a long time ago. Why have the Government looked the other way? Why have they allowed so many people to get addicted to a legal drug and not put any money into services to help people?'[10]

Any lessons which might have been learned were repeated with the SSRIs. Peter Kramer's *Listening to Prozac*, which came out in 1993, was a eulogy, if such a thing is possible about a drug. The book remained on the *New York Times*' bestseller list for 21 weeks, citing case study after case study of patients whose lives had been transformed after receiving treatment. Kramer had captured the popular imagination, much as Freud had in Vienna 100 years earlier with his endless reports of patients being treated with his revolutionary psychotherapeutic methods.

As psychobabble gave way to biobabble, psychopharmacology became more entrenched in the popular mind. Kramer, for example, was writing about 'the transformative powers of the medicine – how it went beyond treating illness to changing personality, how it entered into our struggle to understand the self.'

And millions of people believed him. They wanted to believe, as did most of the medical establishment. But in contrast to such high and avidly received praise, there was a persistent dissent, a sort of static that could always be heard in the distance. It was faint, however, and easily missed, highlighting as it did the risks as well as the benefits of having one's neurotransmitters messed with, particularly if one was only mildly depressed.

In the fall of 1994, when Prozac went on trial for the first time, most of the world's press were covering the main story, which was whether or not O.J. Simpson had killed his wife. John Cornwell, working for the

UK's *Sunday Times Magazine*, was one of only a handful of journalists to sit through all 11 weeks of evidence heard in a Louisville, Kentucky, court at this critical juncture in the drug's fortunes.

Cornwell's job was to make some sense of why a 47-year-old man on Prozac should suddenly return to his former place of work and shoot 20 of his co-workers, killing eight plus himself. What he heard in that courtroom clearly made him wary of the Kramer-type gloss being put out about the SSRIs. Specifically, he objected to how it obscured the inevitable darker side of a medicine that was about to transform not just individual cases of depression, but, as he put it, how people fundamentally saw themselves. In his book of that trial, *The Power to Harm: Mind, Medicine and Murder on Trial*, he wrote:

> Here was the ultimate endorsement for a pharmaceutical product: a psychiatrist who claimed the drug made people feel 'better than normal', and without physical or psychological cost. Here, moreover, was the enthusiastic proclamation of a new vision of human identity for the 21st century: that personhood is a chemical-software program in the brain, and that it is now within our grasp to rewrite that program should it prove defective.[11]

The purpose of the trial had been to decide whether Prozac, the drug Joseph Wesbecker had been taking and which was then still in its first flush of youth, had caused him to commit this terrible atrocity. Prozac was drawing in users at an unprecedented rate for a modern pharmaceutical at that time, and the fortunes of Eli Lilly, the company that made it, were inextricably linked to the drug's fate. Projections at the time of the trial were that [Prozac] would earn Lilly $1.7 billion in 1995, accounting for almost a third of its revenues. 'Winning the case convincingly would give Lilly a powerful promotional gambit to demonstrate to the world that the drug stood vindicated by jury verdict,' wrote Cornwell. 'The consequences of a loss, on the other hand, could be catastrophic.'[12]

Lilly was rigorous in its defence of the charge that it had been negligent in its testing or marketing of Prozac. 'The defence strategy focused on Wesbecker as the product of a dysfunctional family that had suffered from hereditary mental illness in three generations,' wrote Cornwell. 'At the same time, they presented Lilly and its drug-trial procedures as irreproachable.'[13]

Two things perplexed Cornwell enough to spur him to write his book. One was the whole question of responsibility: how a drug that purports to change our brain chemistry when it is being promoted can so easily be stripped of that ability when it stands accused of harm. And second, how the rigour of the legal process fell far short, in his view, of enabling the jury to grasp the full picture of what was happening.

And it certainly got Cornwell thinking about the role of money in influencing people's perception of drugs and the process by which we get those drugs.

> In its determination that Prozac prevail on the market, Lilly showed a consistent pattern of conduct, marked by a tendency to manipulate information to its own ends: according to the judge, even to the extent of influencing the outcome of the Louisville trial with a secret deal.14

Lilly had apparently been able to thwart the plaintiffs' attempts to introduce testimony revealing that in 1985 Lilly had pleaded guilty in a federal court to 25 counts of misdemeanour in the handling of another drug, Oraflex. This was an anti-inflammatory agent used in the treatment of arthritis that was implicated in an estimated 72 deaths in the early 1980s.

> It was not long before I realized that the implications of this case went far beyond the tragic incident and the subsequent postures of the litigating parties. This was a story that embraced new brain science and profound issues of personal responsibility; competitive business practices in contracting markets and endemic workplace stress; the American mania for civil-liability suits and high-stakes contingency litigation. Crucially, it involved the gulf between authentic public health needs and the commercial goals of the pharmaceutical industry; the public's right to know the unadorned truth about medication and the pharmaceutical industry's tendency to withhold secretive information in the interest of corporate aims.[15]

Not long after the trial ended, Cornwell reported that,

> the presiding judge published a motion in his court declaring that he believed Lilly had secured its verdict with a secret payment to the plaintiffs. The judge was alleging that Lilly had paid to withhold the potentially damaging testimony about Lilly's misdemeanours in its reporting on Oraflex, evidence that in the judge's view might have affected the jury verdict. At first, Lilly and the plaintiffs denied any arrangement, but both sides eventually acknowledged, under pressure, that there had indeed been a confidential agreement.[16]

Cornwell sums up what he learned from the incident, which happened not much more than a decade ago. First, he describes it as 'a story of an individual whose community had despaired of helping him except by offering a pharmaceutical remedy which reduced his problems to his brain chemistry. The civil action in Louisville signally failed to discover the community's responsibility in the Wesbecker tragedy; by doing a secret deal with the plaintiffs, and effectively using the court action as a public relations opportunity, Eli Lilly compounded that failure.'[17]

Times moved on and, in late 2001, when the body of evidence about this whole class of drugs had built up considerably, GlaxoSmithKline faced a very different ordeal. The British company was ordered by a Wyoming judge to pay $6.4 million (£4.5 million) in compensation to the surviving relatives of a 60-year-old man, Donald Schell, who had killed his wife, daughter and granddaughter in 1998 while on Paxil (Seroxat in the UK). Like Lilly, GlaxoSmithKline had claimed it was the initial illness, not the drugs to treat it, that caused the tragedy. Unlike Lilly, GlaxoSmithKline lost and immediately appealed.[18]

This was not the only case. Examples of the drugs causing akathisia – severe anxiety which can lead to thoughts of suicide or violence – have mounted steadily over the years. Eric Harris, the 18-year-old American who shot 12 pupils and a teacher at Columbine High School, had been prescribed an SSRI. 'Every single school shooting can be traced to the use of these drugs,' Dr Ann Blake, author of *Prozac: Panacea or Pandora?*, told journalist Sally Eyden in the *Daily Express*.[19]

In 2000, Dr David Healy of the University of Wales College of Medicine did his own experiment by taking a group of 20 healthy volunteers with no record of depression and putting them on an SSRI for two weeks. Two became suicidal. One was a 30-year-old woman who became obsessed with the idea of throwing herself under a car or train. The other was 28, also female, and fantasized about hanging herself.[20]

Support groups set up by people who had had these kinds of experiences flourished and word spread. Ramzia Kabbani, who had been prescribed an SSRI in the aftermath of her fiancé's death from a heart attack, set up the Prozac Survivors' Support Group in 1999, for example. Despite no prior history of mental problems, she began acting recklessly, had suicidal thoughts and seizures, which she remains convinced are attributable to her treatment. Within three years of setting up her group, she had received 4,000 calls from fellow sufferers.[21]

Withdrawal syndrome

Perhaps the worst thing was that once the doubts started and people tried to come off the drugs, a significant minority found they could not. The so-called 'withdrawal syndrome', known about since the 1990s, is devastating. Sarah, a young college student, who was prescribed Seroxat for generalized anxiety disorder (GAD), is fairly typical.

Her harrowing experiences of trying to come off this apparently safe and popular drug made up just one response to a BBC *Panorama* documentary in the autumn of 2002, *Secrets of Seroxat*. Sarah described how she had been initially prescribed Seroxat to deal with a wobbly sensation, as if on a boat, she said, that was bobbing up and down. It was a condition various tests had confirmed was not caused by an inner ear or balance problem. After A levels she started a law degree at Birmingham University and would travel in from Coventry by train each day. 'As the wobbly sensation started to intensify, I worried that I would find myself overcome by it and stranded,' she said.

In November 1997, during her second year at university, GAD was diagnosed and Sarah was prescribed Seroxat.

> When I first started taking Seroxat I noticed no difference to the wobbly sensation, but felt detached from reality and became lethargic. I would frequently experience 'electric shocks', which caused me to visibly jolt. The tiredness and detachment feeling affected my ability to study and travel to university, leading to the second year of my degree being postponed.

After six months, there was a noticeable improvement to the wobbly sensation and Sarah returned to university. By now her weight had started to increase, however, and she needed increasing amounts of sleep. In May 2000, just before her finals, her GP decided it was time she came off Seroxat over a period of two weeks.

> As soon as I started to decrease, new feelings began. My legs were restless and constantly aching, I was nauseous and unable to keep food down, constantly dizzy, aching and feeling like I had the flu. By the time I had finished reducing, I was too ill to leave my bed; I was exhausted and couldn't see clearly, I needed help to get to the bathroom and feed myself. The GP put me back on 20mg of Seroxat and within days I recovered, just in time to sit final exams.

In August 2000, Sarah moved to London and received a call from her father, who was on business in Singapore, to say he had just seen a newsflash about Seroxat. Sarah decided to try coming off again. Her GP recommended a more gradual tapering method and prescribed Seroxat liquid.

> I measured it out with a cup, cutting down 2–3mg each week. By the time I got near 12mg, I was in physical and emotional turmoil. The nausea had returned, along with flu-feelings, aches, blinding dizziness, exhaustion, rapid and painful successive electric shocks and depression. Most disturbing was the onset of suicidal thoughts and violent nightmares, in which I saw members of my family hurt. For weeks, I was unable to leave my bed. Friends would visit me with food parcels and cook for me.

Sarah's GP put her back on 30mg of Seroxat and she made nearly a full recovery. But by June 2002, her weight had doubled from when she had started taking the drug, bringing about all sorts of associated problems. 'I was also requiring increasing amounts of sleep, sometimes 14 hours a night. I found it increasingly difficult to concentrate and was without energy. I decided to postpone my career for a year to try and withdraw from Seroxat.' By May 2003, she was reducing from Seroxat using its liquid form and a syringe.

> It has been a long, hard, painful process. I reached 16mg in the New Year, but the symptoms of withdrawal became overwhelming and unbearable and I had to increase my dose back to 20mg. I am still waiting to feel well again so I can continue reducing, 1mg per fortnight.[22]

Cardiff solicitor, Mark Harvey, was one of many to start challenging new definitions of 'addiction' as he prepared a case against GlaxoSmithKline, the company that makes Seroxat. Harvey told Simon Garfield in the *Observer Magazine*:

> However you dress it up, they're trying to suggest that it's not a major issue. But I've got people who say they've been trying to get off it for four or five years and say, 'My life is a misery.' I've heard this argument about it not being addictive, but I think it's mischievous. What they're saying is that the body doesn't become so absorbent to the drug that you have to keep prescribing larger and larger amounts.
>
> They may well be right. But I have to say that if you're a patient and you read your information sheet that says, 'These tablets are not addictive', then they understand that as meaning, 'If I want to come

> off this drug then I should be able to do so without any problems, like coming off penicillin.' But to say that there's a technical definition to 'addiction' is wrong. It's bad enough doing it to a doctor, but you certainly shouldn't do it to a member of the public.[23]

The worried well

Claims that the SSRIs helped some people but induced horrendous side effects in a significant minority of others had been made several times over the years. Professor Healy of the University of Wales, for example, had acted as an expert witness in another case against Prozac. As such, he had been privy to previously undisclosed research from both Pfizer and GlaxoSmithKline that highlighted holes in the companies' main defence of their products, that it was not the drugs themselves that induced bizarre behaviour but the underlying mental disorder the drugs were being used to treat.

'The Pfizer archives contain healthy volunteer trials that show people became agitated and probably suicidal on Pfizer's sertraline (Lustral) in the early 1980s,' Healy told Simon Crompton in *The Times* newspaper. 'In the GlaxoSmithKline archives, the data showed that they were concerned about people being hooked on Seroxat in the 1980s.'[24]

Most studies looking into the effects of SSRIs on healthy volunteers had never been published. In the case of Prozac, just 12 out of 53 had been reported on. These unseen trials were important because most published studies had used data looking at the effect of Prozac not on healthy volunteers, but on people hospitalized with depression. 'But for years,' Crompton pointed out, 'Prozac and the like had been doled out to mildly depressed people – whose brain chemistry was likely to be different from that of severely depressed people in hospital. No one had published studies about the side effects on Joe Public.'[25]

This was where the significance of the *Panorama* programmes became apparent. They vividly portrayed, for the first time, the widespread and harrowing effects of the drugs on the general public. Any hopeful assumptions that since the claims against the SSRIs were so serious they must have been fully checked out by the regulators were instantly crushed.

Indeed, the response to the first programme was so overwhelming that a second broadcast was scheduled the following spring, called 'Emails From the Edge'. Around 1,370 people like Sarah had contacted the programme makers to report similar withdrawal reactions. What no one knew, and what the programme revealed, was that these side effects were not being looked into. Despite all sorts of official reporting schemes whereby doctors flag up side effects for the benefit of the public good, no one at the MHRA was following them up. The MHRA stood charged on public television of failing in its duty as a public body responsible for the safety of prescribed medicines. People had tried to tell their GPs; others had written to the MHRA direct. But no one was listening. Even GPs who took the time to report how their patients were reacting to commonly prescribed drugs were not taken seriously.

To substantiate the claim, as if the facts hadn't spoken sufficiently eloquently for themselves, the programme makers commissioned a report analysing the 1,370 emails that had been sent in by viewers plus another 862 messages on a similar theme addressed to a website discussion group. Based on this evidence alone, and published in the *International Journal of Risk and Safety*, the report links Seroxat to 16 suicides, 47 cases of attempted suicide, 92 people who had thoughts of harming themselves or others, and 19 children who had suffered serious side effects.

And this was only the beginning. The *Observer* newspaper reported:

> The outcry that followed forced GlaxoSmithKline to make a stunning admission. In June 2003, it corrected its prescribing instructions for Seroxat, revising its estimate of the risk of withdrawal symptoms from one in 500 to one in four.[26]

But perhaps the most telling insight into the inner sanctum of the MHRA came in a third *Panorama* programme, when its chief executive Professor Alasdair Breckenridge appeared before the cameras himself. His performance, apparently stonewalling the interviewer about important questions regarding the drug's safety, was recalled with some embarrassment when he gave evidence to the parliamentary inquiry. And although he insisted that several hours of interviewing had been edited down to a few minutes the fact remains that his only response as to why the agency had taken so long to investigate mounting evidence of harm was that his staff was awaiting the results of more studies to confirm the extent and nature of that harm.

The irony of a delay being used to justify a delay was not lost on the viewers. The *Observer* report continued:

> The events that led to Seroxat's exposure would seem to suggest that it was television power that forced GlaxoSmithKline to recant. But it was really the internet that allowed public health activists to do an end run around GlaxoSmithKline's and the medical authorities'

> denials of the drug risks. An explosion of websites dedicated to vivid accounts of antidepressant reactions told these campaigners about hundreds of thousands affected by a problem that officially did not exist. The internet was groaning with evidence; over time, the 'cover-up' became more obvious as the weight of scientific evidence got stronger and public protest grew.[27]

Professor Healy sums up the sorry episode well. When asked at the parliamentary inquiry about whether waiting for ten years before conducting a thorough review of the SSRIs represented a good track record, he said, 'In actual fact, here in the UK we track the fate of parcels through the post 100 times more accurately than you track the fate of people who have been killed by SSRI or other drugs.'[28]

Meanwhile, over in the US, the feud over pharma companies not revealing the full warts-and-all picture of their products by only publishing good data was moving out of the realm of the unethical and into the illegal. In June 2004, New York attorney general Eliot Spitzer accused GlaxoSmithKline of 'repeated and persistent fraud' for concealing vital safety information when Seroxat, or Paxil as it is known in the US, is used in children.

According to the FDA, 2.23 million prescriptions for Paxil had been dispensed to people under the age of 17 in 2002 for a range of conditions that include depression, attention-deficit disorder, anxiety and other mood disorders.[29] Spitzer's contention did not concern whether the drug was good or not, only that information had been withheld from the assessment process. To that end he cited New York Executive Law 63 (12), which allows the attorney general to obtain compensation and damages from companies who make 'any deception, misrepresentation, concealment or suppression' of material fact.

Spitzer pointed out that the company had done several studies, only one of which generated the results it wanted to use in promoting the drug. Its 'efforts to suppress the other studies was harmful and improper to the doctors who were making prescribing decisions and it violated the law,' he said.[30]

In one study that was not published, for example, 7.7% of the young people taking Paxil had suicidal thoughts, compared with just 3% of the placebo arm.[31] The British company did not come out well, and chose to settle the affair with a one-off $250 million fine, which for an organization its size was not a lot of money. But it also agreed to set up a public register of all clinical trials on all of its drugs. This breached a long-standing convention, vigorously upheld by the regulators, whereby clinical trial results were regarded as company property and commercially confidential.

One bit of particularly damning evidence was an internal company memo published in the medical journal, the *Lancet*, and cited by Spitzer. 'It would be commercially unacceptable to include a statement that efficacy had not been demonstrated,' it said, before going on to recommend the company prepare and publish a full article on the one study out of five that had some favourable conclusions.[32] That study was published in the *Journal of the American Academy of Child and Adolescent Psychiatry*, authored by two GlaxoSmithKline scientists.

Meanwhile, field sales forces had received a memo from Paxil's product manager, Zachary Hawkins, which said, 'Paxil demonstrates remarkably efficacy and safety in the treatment of adolescent depression', a claim Spitzer said in the lawsuit was completely untrue.[33]

The FDA has since commissioned a study by experts in suicidal behaviour from the University of Columbia to build a better picture of the links between children being prescribed antidepressants and any subsequent suicidal behaviour. But studies, however many are conducted, cannot dispel doubts if people remain unconvinced of the impartiality of those conducting and analysing the findings. Indeed, when the results of that two-year study Breckenridge had referred to were eventually made public in December 2004, critics had a field day. The trouble was the sheer volume of data, with unpublished trials of all the SSRIs on adults outnumbering published results by eight to one. Most of the data used had been supplied in the form of drug companies' summaries, plus some individual case reports.

And tellingly, when what should have been the final verdict on this incredibly popular class of drugs was announced, there was no representation from either the Royal College of Psychiatrists, or the leading mental health charity MIND. Indeed, Richard Brook, chief executive of MIND, had resigned from the MHRA expert committee charged with assessing the SSRIs before this final verdict, saying the regulator had been sitting on evidence that Seroxat had been prescribed in unsafe doses for ten years.[34]

Ushering in changes

The train of events that had so battered the reputation of its US counterpart, the FDA, was being replicated on the other side of the Atlantic as measures were instantly taken to restore public confidence in the whole process of medicines regulation. What was revealed in the process showed just how closely aligned the aims of the regulators and the industry have become.

The Association of the British Pharmaceutical Industry (ABPI), according to one national newspaper, didn't much care for the changes that had been ushered in, which include a new 18-strong commission to advise ministers on the safety and effectiveness of medicines. This new body replaces both the Medicines Commission and the Committee on Safety of Medicines and, to help prove impartiality, includes two members of the public and no industry representatives.

Industry used to have three people on the ministerial advisory board and two on the Medicines Commission, the drug licensing appeal body. In a letter of protest before the changes were announced, ABPI president, Dr John Patterson, wrote to Professor Sir Alasdair Breckenridge of the MHRA in January 2004, saying:

> We remain concerned at the lack of representation of the pharmaceutical industry at board level within the MHRA ... As the only regulatory agency that is fully industry-funded, we believe it is essential that we have a say on a variety of issues, not least financial matters relating to fees and service levels.[35]

As an important NHS partner, industry had become accustomed to having some say in matters relating to drug policy. And after more ABPI pressure for greater representation, 'Roy Alder, a senior MHRA official, suggested in March 2004 that "there could be scope for industry to make a similar input to MHRA business and operational policy" through other ways.'[36]

How this new set-up will pan out remains to be seen, especially in the light of what the parliamentary inquiry into the industry found. The summary of the final report noted:

> The [MHRA] has been too close to industry, a closeness underpinned by common policy objectives, agreed processes, frequent contact, consultation and interchange of staff. We are concerned that a rather lax regime is exacerbated by the MHRA's need to compete with other European regulators for licence application business.[37]

Big pharma's big money affects the regulation of the medicines business at every level and in all countries. Even if cutting-edge experts who have no connection with industry can be found, and even if those experts are prepared to wade through the full warts-and-all disclosures of drug company research that are being called for (and promised in some countries), real change to any regulatory system can only come from greater involvement of the people in the systems that have been set up to protect them.

This won't be achieved by a couple of lay people being invited to sit on a few committees, nor by all data informing every single licensing decision being up for scrutiny, as has also been promised. Things will only change substantially when the whole process can move to reflect the climate of the times, which has changed considerably since the post-war years when most systems were set up.

The wider significance of the SSRI story is, as Collier says, that it shows how people's experience of medicine has to be listened to in the end. It doesn't go away, and the wall in the minds of doctors and regulators who had stopped listening was forced down eventually. In a sense, what has happened is not so dissimilar to what many people in Leipzig, in former East Germany, believe was achieved by their silent protests year after year before events finally turned and started to lead to the dismantling of the Berlin Wall in 1989.

The Berlin Wall of healthcare is to be found in systems that were created when patients were far more passive than they are now, when doctors were more revered than they are now, and when, perhaps most importantly, no one dreamt for a second that medicines could ever be prescribed for anything but the public good. It exists primarily in the authority of medicine that people must buy into at some level for the system to work. As time moves on and, quite rightly, people want more say in how they are treated, the systems supporting this authority have proved too rigid and certainly too inaccessible.

In the past it didn't seem to matter that the voices of patients weren't heard because of a basic trust that doctor knew best. If nothing else, the SSRI story has shown that the patient voice does matter. To what extent regulatory systems can respond remains to be seen.

7

A crisis in medicine

The stories of the Cox-2s and the SSRIs are not the first examples of medicines regulation going awry, nor will they be the last. They are the ones that got told because enough doctors with enough clout decided to speak up at a time when enough people were already wondering about the extent of the commercial influence in medicine.

The regulators tightened their procedures but saw it more as a time for reflection than wholesale change. Nothing had gone awry in their book because this is largely how the system works. No one wants the public to be prescribed seriously bad drugs, least of all drug companies who would have to pay significant sums in compensation. Vioxx is as good an example as any of the amounts involved. In August 2005, the legal claims facing Merck were put at $18 billion (£10 billion) after a Texas court awarded $253.4 million to the widow of Bob Ernst, a 59-year-old produce manager for the retailer, Wal-Mart. Ernst had died in 2001 having taken Vioxx for eight months and for reasons that will continue to be debated in the courts, because Merck has stated its intention to defend itself aggressively case by case.

And, of course, early decisions affect all the others. Benjamin Zipursky, a professor at Fordham School of Law in New York told *The Times* newspaper, 'A Merck loss means the jury believes the plaintiff's story about the company's wrongful conduct. That carries into the future.'[1] With more than 4,000 cases filed in the US alone, the company's $675 million fighting fund suddenly seemed rather inadequate and its shares took a nearly 8% dive on the news.

Even if the Texas decision about Vioxx – and all it implies in terms of how the medicines business affects people – does suggest a deeper crisis in the relationship between science, commerce and politics, it is not at all clear how to deal with it. One response to the Vioxx drama in the US was, as we have seen, to close ranks and find ways of resolving internal disputes before the public has any reason to know anything is amiss. And the US is more open than most. Many countries don't have the kind of whistle-blower protection that enabled Graham to express his concerns about the drug. The staff in regulatory authorities around the world routinely sign confidentiality agreements that serve two purposes. One is to protect the commercial interests involved in the drugs they are investigating, and the other is to shield the public from the alarm that inevitably follows safety concerns about popular drugs that have been communicated irresponsibly.

But paternalism can be taken too far, and one effect of the recent regulatory scandals has been to highlight how layer upon layer of protection for the public has also isolated them almost entirely from any serious debate about how the medicines business operates. Another is that despite welcome new pledges of transparency, full disclosure of trial results and no more conflicts of interest, the public is still largely peripheral to the process and still rightly concerned about any other regulatory failures in the pipeline.

Even when they are invited to sit on regulatory committees, as is increasingly the case, they can be little more than a token presence. This is not to negate the value of the increasingly fashionable 'patient representative', rather to point out how it is rather more convincing in theory than reality.

One reason is that truly representative people don't speak the language of science, which is an important tool to work through the labyrinth of rules designed to balance commercial and public health interests. Second, any contenders who are genuinely interested in getting a better deal from the politics of health, usually find they can use their time more effectively elsewhere. One is left therefore with people with a stake in the pharmaceutical model, either because they suffer from a chronic condition themselves or because they have been paid to put themselves forward by industry.

Meanwhile, all this protection for the public is not well equipped to resist commercial influence. When the stakes were sufficiently high, the rules failed to prevent catastrophe. And in the absence of any real surveillance from the public, or a significant narrowing in the gap between private and public sector science, there doesn't seem to be much in place to guarantee similar scandals won't happen again.

This single structural problem doesn't just lead to occasional regulatory disasters; it can also be shown to contribute to inappropriate prescribing, a progressive collapse in public faith in doctors, and an inherent bias away from non-pharmaceutical approaches to healthcare.

In the UK, the regulators' £65 million ($117 million) annual budget is funded entirely by industry (60% via licensing fees for drugs seeking approval and 40% via an annual service fee). This money goes to paying its 750 staff, whose job is to interpret the laws that have been passed for our protection.[2] Moreover, the lion's share, the money that comes from licensing fees from Europe-wide applications for new drugs, is hotly fought over among Europe's other national regulatory agencies.

It is against such a background that the rules that protect our interests are interpreted. These say, for example, how much testing a drug must go through to get a licence, the extent to which animals are used, the size of the trials, how they are presented, and so on. Standards that require a high level of testing also have the effect of barring companies that don't have the money to fulfil the obligations of entry into the big pharma markets. But it seems that whatever level of protection is erected by law, there is no guarantee within the system that the trial results insisted upon are scrutinized in anything like the detail necessary for effective regulation. The UK parliamentary report found, 'The MHRA relies on company data, presented as a series of detailed assessment reports, in its decision whether or not to license a drug. Raw data are very rarely analysed.'[3]

Dr John Griffin, a former chief medicines regulator for the UK's Department of Health, is one who thinks the rules could go further.

> Drug regulation is largely a paper exercise and it relies on the honesty and integrity of the person making the application. If there are problems with non-disclosure of information, as there have been in at least half a dozen cases in recent years, then there will be problems with the subsequent labelling and usage of that drug.[4]

He suggests, for example, how regulators could conduct their own small-scale studies to confirm results if there is reason to believe it is in the public interest so to do.

The public might go further still, requiring regulators to have a mandate to conduct independent exercises if they thought it was in their best interests to do so. Yet no one knows what the public want because there is no way of knowing. No other industry, except perhaps financial services, is so bound by red tape, so restricted by law in what it can and cannot do; no other industry requires such high standards of proof; and for no other industry is the goodwill of its political paymasters more critical, because they pay the drugs bill at the end of the day – not to mention their obligation to protect public health.

But all these rules have the effect of distancing the regulators (the police if you like) from the very people they are trying to protect. Their world operates from a modern-day citadel that has few windows out and even fewer routes in. The medicines regulator could be on another planet for the amount of coverage it gets in the mainstream press. Even when serious safety concerns are raised over commonly prescribed drugs, the issues are rarely debated outside the financial pages of the more serious papers, and then only to cost the damage.

Besides, as veteran commentator on the business, Dr Philip Brown, points out:

> Laws provide little protection against risk. What they do is put people in place who are supposed to protect the general population from risk, without due regard to the degree of protection desired by those who are being protected. Whenever there is a hazard, the authorities get it wrong; either they exaggerate the risk or they dismiss it. They never get it right, because they have no idea what the population at large thinks and does.[5]

The private market is virtually the only channel that has been created whereby people can react to either the drugs industry or its close ally, the regulator. They can walk away from drugs and try the complementary approach, of course, as people are doing in ever-increasing numbers on both sides of the Atlantic. But as citizens who are not ill, they have no way of expressing their appreciation for the likes of Topol or Graham, for example, who took some professional risk to speak up on their behalf.

Trust slips away

Trust in medicine falters gradually, almost by default, leading to something of a crisis where, on the one hand, regulators seem to work more closely with industry than with the public they serve. And, on the other, equally abundant evidence shows how people are openly defying what the regulators do and say. Fears over the MMR vaccine in the UK, for example, prompted a mass rejection of national health policy, despite the best clinical evidence that could find no justification for those fears. Meanwhile, health stores transparently avoid complying with labelling regulations by not making any claims for their products on the labels at all. And of course, patients themselves, in increasing numbers, are choosing to pay out of their own pockets for untested treatments rather than use those that have gone through the whole gamut of regulations and can be had for free.

Trust in medicine and in the medicines regulator is both crucial and at an all-time low, prompting regulators on both sides of the Atlantic to jump to attention in the wake of the Vioxx and SSRI investigations. Communication with the public rose to the top of the regulatory agenda, along with an insistence on greater transparency throughout the development and marketing process.

But there is nothing the regulators can do to halt the machinations of the medicines business. They can't stop Pfizer denying people level access to what could be an important new drug, for example. This happens because the company finds it commercially advantageous to bundle its brand-leading Lipitor up with the new drug in one combination pill. The new drug is not made available on its own; it only comes as part of a package deal.

As the company embarked on clinical trials for this, Dr Jerry Avorn said in the *New England Journal of Medicine*:

> The current trial designs may not optimally meet the scientific needs of prescribers, the clinical needs of patients, the economic needs of payers, or the regulatory needs of policymakers. But they superbly meet the business needs of the sponsor – to create new knowledge in a way that will protect the market share of the largest drug company's most important product.
>
> A more science-based or patient-centered research design would not have accomplished this goal as well; indeed, any Pfizer official who signed off on such a study might be accused of compromising his or her fiduciary responsibility to the company's shareholders. This is the predictable consequence of an industry-driven approach to defining the nation's drug-research agenda.[6]

Mammon is everywhere in medicine. And whatever rules are put in place to address the inevitable conflicts of interests between private profit and public good, the forces of commerce carry on working regardless to blur the edges between them. That is their essential nature; pharma works in partnership with doctors and patients when it is in its interests to do so, but when it comes down to ownership, it operates alone.

The ownership of knowledge

The boundaries between the private and public sectors are clear when it comes to the ownership of knowledge. Science needs money to acquire knowledge. Industry, meanwhile, needs a reliable base of knowledge on which to make money. The way it gets to own that knowledge is via the patent system. This set of rules is crucial to industry, but again, as with the rules that govern its general operation, they are social contracts with virtually no way for the public to strengthen its side of the bargain by becoming engaged with the issues.

The boundaries as to what is and what is not innovation are set by law, and are under constant challenge from the legal teams of the pharma and generics companies as they battle out cases that can be worth tens or hundreds of millions of dollars. Viagra, arguably the world's most famous drug, had its patent stripped in the UK courts a few years ago on the grounds of obviousness, for example. This is the very opposite of innovation, what we pay our drug companies for. And it only came to light in a case brought about by two pharma companies, Eli Lilly and Icos, that had teamed up to form a joint venture to develop Cialis, the so-called 'weekend' answer to Viagra.

The case hardly raised a mention in the mainstream press, but it explains the intense battle we now see between broadly similar products fighting for a slice of the growing erectile dysfunction market. The science, how the PDE-5 inhibitors work, had apparently been sufficiently written up in the medical literature to strip Pfizer of its 20-year monopoly on how that science is deployed. Pfizer argued, naturally enough and with a pretty solid case one would have thought, that if it had been so obvious why hadn't anyone else done it? It took the risk and should, it said, be entitled to the full rewards for creating what went on to become the world's most famous drug.

Diana Sternfeld, an intellectual property lawyer reporting on the case, pointed out some common misconceptions regarding patents serving the public good, at least as far as UK law is concerned:

> When deciding whether an invention is obvious, the Courts do not ask whether the patent gives the public something which is 'good enough' to deserve the monopoly. The test for obviousness is objective but it is also qualitative and quantitative. There are no units of degrees of inventiveness. Each case has to be looked at on its own facts and circumstances, which is why it is difficult to predict the outcome of a dispute about inventiveness.[7]

Where there is speculation there are also hefty legal fees. And indeed, the money spent by pharma on intellectual property lawyers has long been rising faster than that spent on basic research. An article in *Science* found around 46 intellectual property lawyers employed for every billion dollars of R&D expenditure in 1987. Ten years later, in 1997, there were 75 for the same billion-dollars' worth of medical research.[8]

The secret of life

Like the broader regulatory system governing the medicines business, the rules on ownership only change when sufficient pressure is brought to bear, usually by doctors, who say enough is enough. This happened in the field of molecular biology after irresistible opportunities for private money had been created on the back of the work by Francis Crick and James Watson on the structure of DNA, and specifically, how it answered the question that had baffled biologists for years: how does life reproduce itself?

Commercial interest wasn't awakened immediately because there wasn't any money to be made immediately, but the significance of that work explains the extraordinary battle 50 years later to claim ownership of our human heritage contained in our genome. Once the secret of life was out and once people had developed the tools to start making sense of it, they also started to lay claim to slices of it, as expressed in individual genes or gene sequences.

The politics of patenting life became a clear fight between private interest and public good, and it garnered enough pressure for policy makers to look more closely at how the rules that determine the ownership of science work. Academics such as Martin Bobrow, professor of medical genetics at the University of Cambridge, charged that science as a discipline was being brought into disrepute. Speaking in the early days of the biotech boom in 2000, he said broad patents on minor inventions were encouraging sloppy science that led to a gambling mentality in the investment community.[9]

DNA sequences, he said, could not be treated in the same way as chemical molecules because they were inherently different. 'My view is that it is a false analogy that will lead to false and senseless conclusions because the DNA molecule itself is unimportant chemically. What is important is the information if contains and how this applies to the cells of the body. To claim a patent on the sequence of a gene is the same as claiming copyright on a page that has been ripped out of a book. It makes no sense.'[10]

The EU biotech patenting directive was being debated at the time, but Bubrow's pleas fell on deaf ears because of the overwhelming commercial arguments in favour of genetic material being used for private gain, at least for the 20-year patent term. And they weren't just about economic gain: more money makes the science move faster.

But only in a commercial direction. Patents laws can inhibit innovation, Bobrow said, while pointing out that the public scientist doesn't usually have the resources to play to corporate rules. Unravelling the interlocking and overlapping patents takes time, even with all the legal concessions that exist for academia.

> Someone finds a use for a gene and then finds they are in a big court dispute with the initial innovator. The villains in all this are not the patent lawyers, the academics or the companies. And the problem is not patenting as such but the system we have adopted.[11]

In the EU, a directive was eventually passed that introduced a distinction between genetic material that is in the body and that which has been extracted, the latter being patentable while the former is not. But the cases fighting out this out in the courts never really happened because the entire human genome was soon in the public domain anyway and the initial promise of what one could earn from genetic material was swiftly crushed.

In the US patent office, the initial fervour for gene patents caused the rules to be tightened to insist an inventor shows a clear utility for any invention. It wasn't enough just to identify a gene sequence and slap a patent on it like a prospector might have done on a piece of land in the Californian gold rush. The patent applicant also had to have a pretty good idea of what useful purpose that knowledge might lead to.

As the biotech boom and subsequent bust has shown, finding uses for genes is far from easy. What Crick and Watson had done back in April 1953 was to show the basic mechanism by which life passes from one generation to another, that enables an acorn to grow into an oak tree or a rabbit egg cell to become a rabbit. The secret of life, they said, was contained in the DNA at the heart of each of nature's trillions of kinds of cells. What Crick and Watson revealed is that life is indeed a thread. And within the strands of that coiled thread are the precise instructions to create life and to order it. DNA is that thread. It is structured as a double helix, a sort of spiral staircase whereby information, structured in the banisters of each step, is translated into instructions to build proteins via the step-rungs in between.

Life is extraordinarily simple at one level and worth grasping if only to comprehend the importance of Crick and Watson's discovery and how it was to take medicine into an entirely new era. It consists of the interplay between two kinds of chemicals: proteins and DNA. Proteins, says Matt Ridley in his book, *Genome, the Autobiography of a Species*, represent chemistry, living, breathing, metabolism and behaviour. They are responsible for almost every chemical, structural and regulatory thing that is done in the body. They generate energy, fight infection, digest food, form hair, carry oxygen and so on. 'DNA, on the other hand, represents information, replication, breeding, sex. Neither can exist without the other. It is the classic case of chicken and egg: which came first, DNA or protein?'[12]

The understanding of how life reproduces itself was supposed to make it easier to discover new drugs because it provided the prospect of an astonishingly detailed blueprint for how everything in the body works. Every single protein in the body is made from a gene by a translation of the genetic code that is DNA. That code is a code of chemicals. DNA is a long thin molecule made up of four base chemicals called adenine (A), cytosine (C), guanine (G), and thymine (T). 'It is almost too good to be true, but the code turns out to be written in a way that we can understand,' says Ridley. 'Just like written English, the genetic code is a linear language, written in a straight line. Just like written English, it is digital, in that every letter bears the same importance. Moreover, the language of DNA is considerably simpler than English, since it has an alphabet of only four letters, conventionally known as A, C, G and T.'[13]

Another stunning revelation was to come. The three-letter words of the genetic code are the same in every form of life. 'CGA means arginine and GCG means alanine – in bats, in beetles, in beech trees, in bacteria. Until the genetic code was cracked in the 1960s, we did not know what we now know: that all life is one; seaweed is your distant cousin and anthrax one of your advanced relatives. The unity of life is an empirical fact.'[14]

The processes by which life comes into being are also largely similar. When a plant grows a new leaf, for example, it is because certain genes are expressing themselves in certain cells such that the leaf naturally takes on the colour, feel, shape and form of all the other leaves on that plant. The growth process follows a detailed series of instructions, in other words, that order the production of new cells in a human body like they do new leaves in a plant.

Genes within DNA instruct the body to build proteins. The next stage for scientists was to reduce the definitive knowledge on proteins to a form that could speak the language of genes. Proteins, in school biology, are described as the building blocks of life. But they are flexible entities that change their shape, and therefore their function, under a bewildering array of circumstances. When an egg is boiled, for example, and the white solidifies, that is because the protein, albumin, has changed structure with the heat.

Mostly, we can't detect the changes, but it is understood there are around 100,000 proteins in the human body. Unlike genes, which consist of different combinations of four bases, proteins are made from 20 amino acid building blocks. In addition, the set of proteins a cell uses is in constant flux. Some proteins are broken down and their components recycled in minutes, while others can persist in the cell for days. The confounding factors in trying to map out all the trillions of permutations are influenced by the time of day, what people eat, their age, even their mood. This extraordinary complexity lends credence to the holistic view that there is some process whereby harmony as a whole is maintained and indeed, that balance is the most important determinant of health. The heart of the problem, as pointed out in the opening chapter, lies in the fact that we are dealing not with a chain of causation but with a network that is a system like a spider's web in which every perturbation at any point of the web changes the tension of every fibre right back to its anchorage in the blackberry bush.

Medicine was suddenly being cast within an infinitely vaster framework and new bodies of knowledge began emerging. The word proteomics, for example, was coined as recently as 1994, at a meeting in Sienna, to convey a branch of science that identifies and characterizes proteins.[15] Proteomics companies might compare the tissue of healthy people with those who have a particular disease, for example, isolating those proteins that only show up in the latter. Or big pharma might employ a proteomics company to find biological markers that define the various stages in the development of a disease. Alzheimer's research provides an example where tests to identify the early stages would have considerable commercial potential.

A third avenue builds up maps of cellular pathways and interactions that may be important either in a disease process or in the mechanism of action of a drug. This has led to the emergence of yet another new breed of person, the bioinformaticist, who integrates data on gene expression with those on protein pathways to find patterns no one had previously been able to see.

These patterns relate to how every function in our bodies is maintained and regulated: how we know when to eat and sleep, how we translate food into energy, fight off attack from foreign invaders, organize thoughts and so on. This, more usually known as the *milieu interieur*, consists of a whole host of protective forces that combine to ensure 'a steady state' in mind and body. It is what prompts us to maintain regular rhythms not only within our own lives but also in keeping with those around us in nature, where the passing of day into night, for example, has always determined our sleeping patterns.

Fantastically exciting as this is for the scientific community, it took some time for the private market to kick in. 'It was only at the beginning of the 1980s that biotech began to develop a business edge, and the commercial application of Crick and Watson's discovery has proven more difficult than expected,' says biotech expert Lisa Davies.[16]

Even before the biotech industry got started in earnest, the so-called new science had a dramatic effect on public funding. From the 1970s, as the political climate became more centred on the individual and away from broad collective enterprises, a whole series of laws was passed in the US that made the federally financed National Institutes of Health cooperate with the private sector. Similar laws were passed elsewhere as everyone cheered on the new knowledge and the new medicines it was thought would pour out of the pipeline on the back of it.

Universities, says Sheldon Krimsky, physicist, philosopher and policy analyst at Tuft's University School of Medicine, were transformed at a stroke into little more than instruments of wealth, and any notions of knowledge as human welfare were abandoned in the pursuit of profit. The US National Research Council found that the number of patents held by universities increased by a factor of 15, from 96 to 1,500 from 1965 to 1992, whereas the total number of patents only increased by 50% over the same period. By 2000, universities had been awarded more than 3,200 patents.[17]

'Entrepreneurial scientists no longer identify themselves as having a commitment to investigate public-interest problems *per se*,' says Krimsky. 'The choice of problems is dictated by commercial not social priorities.'[18] He cites biologist and Nobel laureate Philip Sharpe who points out that as universities become more identified with commercial wealth, they are no longer seen 'ivory towers of intellectual pursuit and truthful thoughts, but rather as enterprises driven by arrogant individuals out to capture as much money and influence as possible.'[19]

According to Walter W. Powell and Jason Owen-Smith in their book *To Profit or Not to Profit*:

> The changes underway at universities are the result of multiple forces: a transformation in the nature of knowledge and a redefinition of the mission of universities by both policymakers and key constituents. These trends are so potent that there is little chance for reversing them – nor necessarily a rationale for doing so.[20]

The Human Genome Project

The general current in favour of using private money to fund what was, and is, a breakthrough period in medicine, was helped in no small measure by the Human Genome Project (HGP). This was a vast publicly funded international collaboration that was started in 1990 to decode the entire human DNA sequence and make the information freely available to the scientific community.

Think of the human genome as a rather odd book. Since 97% is apparently blank, we are talking only about the 3% that contains information. This is arranged as chapters, each representing the chromosomes we get from each of our parents. Our 30,000 individual genes are to be found within these chapters. And each, in truth, is a mammoth encyclopaedia in its own right with a mine of lucrative information in terms of what biological events genes give rise to and in which cells they find expression.

Genes not only give us the physical characteristics of our parents but, more importantly, help explain how the 100 trillion cells in our bodies are ordered and regulated, how the cascades of events that lead to illness are triggered, and, by no means least, how awesomely complex it all is.

With the results of the HGP being posted on the Internet for anyone to see, more private money was encouraged in. It was thought that once this key component had been broken down into information it could be manipulated, together with that on other databases, for new answers to old problems.

There were lots of things for these new biotech companies to do. Often, they were just a couple of scientists from a university department trying their luck on the open market by adding value to what was building up in the public domain. No one had ever dreamt they would have so much information, and technologies that could make sense of what was being thrown up were in big demand. Within five years, knowledge of the genome and the technologies to work with it had developed to such a point, US biotech company Celera Genomics in Rockville, Maryland was in a position to challenge the international consortium to a dramatic race to completion. Its slogan was 'Speed matters. Discovery can't wait.'

The press naturally focused on the race, which provided considerable momentum. But there was another aspect to the discomfort that many involved in the public effort felt. John Sulston, director of Cambridge University's Sanger Centre, who received a Nobel Prize in 2002, was leader of the British arm of the consortium. He said that the most important thing was that the knowledge should be available to the whole biological community. 'No single individual or group can credibly claim that they have the expertise to deal with it,' he wrote in his fascinating book, *The Common Thread: A Story of Science, Politics, Ethics and the Human Genome*.

> When the commercial company that became Celera Genomics was launched in May 1998 with the stated aim of becoming 'the definitive source of genomic and associated medical information', the whole future of biology came under threat. For one company was bidding for monopoly control of access to the most fundamental information about humanity, information that is – or should be – our common heritage.[21]

This event triggered an intense political drama which illustrates well the battle between public and private interests in health. The public collaboration described it as a fight to stop fundamental knowledge about our heritage passing into private hands. The other side of the argument was that it took private money to move it along. James Watson, who had been so instrumental in making either project possible, was incensed. According to Sulston, 'he compared [Celera CEO] Craig Venter's attempt to take over human sequencing with Hitler's invasion of Poland, and demanded to know whether Francis Collins [the head of the HGP] was going to be Churchill or Chamberlain.'[22]

At that time, 1998, a lot of companies were trying to patent anything they could on the genome because finding out the functions of individual genes, or providing the tools to do so, became a way of making a lot of money, or so everyone thought.

The rewards of ownership could be seen, for example, in Myriad Genetics of Salt Lake City in Utah owning a series of patents on the *BRCA1* and *BRCA2* genes that are used to assess a woman's chances of developing inherited forms of breast or ovarian cancer. These patents caused a big fuss a few years ago. According to an editorial in *New Scientist*:

> A company owning such patents could earn lucrative royalties from university labs – and, possibly, other companies – that develop tests for the patented genes. But instead, Myriad wants to be the world's sole provider of comprehensive tests on these genes, and is trying to stop anyone else carrying them out.[23]

In 1998, the University of Pennsylvania's genetics laboratory had to shut down its breast cancer testing programme when Myriad Genetics threatened it with patent infringement if it used the *BRCA* genes. And, according to Krimsky, the NHS was faced with a price hike from £960 to screen for the two genes in 1997 to the £2,400 ($4,320) Myriad Genetics was charging the following year.[24] As it happens, the company never enforced its rights.

Nevertheless, the stakes were high, and people like Sulston were astounded public opinion should not be overwhelmingly with the public camp. Much public money had been invested in the project and the results were a great help to Celera and the private sector who kept their data for themselves and were intent on profiting from it. The battle was portrayed in the wider non-academic world as a lone and struggling entrepreneur in Celera up against a federal goliath intent on stifling private enterprise.

In the UK, the *Economist*, for example, applauded the private initiative.

> The founders of Celera Genomics found a way to profit from the genome – or, to be more accurate, from carefully annotated and ingeniously packaged descriptions of bits of it, which drug companies were happy to buy. As a result, they got a move on. They did their work faster and in some ways better than their public-sector rivals – who would probably still be plodding towards their goal had they not had the spur of competition. The public researchers complain that Celera drew on public knowledge in order to advance their private goals. So it did – that is what public knowledge is for.[25]

Sulston recalls it rather differently:

> Celera was much more powerful than it appeared. Representing private enterprise, the company could count on the backing of many in Congress who were philosophically opposed to state-funded projects. By repeatedly hinting that the government was wasting its money, [Celera] clearly aimed to influence congressional policy on the funding of the Human Genome Project, if possible to the extent of shutting it down.[26]

According to Bobrow, Celera's scientists were not doing anything significantly differently from the public endeavour; they just had a few powerful computers, the good tailwind created by the international effort, and an awful lot of influence to push the collective cause of public support for private science. Meanwhile, the patenting of gene sequences had reached fever pitch. Celera alone announced in October 1999 that it had applied for patents on 6,500 new genes.[27] And although these were provisional applications, with the company claiming it would pursue only 200–300 of them, they potentially gave Celera title to a great deal more biological information than had been suggested when the company was launched.

Patent offices not only operate in the same kind of isolation as the regulators, but they also work several years behind the current state of knowledge. Their job is to decide if something was innovative when the application was first made, which might have been years before the patent decision is taken. It would be irrelevant that the sequence of the entire human genome was on the Internet at the time of the patent decision, for example, if a patent had been filed earlier. Moreover, legal precedents had been set about the patenting of natural substances. Strains of yeast had been patented, for example, to protect a company's brand of beer, opening the way for our genes to fall into private hands. 'The rules had been changing over the years by a gradual creep effect,' Bobrow said. 'The rights being granted on some sequences were very extensive and many scientists felt that with human genes, a line had been passed and there needed to be a stronger protest because it was clearly a policy issue that couldn't be left to lawyers alone.'[28]

That protest, along with arguments between the two sides as to how far they had got, who said what about whom, and so on, became such an embarrassment, that US president Bill Clinton appointed an impartial broker in Ari Patrinos from the Department of Energy to get the two sides to at least pretend to be collaborating. 'The White House wanted something nice to happen about the human genome, which was now getting a lot of press attention,'[29] recalls Sulston.

After a few sessions over beer and pizza, the two heads, Craig Venter and Francis Collins, agreed to a joint statement about the completion of the sequence, simultaneous publication later in the year and a truce in the war of words about who had done what. On 26 June 2000, UK Prime Minister Tony Blair and Bill Clinton announced the secrets of the genome would be freely available to all researchers and patents on individual genes banned.

The bubble bursts

Having two heads of state identify themselves with a single scientific advance is almost unprecedented and is some indication of the political capital tied up in the HGP. And the victory seems rather hollow now all the hype about the fantastic potential of genes has faded somewhat. Dazzled by its potential and underplaying the real difficulties of making sense of so much new information, the biotech boom very quickly went bust.

In the months before Celera and the international consortium published the first draft of the human genome, the company's share price had soared to $250, valuing it at more than $15 billion. Within a few years that valuation had dwindled to just $720 million, Venter had been pushed out, and the original business plan to sell packages of data to pharma companies had very few subscriptions.

The boom that had attracted no less than $44 billion in private investment between mid-1999 and mid-2001 (more than for the whole of the previous decade) had been punctured by a hefty dose of realism, Geoff Dyer said in the *Financial Times*. 'Just as the Internet has brought countless changes to modern business, so genomics is proving hugely influential in drug discovery. Yet investors have come to realize that the impact on human medicine will not be felt for many years.'[30]

The withdrawal of so much private money was something of a jolt, as scientists had come to accept, and in many cases enjoy, their enhanced status as entrepreneurs. Few noticed that while universities had been happily reinventing themselves as corporations, there had been a steady drain of people working for the public good and there was now less chance than ever they would be replaced. According to Avorn,

> Growing deficits in the federal budget now place considerable pressure on publicly funded medical research, which will further limit the ability and the willingness of the National Institutes of Health to support applied studies of drug efficacy and safety in the future. Thus, the scientific questions that are asked in both domains will increasingly be defined by the pharmaceutical industry.[31]

And indeed, the international consortia of scientists that are doing the groundwork on the proteome in same way the HGP did with the genome, have taken collaboration rather than competition as the starting point. The necessity of attracting private funding means that most research efforts are hybrids of public and private enterprise. Conflicts are perhaps inevitable, said Dr John Yates of the US Scripps Research

Institute and a member of the global advisory council (known as the Human Proteome Organization or HUPO) which coordinates the work, adding that these are the responsibility of the universities to sort out.[32]

Universities must survive in a commercial world and private money is usually something of a godsend. Vice-rector at the University of Geneva in Switzerland, Professor Jean Dominique Vassalli, sees no conflicts of interest now or in the future. His university owns one of the world's largest protein databases, SwissProt, which was created from the work of its academics. In 2001, SwissProt received a $43 million injection of cash from pharma company Novartis. The dividing lines, Vassalli says, are clear. 'GeneProt is not generating basic science. Its business plan is to generate proteomic information. This is applied science.'[33]

Without knowing the terms of the licence agreement, it is impossible to know whether Novartis or the university gets the better deal. But the example illustrates well the extent to which science needs private money, and vice versa. If the goals of the bioinformatics people are ever to be realized, private money is essential. 'The goal of a complete model of human biology is vast, arguably unachievable,' say Stephen Warde and Dr Scott Khan of the global computational science company, Accelrys. 'But, in pursuing it, a picture is built that enables more informed discovery. And the more of that picture scientists have, the better, whether built bottom-up, top-down or – via approaches like proteomics – from all sides.'[34]

The danger of too much private money, of course, is that academic institutions start putting pressure on their staff to prevent them speaking up in the public interest because they fear that doing so would adversely affect their chances of commercial funding.

The oft-cited example is of a scientist called Nancy Olivieri who worked at the University of Toronto and the city's Hospital for Sick Children on a drug for a rare blood disorder called thalassaemia. Her work was sponsored by the Canadian Medical Research Council and a pharma company called Apotex.

When Olivieri found the drug wasn't as good as she first thought, she wanted to publish her findings and inform the patients in her care of its apparent dangers. But a clause in her contract gave Apotex sole right to communicate the data for a year after the trial had ended.

> The hospital began an inquiry ... astonishingly, she was fired. All this went on while the university was itself engaged in discussions with Apotex about a $12.7 million donation by the company to the

> University of Toronto. The president of the university was lobbying the Canadian government on behalf of Apotex.[35]

In 1998, the university and Apotex agreed to suspend discussions about the multimillion-dollar gift until the dispute with Olivieri had been resolved. By the following year it had withdrawn the offer, Olivieri had been reinstated and her reputation cleared of all wrongdoing.

Then David Healy had a similar experience after being offered a $250,000-a-year job as professor of psychiatry and clinical director of the Centre for Addiction and Mental Health at the same University of Toronto. In November 2000, before taking up the position, he gave a talk stating that Prozac could cause patients to commit suicide. Eli Lilly, Prozac's manufacturer, was a major donor to the hospital. A few weeks later, Healy learned his job offer had been rescinded. He immediately filed a lawsuit, alleging his academic freedoms were being denied. This was settled for an undisclosed sum and Healy took a different job, as visiting professor of its faculty of medicine.

> The pharmaceutical company may indeed have played little or no role in deciding the fate of Healy [says Krimsky]. Its values and interests may already have been internalized by the administrative heads of the hospital and university, who needed little prodding to understand their sponsor's concerns.[36]

These examples, and there are others, show the inevitable result of an almost universal assumption that private profit and public good are one and the same in medicine. The impending crisis, if it has not already arrived, is blindingly obvious once one appreciates what it is that is being systematically stripped away from our healthcare infrastructures.

> Sustaining some form of non-instrumental science – which in practice means not routinely applying the litmus test of wealth creation to every new idea or hypothesis – is important not only for inquiry into fundamental theoretical questions but also because society needs a model of independent critical rationality for the proper conduct of democratic debate, judicial inquiry and consumer protection.[37]

Most of all, disinterested science is important to sustain public trust in the whole enterprise. If researchers, increasingly motivated by financial gain and hamstrung by sponsorship deals, are forced to trade their discoveries with the rest of the community only under the protection of patent law or commercial secrecy, people will look on the public deal with pharma – in particular, its unimpressive record in finding new drugs – rather differently.

Could pharma's massive influence over healthcare actually be thwarting the scientific community's ability of make sense of the new science by directing effort according to its own rather narrow agenda? To find out, we need to follow the counter-argument, which is that the private market is perfectly capable of directing research funds to where they are most needed. The place to start is the battle against cancer.

8

A bit of a lottery

Erbitux, the drug that caused Martha Stewart's fall from grace, is a good example of how cutting-edge science will always be something of a lottery. The US style guru had been advised to sell her shares in the company that developed it, ImClone Systems, because it was not expected to get FDA approval. As a result of how she came by that information, she was sent to prison. But in a bizarre and subsequent twist, those shares went on to rocket, because the drug went on to become one of an exciting new generation of cancer therapies.

The jitters caused by the uncertainty over the product's approval prospects affected not only those in the ImClone camp. Pharma company, Bristol-Myers Squibb (BMS), was also thrown into some disarray because it had paid $2 billion for a 20% stake in ImClone plus the US marketing rights to Erbitux, the jewel in its crown. Even with all the due diligence a company the size of BMS can afford, still pharmaceuticals are a seriously risky business.

All that changed, of course, when the concerns to do with the study design had been ironed out and Erbitux did get its first licence. It has since become an important new therapy in colon cancer, a disease that is estimated to affect more than a million people in the US and around 275,000 in the five major European markets: Germany, France, Spain, Italy and the UK.[1] The market for colorectal cancer alone is estimated to be worth in excess of $750 million.[2] It is now being tested in six other cancers.

Erbitux is just one of several drugs that exploit new knowledge of how cancers are formed. This one works by blocking a specific molecule that tells cancer cells to proliferate. Another kind of drug, Avastin, again initially for colon cancer, blocks a protein that encourages blood vessels that grow specifically to feed a tumour, thus starving it of another source of growth. The genius of yet a third kind is represented by Glivec, which identifies, and then reverses, a genetic flaw which, in this case, turns on an enzyme that causes a rare form of blood cancer.

These are real advances and doctors love them. They don't care what they cost because the results in some patients are fantastic and, on the whole, they are well tolerated. Earlier chemotherapies could not help but poison healthy as well as cancerous cells, leading to horrendous side effects. Moreover, the new drugs are a major stride in what has been steady upward progress. In the UK, the *Observer* newspaper notes, 'For women with breast cancer, their five-year survival rates have been increasing by 6% every five years since the mid-1980s.'[3]

This is how medicine moves forward: in small, incremental steps. The latest drugs are able to mimic the body's immune system by targeting drugs to highly specific communication lines where they sit on equally specific receptors that serve as biological messengers in the development of cancer. The idea is to foil the communication by producing a drug to block the fatal messages. The trouble, writes Sharon Begley in the *Wall Street Journal*, is that tumours seem to have more pathways than there are field mice in a meadow. In breast cancer alone, there are at least two dozen. You have to find the one the tumour depends on, which isn't easy.[4]

Erbitux, for example, binds to epidermal growth factor (EGF) receptors on both normal and tumour cells, preventing EGF, a molecule that helps trigger cell growth, from transmitting signals for cell proliferation. Some studies have suggested 25% of colorectal cancers overexpress EGF receptors, others that 82% do.[5]

'But Erbitux won't work if the pathway it hits isn't one the tumour is dependent on,' New York oncologist Dr Leonard Saltz told Begley.[6] Which explains why, in trials, Erbitux shrank colorectal tumours by more than half in only one-fifth of patients. Tumours in the other patients presumably used different pathways. Geoff Dyer in the *Financial Times* reported on one trial which showed that when the drug is used on its own (cancer therapies are often given in combination), only 11% of patients responded to Erbitux.[7]

The problems don't end there. Tumours can switch course if they find a drug blocking a preferred pathway. Iressa only shrinks tumours in one in ten cases of lung cancer, according to scientists at Massachusetts General Hospital in Boston. 'In the other 90%, Iressa is like a square peg aiming at a round hole,' says Begley.[8] Moreover, it had been assumed that having an effect in one in ten cases would mean a statistically significant increase in overall survival. But a large study, made public in December 2004, showed the drug did not prolong survival any more than placebo. Unsurprisingly, patients still wanted Iressa, if only for that placebo effect. The results (coupled with other bad news) triggered a $3 billion dive in the company's value.[9]

A further potential problem is illustrated by Glivec – it is now known around one in five patients become resistant to it within three years because the enzyme it attaches itself to changes shape. Nevertheless, for the person concerned and their loved ones, three years' extra life is priceless.

An expensive business

Fighting cancer is an expensive business. These drugs take medicine into a whole new pricing league. When Genentech announced in February 2004 that Avastin would cost around $44,000 per patient per year, it was more than double some analysts' predictions.[10] The price in the UK, at £24,000 ($43,200) per patient per year, either reflects a very strong pound or is very slightly cheaper. Erbitux costs $10,000 a month, meanwhile. These prices differ only marginally around the world.

Then there are the actual gains to consider. 'For all the hype surrounding Avastin, it only extended the life of patients for five months more than those taking standard chemotherapy,' said Dyer.[11]

As such, the drugs are proving to be as much a lifeline to the industry as to the people they treat. The health gains may not be great, being measured in months rather than years, but the drugs do extend life and that's what matters most in medicine. Besides, costs naturally come down once the patent term has expired, and for now they are delivering results, the importance of which cannot be overstated.

CEO of Novartis, Dr Daniel Vasella, said he wrote the book, *Magic Cancer Bullet: How a Tiny Orange Pill Is Rewriting Medical History*, to capture the moment he saw the results of an early trial with Glivec. These showed the white blood cell counts of all 31 patients with the blood cancer, chronic myeloid leukaemia (CML) had returned to normal, indicating a quite spectacular recovery.

> The data, my intuition and thoughts about the patients led me in only one direction. The quality of the drug was simply too overwhelming. A moment like this comes perhaps once in a lifetime. It made no sense to miss out by being overly conservative.[12]

Vasella went on to pull off a scientific and management triumph that saw an application for a licence being filed only 32 months after the first dose had been administered to a human being. This more than halved the six years it typically takes to develop a drug. And with agency reviewers giving up their evenings and weekends to get it out to patients as quickly as possible, it was approved by the FDA in a record two and a half months.

But the tiny orange pill quickly became known as much for its cost as its status as one of the world's first rationally designed cancer drugs. Aimed at such a small market – the company says just 75,000 people are eligible for treatment worldwide – the price, at $27,000 a year, was the first real venture into the new pricing stratosphere that was being opened up.

Immediately, the company found itself at loggerheads with governments around the world, particularly those in middle-income countries, such as South Korea and Brazil. From the industry's perspective, these countries have large middle-class populations that can afford to buy brand-name pharmaceuticals. It was important therefore that battles over pricing be strenuously fought, and not altogether surprising to find the US government in industry's corner.

'After heavy pressure from the US, South Korea agreed [in 2003] to pay a price for new drugs equivalent to the average of their cost in the G7 countries,' said Geoff Dyer in the *Financial Times*.[13] This was the $27,000 a year price in December 2001, equivalent to $19 for each 100mg capsule of the drug. In contrast, Japan paid $25; France and Switzerland paid $20; Germany, Italy and the UK also paid $19; and Brazil just $13. The US, somewhat unfairly given its strong-arm tactics, paid only $16 per capsule.[14] Jamie Love of the Washington-based lobby group, Consumer Project on Technology, told Dyer at the time, 'The US government does not control the price of drugs in its own country but it is telling Korea what it should charge.'[15] What the US is actually telling the world is that no one should meddle in the companies' drugs-pricing mechanisms.

High hopes, high prices

Cancer drugs are one of pharma's success stories in recent years, although this has to be set against the increase in the numbers of cancer cases, the reasons for which are largely unknown. In the UK, where the first national cancer tsar, Professor Mike Richards, was appointed in October 1999, a report was issued to show that at any one time there are more that 225,000 cases and more than 120,000 people dying from cancer in England alone.[16]

It also shows that the rise in overall incidence is rather lower for men than women. Although the increase across the sexes was a third over the past generation or so (1971–2000), it broke down to 21% for men and 39% for women. Moreover, the extent to which cancers kill has gone down by 12% and this again looks better for men (down by 18%) compared with just 7% for women.[17] Why the statistics show women to be faring so badly compared with men when it comes to cancer is not known. Nor why wealthy health-conscious women get breast cancer at greater rates than those lower down the social scale. Nor a million other questions people ask about this number one source of modern angst that one in three UK people can now expect to be diagnosed with at some point in their lives. The good news is that the diagnosis is less likely than ever to be an automatic death sentence.

The price of that good news is that governments are being asked to pay prices that are generally recognized as test cases for what societies can afford. 'How much do people want to live?' companies ask. Professor Karol Sikora, professor of cancer medicine at Imperial College School of Medicine, told the *Observer* newspaper, 'We have around seven new therapies coming along which cost around £50,000 a year per patient, once you've taken all the associated costs into account. Patients are increasingly well informed, and naturally they want them. There seems to be no real debate happening about how we're going to pay for this. Do we make all the drugs available to everyone, regardless of their age, or do we have to be more selective about who gets them?'[18]

Another report from the cancer tsar shows that deciding which patients get the drugs already depends very much on where they live. Working with the strategic health authorities in England, the 34 cancer networks and the pharmaceutical industry, the report found that at the narrowest end of the range of availability was Mabthera for non-Hodgkin's lymphoma, with a 2.6-fold variation, and the widest was Temodal for brain cancer, which has an 11.6-fold variation between health authorities.[19] This means that for every patient that qualified for Mabthera in the most drug-abstemious authority, 2.6 did elsewhere. And where one patient gets to use Temodal in one area, more than 11 do elsewhere. If these drugs are as good as everyone says, that is reasonable cause for concern.

Intriguingly, the report said funding was not the reason for the variation in take-up rates, which should anyway follow centralized clinical guidelines. Nor were variations in incidence of cancer to blame. Mabthera, produced by the Swiss drugs company, Roche, is an antibody that targets tumour proteins in the lymphatic system. According to the UK's National Institute for Health and Clinical Excellence (NICE), which assesses the value of new drugs, it costs the NHS £4,900 ($8,820) for a single course of treatment (plus another £1,600 [$2,880] in associated costs), and treatment is restricted to people whose cancers have progressed to the third and fourth stages of the disease.[20]

The variance in prescribing was the lowest of the 16 cancer drugs that have been reviewed by NICE and were surveyed in this report. Nevertheless, even with some health authorities using it more than twice as much as others, the report insists the differences are not to do with funding restrictions. 'Instead,' it writes, 'the main impact on usage seems to be constraints in service capacity and differences in clinical practice.'[21]

That doesn't explain the storm that ensued once the Scottish equivalent of NICE, the Scottish Medicines Consortium (SMC) approved the drug's use in earlier stages of the disease. In the capital, cancer consultants had also recommended its earlier use to their Trusts, which are the funding bodies. 'For the rest of Britain, the situation is bleak,' said Revill.[22]

Everyone else has to wait until NICE has made its decision. Such decisions run, on average, 18 months behind the SMC, says NICE spokesperson, Phil Ranson. If decisions clash, he says, the more in-depth NICE appraisal tends to take precedence. Again, one finds public opinion, in almost total denial of the politics behind drug pricing, urging greater spending. 'Many doctors see the need for an intelligent debate about what should be affordable within the NHS,' the *Observer* says in its editorial columns. 'Cancer drugs form part of that debate and there is no doubt that we significantly underspend on them.'[23]

The column developed its argument on grounds that tell only part of the picture. 'Some £380 million a year is currently spent on cancer drugs [in the NHS],' it went on. 'But when you consider that, in the same period, the NHS overspent by nearly £1 billion on procuring a new IT system which has not yet been introduced, that seems pretty small beer.'[24]

If it is hard now to come to grips with the debate and reconcile the variances in access to these drugs, it will only get worse once they have been tested in different markets and in different combinations to recoup more of their investment costs. The combination treatment theories are attractive because they increase the chances of doctors being able to hit the spot, so to speak. But they cost twice as much and what is spent on one clinical area takes it away from others in most fixed-cost state-funded systems.

Nevertheless, top oncologists such as Dr John Hainsworth of the Sarah Cannon Cancer Center in Nashville, Tennessee, told the American Society of Clinical Oncology at its 2004 meeting that combinations were the future. He went on to present positive findings in kidney cancer, a traditionally hard tumour to treat, using Avastin and Tarceva.

'The rationale was to try to build on the biology by blocking more than one signalling molecule within these cells,' he said.[25] That same combination of drugs has also been shown to be effective in non-small cell lung cancer. So far the improvements are modest but it is early days. If they are shown to stop progression of the tumour for 18–24 months rather than 12–14 months, says Hainsworth, they will be hard to resist.

Dr Bob Mass, Genentech's director of bio-oncology, told *Scrip Magazine* there was a clear incentive to push the idea of people taking several drugs at once. 'More people on a double therapy could make a real impact on sales,' he said.[26] What people are prepared to pay, on the other side of the equation, is almost impossible to know. The costs soon add up, however, if people take two or even three drugs at a time. And while it is comforting to know doctors can block deadly messages that tell cancer cells to grow or divide, or that cut off the process of building a blood supply to the tumour, it is baffling to know why tests are not developed to know if a patient has the pathways the drugs work on. Some say the knowledge is not there yet, except in some breast and prostate cancers. But others have argued that where the knowledge does exist, governments should take the initiative on the grounds that they pay. 'The Medical Research Council could set up tests for the likely efficacy of a product,' says Joe Collier, adviser to the recent parliamentary report into the pharma industry. 'I think it's a good idea.'

Death is not a pricing issue

Anyone who has lost someone close to them from cancer will know that price is not the only issue. To take one example, a man in his 70s recently chose to buck the trend for longevity when he was offered a drug that promised to extend his survival from cancer by between three to six months. This was a new drug offered under the NHS. For some reason, this patient didn't fit the NHS criteria, but he was offered the chance to buy it privately at NHS prices.

Consider what is involved in deciding whether or not to take Chiron's Proleukin, a new drug for advanced kidney and skin cancer patients. It is a drug that costs the NHS £140 ($250) a vial ($700 in the US), and takes 18 vials for a full course of treatment. Patients tolerating the initial course are given a second, with some discounts. The man thought about it for a while, because what else could he spend his money on? Besides, the cost wouldn't matter if the drugs offered some comfort in his final days. Then he read a report which said that in the US, the extra hospital costs to monitor the patient in an intensive care unit, and supply fluids, pressors and drugs to counteract the toxic side effects – sickness, capillary leak syndrome, heart attacks, cardiac arrhythmia and infection – bring the final bill to more than $50,000.[27]

Although he was not being asked to contribute to the hospital costs, he chose to die a few months earlier but at home surrounded by all the many comforts a loving family can afford. The issues involved in the medicines business are complex but they are essentially human, revolving around how people want to live and, equally crucially, how they want to die.

Valuing medicine

How people want to have sex has more recently found itself on the medical agenda. Of all the things Viagra is famous for, changing drug-pricing regimes is probably not the one that springs instantly to mind. But at the time of its launch in 1997, the era of blockbuster medicine had been going for some years and budgets were stretched. Pfizer's calls for healthcare systems around the world to reimburse Viagra's cost as it does other drugs led to the press speculating that the entire NHS drug budget would be spent maintaining erections if rationing wasn't confronted upfront, and soon.

Pfizer was serious. Its legal challenges against both the UK and Australia for trying to restrict access to the drug only died down when it became clear men were happy enough to buy it themselves. But that was after new ways of dealing with rationing had emerged, transforming our sex lives into an economic and political issue that challenged the most committed rationalists. Even those who believe there is nothing that cannot be measured admitted defeat when it came to finding some way of delicately rationing Viagra's use. In Ireland, a quantity limitation (four tablets a month) was introduced into the medicines rule book for the first time to deal with the expected demand. In Sweden, meanwhile, men could get as many as they wanted, which was largely because Pfizer had reached a price–volume agreement with the National Social Insurance Board which had not yet hit the ceiling. In the UK, it could be used, but only for men with diabetes or who had real erectile dysfunction problems. And so on.

Slowly it dawned that Viagra was only the latest and most celebrated drug to highlight how overprescribing was rife. Doctors were either overtreating symptoms that couldn't be measured or being unduly influenced to lower the thresholds of those that could. The medical profession were the brakes in the system, the mechanism that should keep the level of prescribing at least in proportion with clinical need. Their refit involved erecting an entire infrastructure for issuing guidelines to doctors as to appropriate use.

A trend for greater clinical evidence in medicine had been gathering pace for some years and this helped build momentum for formal and accepted ways of assessing medicines financially to become established. In the late 1990s, the UK's NICE was set up, a public body of experts charged with assessing medicines, and now spearheads a growing movement. At the start of the 'noughties', mandatory programmes for certain (usually expensive) drugs were in place in Australia, New Zealand, Canada, the UK, the Netherlands, Finland, Portugal, Norway, Ireland, and many managed care organizations in the US.

Some countries told pharma that cost–benefit data on their products would help the pricing negotiations; others that data would be accepted on a voluntary basis. With the writing on the wall, companies began preparing for what was being dubbed the fourth hurdle. After proving safety, efficacy and quality in getting a drug approved, now companies would have to show their drug was cost-effective before it would actually be used.

A minefield opened. How much is Viagra worth to you? And that's easy compared to some drugs. At least with Viagra it is clear what it's supposed to do. Consider a disease like Alzheimer's, which is diagnosed by questionnaire and then by a process of elimination rather than clear tests of organic functions. Reactions to treatment are as variable as the symptoms are subjective. Even if drugs don't work, people can think they do. Given the right circumstances, like the run-up to a general election, these views can crush the most scientific of studies that say they don't.

What is interesting is that, for the first time, the processes by which drugs are valued are being set down. This means that ordinary people, particularly those who have a family member with Alzheimer's, can challenge any threat to drugs they so desperately want. The same is true, of course, for the cancer drugs, prescribing guidelines for which have also been clearly laid out by NICE.

Just before NICE produced its consultation document about the value of Alzheimer's drugs to the NHS, health minister Dr Stephen Ladyman told the *Observer* newspaper he would personally ensure NICE should find in favour of them. 'I can understand why the public is so worried,' he said. 'If you have someone in your family who has a form of dementia and you have drugs which do work, then you are going to find this decision baffling.'[28]

Being one of the more publicized squabbles over whether drugs provide value for money, it serves well as a starter lesson in the fiendishly difficult matter of assessing the value of drugs. The principles are straightforward enough. First, you decide the clinical effectiveness of a drug. Then you take its cost. Cost-effectiveness is the clinical effect divided by the cost. So far, so good.

Except you immediately start running into problems. First, for most medical interventions, there simply isn't a consensus on their effectiveness. And the Alzheimer's drugs, the cholinesterase inhibitors – Aricept, Exelon, Reminyl and Ebixa – are a classic example. Now a $1.8 billion business, they work by boosting levels of acetylcholine, a neurotransmitter believed to be important in memory and learning processes. But while these drugs do help this memory-robbing disease initially, eventually they become less effective. Also, because they don't act on the plaques and tangles in the brain that are thought to lead to Alzheimer's, the disease continues its grim progress.

'Scientists aren't sure why the drugs seem to stop working,' says Andrea Petersen in the *Wall Street Journal*. 'Some say the brain may get used to the effects of the drugs and stop responding. Another theory is that the disease may progress to the point where too many neurons have died or acetylcholine levels have fallen to the point where the drug won't do any good.'[29]

In the US, recognizing the downsides of the drugs (weight loss, upset stomach, as well as their cost), the debates have tended to focus on how long patients should remain on them, not whether they should be prescribed in the first place. Evidence that suggests new benefits from longer use is closely scrutinized. Much of this new research, says Petersen, comes from 'extension trials' funded by the drug makers to look for additional benefits to approved drugs. In extension trials, patients know they are taking a drug and there is no placebo arm to compare the results with. What you get is a measure of patients' perception of how well the drug is working, something that is notoriously difficult to assess, particularly in a degenerative disease.

'Often the drugs don't improve a patient's cognitive function,' Petersen continues. 'Instead people may decline at a slower rate than they would without the medication. But that is a benefit that is impossible to measure in an individual.'[30]

If that is hard, it is nothing compared to the second problem one runs up against when evaluating medicines. That is to find some common currency, some agreed formula by which clinical effectiveness can be determined. That currency is life itself. The next problem then lies in finding ways of measuring the quality of life in some average NHS person. The measure most commonly used is the 'cost of quality-adjusted life-year gained' (CQG). In layman's language, the CQG can be seen as the cost of replacing a year of what an illness or a condition or a syndrome has deprived a person of: normal life. Same problem. What's a normal life? To calculate this impossibly indeterminate sum, questionnaires are specially designed by experts to measure quality of life in basic tasks such as walking, hearing, remembering, and so on.

A treatment that gives an extra year of life but at only half of full health, would represent half a quality-adjusted life year. If that treatment cost £500 ($900), then its CQG would be £1,000 ($1,800). So far, so good still (I hope). The devil, as usual, is to be found in the detail. And with so much debate over the values of various human tasks and so many different ways to measure quality of life, the devil has ample room for manoeuvre. It can be hardly surprising to find that CQGs for any drug will vary. In the case of Roche's obesity drug Xenical, for example, NICE's independent review estimated a CQG of £46,000 ($82,800). Translated, this represents a cost to the NHS of £46,000 a year to bring the patient's quality of life up to that of someone who was not obese – which would be cheap if it actually delivered on its promise, but that is not the point. Roche, meanwhile, had arrived at a CQG of just £10,000 ($18,000).

Where the Alzheimer's drugs were concerned, the discrepancies were greater. Studies into the cost-effectiveness of Aricept, for example, came up with CQGs ranging from £21,000 to £139,000 ($37,800–$250,200). With Exelon, they ranged between £16,000 and £46,000 ($28,200–$82,800). Those conducted by the NICE secretariat itself found a range from £32,000 to £52,000 ($57,600–$93,600), leading it to conclude the drugs were outside 'the range of cost-effectiveness that might be considered appropriate for the NHS'.[31]

Such a squabble could have been predicted the moment the first significant trial in Aricept that had not been sponsored by the industry was announced in June 2004. According to Clive Cookson, science editor of the *Financial Times*, 'The participants were selected to represent a range of patients with mild to moderate Alzheimer's in a real clinical setting, as opposed to the refined selection criteria used in trials sponsored by drugs companies.'[32]

This was one of very few studies to be paid for by the NHS and the results, published in the *Lancet*, concluded that the drug produced a slight, temporary improvement in memory test performance but failed to improve quality of life or delay the progress of dementia. '[It] is not cost effective, with benefits below minimally relevant thresholds,' the final report said.[33]

Although the Alzheimer's drugs are not expensive by recent pharmaceutical standards, costing the NHS around £2.50 a day (£75 a month, [$135]) per patient, or £54 million ($97.2 million) a year in total, what is interesting is how the public voice is beginning to filter through. Ladyman got involved, partly because he was in a marginal seat and partly perhaps because he had talked to his elderly constituents, looked at the evidence, and thought, why not up the ante for these suffering families.

How much real benefit patients and their carers get from the drug will always remain a moot point. But the scientific foundations on which it was built will continue to be challenged by people's experience of their own and others' illness. Susan Wandell, a business consultant in Minneapolis, told the *Wall Street Journal* that her father was on Aricept for more than ten years, until a month before he died at the age of 85. 'It took a long time before Dad got really bad. In my gut I believe it [the medication] helped my Dad.' Increasingly, that is what counts, despite the best efforts of science.[34]

My father, your father

And if it was your father, you would probably want the drugs too, because the value placed on a declining memory is totally subjective. Gut feelings are what we will pay for if rationality does not finally win the day. The Alzheimer's story shows that for prices to become affordable, the critical benchmark, beyond which a drug becomes too expensive for the NHS, must be raised. This figure has always been contentious because it reveals how much a year of regular life is worth in the eyes of the NHS, ruffling all sorts of feathers in departments where things can cost a lot more, and less, than this.

In the summer of 2001, NICE chairman Professor Sir Michael Rawlins appeared to confirm a ceiling to the worth of the NHS life of around the £30,000 ($54,000) a year mark,[35] and since then similar figures have been mentioned at conferences by NICE personnel. If that is the case, then a positive decision on the Alzheimer's drugs would raise the bar. And continued pressure to make drugs more affordable, because we as a society value life more highly, will inevitably push that ceiling up further and further.

At the time of writing, July 2005, NICE seemed to have taken the decision that the drugs are too expensive, not by saying as much but by asking the drug companies involved for unpublished data about effects on particular patient groups. 'It is a sure bet that none will be forthcoming,' said *The Times*' science correspondent, Mark Henderson.

> Firms have been caught before sitting on results that do not suit their marketing strategies but are unlikely to have suppressed work that supports their interests.
>
> Ministers have overruled NICE before – on beta interferon for multiple sclerosis and on offering one cycle of free IVF infertility treatment instead of the recommended three – but the choice to step beyond dispassionate cost-benefit analysis and introduce other factors to the mix is a political one.[36]

Who knows what will happen? Ministers may intervene, thus opening the political route to spending greater amounts of money on a course of diminishing returns. *BMJ* editor Richard Smith, in a special edition devoted to whether society had become overmedicalized, wrote:

> Presumably no one wants to keep cutting back on education, the arts, scientific research, good food, travel, and much else as we spend more and more of our resources on an unwinnable battle against death, pain and sickness. And do we in the rich world want to keep developing increasingly expensive treatments that achieve marginal benefits when most in the developing world do not have the undoubted benefits that come with simple measures like sanitation, clean water and immunization?[37]

Paying for science

The innovation pipeline is expensive to maintain, and while public protests over access to Alzheimer's and cancer drugs can be heard, few people question how the prices are set. We heard earlier about how the *Observer*, for example, had wondered if UK taxpayers' money might be better spent on lives than computer contracts, but it didn't question why the prices of cancer drugs are so high in the first place. Those reasons don't only apply to the UK, but globally, because what we are talking about is the value of a human life.

According to Professor Joe Collier, chief adviser to the recent parliamentary enquiry into the pharma industry's influence, the prices are almost entirely arbitrary. 'They could be £1,000 a year or £10,000,' he says. 'They are set at what it is thought the market will bear.'[38]

Going for what you can get makes commercial sense. In pharmaceuticals, however, the limitations are not obvious or transparent; they are set not by consumers making a series of sound well-informed judgements as they might in the supermarket. In the UK and most state-funded healthcare systems, they are set by budgetary constraints. The patient has – until recently – had no way of knowing, nor any need to know, if prices are fair.

But with significant improvements occurring across a broad range of cancer areas, that is changing. When a trial showed the latest breast cancer drug had beaten the gold standard tamoxifen, a British newspaper wrote:

> The announcement will trigger great demand for the drug, anastrozole, in Britain and inevitably lead to a big hike in the NHS drugs bill once it is licensed. Tamoxifen costs around £25 to £30 a year per patient, compared to £1,000 for anastrozole. With at least 100,000 women taking tamoxifen at any time, the switch could cost £100 million.[39]

Tamoxifen shows how if medicine moves forward in small, incremental steps, prices take strides in an ever steeper ascent. The drug is a British invention that has been used for more than 20 years with huge success, cutting in half the number of women whose breast cancers returned after treatment. Its performance is now outclassed on virtually every measure by the latest so-called aromatase inhibitors, of which anastrozole is just one. According to Sarah Boseley in the *Guardian*, anastrozole increased the time to any recurrence of cancer by 20%, reduced the spread of cancer to other parts of the body by 14% and cut the chances of it recurring in the other breast by 40%. On the downside, it caused more bone fractures.[40]

Anastrozole could have been compared with later breast cancer drugs, such as Herceptin. This costs £20,000 ($36,000) a year and works spectacularly well in the one in five women that carry the particular genetic flaw it addresses. So well in fact there are calls for women who are known to have this flaw, as expressed in a protein known as HER2, to take it at much earlier stages, putting more strain on limited budgets.[41]

If the comparison had been with Herceptin, anastrozole would not have looked so good. But Tamoxifen gives a more direct comparison to glean what we are paying for: £100 million ($180 million) for the advances since Tamoxifen as outlined above. In affluent countries, that may seem like a good use of taxpayers' money, because what is more precious than health? But no one knows what taxpayers think because there is no way of knowing and very little serious debate beyond simply demanding greater access to life-saving drugs. That money would also buy an awful lot of nutritious school dinners, for example, as part of a cancer prevention campaign.

The real problem lies in finding some way of valuing innovation, which is how companies are rewarded in the broader scheme of things. Pharma's traditional method of justifying its prices has been the cost of its research, which, as we have seen, must take into account the research costs of drugs that fail as well as those that succeed.

In an area like cancer, it should perhaps also take into account the public input into science. The US National Cancer Institute, for example, has established the Cancer Genome Anatomy Project, which draws together information about the molecular anatomy of cancer into public databases. Anyone, single researchers or multinationals, can use this information.

Where the pace of development is fast, as in cancer, public science suits these young companies. The new molecular approach means dynamic hives of activity are created and this is where the ideas are coming from. But while youth has the advantage of having no old ways of working to let go of, nor hierarchies to observe, these companies have not got much money and are dependent on their ideas being picked up by pharma for development.

If they do well, however, they can do very well indeed. Genentech, for example, has developed a number of new cancer drugs, including Avastin. In a letter to stockholders in its 2004 annual report, CEO Arthur D. Levinson boasted how total operating revenues had increased to $4.6 billion, more than doubling since 2001. 'Our financial position also remains strong, with approximately $2.8 billion in unrestricted cash and investments,' he added.[42]

One of the reasons Genentech, which is now 60% owned by Roche of Switzerland, has done well is that it takes risks to nurture creativity. Napoleone Ferrara, Avastin's originating scientist, said he was only able to discover how new blood vessels grow to feed a tumour with nutrients because he had been given the time to do so,[43] describing how it is company policy that a quarter of researchers' time should be spent on projects of their own choosing. Avastin's launch was the most successful in US oncology history, earning $545 million in its first ten months on the US market. 'This exceeded the first full-year revenues of any other product in this therapeutic category by approximately $175 million,' said Levinson.[44]

The larger companies, meanwhile, from the first germ of an idea to the fanfare of a major launch, seek to minimize risk. They keep an eye on the early research but generally only move in to buy at the latest possible opportunity, which puts the onus on the smaller companies to have shown proof-of-principle in the science and whether the product can make billion-dollar revenues within pharma's 20-year framework.

Inherently conservative by nature, pharma is anyway not suited to such a dynamic environment. Its size, for a start, works against it. Some multi-merged companies, such as GlaxoSmithKline, have created small, autonomous R&D units in an attempt to keep the creative spirit alive. But, says industry commentator Brown, there is still an overriding bureaucracy and one can't see any real productivity gains.

Freedom works best at the cutting edge, and biotech companies, used to bowing to every pharma whim, find the balance of power tilting in their direction. 'Biotech is commanding an increasingly large share of the potential upside, and is pushing for equity stake investments and innovative options such as co-development,' said Karen Beynon and Jacob Plieth in a review of pharma's deals in 2004.[45]

Changing the parameters of business with pharma is no mean feat and such changes can be taken as some indication of the deep water it is in and why the cancer drugs are such a lifeline. According to Brown:

> Big pharma is locked into a box where it sees it has 20 years to develop a drug, register it, market it and get their money back. That creates a kind of neurosis or anxiety where, although naturally risk-averse, pharma finds itself taking decisions that have led to problems.[46]

Costing innovation

The obvious way out is to increase the size of the box by charging more for its drugs. The figure used since 2001 to cost innovation, thereby justifying high drug prices, has come from Tufts Center for Drug Development in the US, an institution heavily supported by the drugs industry. A group of economists, led by Joseph DiMasi, conducted a complex study that year which officially valued the research input of pharma at a staggering $802 million a drug, an amount that was greeted with some scepticism even by those close to industry. 'When people come up and in a macho kind of way say it costs $800 million to develop a drug,' says Brown, for example, 'I just think that must be very inefficient. It shouldn't have to cost that much.'

Companies are already offered incentives to do research. In the US, for example, R&D expenses are tax-deductible. And in the UK, where the Department of Health controls pharma company profits, rather than prices, companies can offset 20–23% of the value of their NHS sales against their R&D costs. Moreover, the terms of reference in the DiMasi study are almost as elastic as the boundaries of disease, and impossible to justify because so much of the data must be assumed since companies are allowed to keep them close under cover of commercial secrecy. But even using the total R&D figures supplied by the pharma industry association in the US, averaging them out over the same decade DiMasi used, and making allowances for the long drug-development times, the US consumer advocacy group Public Citizen could only come up with a figure of $100 million.[47]

The $802 million figure only applies to a sample of highly selected and very costly drugs produced during the 1990s. It is limited to what pharma has developed in-house rather than licensed in from smaller companies, which is what they normally do because it is so much cheaper. Moreover, the DiMasi selected drugs are new molecular entities (NMEs). 'In 2002, only 17 of the 78 newly approved drugs were NMEs. And of these NMEs, only a fraction are developed entirely by the companies themselves,' says Angell.[48]

But the more intriguing reason this figure is wildly inflated is that it doesn't just account for 'out-of-pocket' money spent; it adds in what that money could have earned if it hadn't been spent on research.

> That [out-of-pocket] cost was $403 million per drug. The $802 million is what the authors call the 'capitalized' cost – that is, it includes the estimated revenue that might have been generated if the money spent on

> R&D had instead been invested in the equity market ... That accounting manoeuvre nearly doubled the $403 million to $802 million.[49]

Before long, the figures had doubled again, this time to $1.7 billion, which is equivalent to the gross domestic product of Guyana. This latest calculation, released in a paper entitled, 'Rebuilding big pharma's business model', came from pharma consulting firm Bain & Co. in November 2003, and forms the basis of the US argument that the rest of the world should pay more for their drugs.

Two reasons are offered for the latest steep rise, both of which are enlightening because they reveal how the report's authors see the main forces raising drugs costs. One is that it includes the costs of marketing drugs after approval, adding another $250 million per compound. It's official: marketing is now considered a part of research. The second is that the success rates are much lower than those accounted for by Tufts, as Bains used a much more recent time period, 2000–2002. It's official: more drugs are failing.

The failures are not necessarily explained. When pharma decides to kill a drug, it is in response to the level of proof that must be provided by law and the time frame in which it has to make money. Despite the increasing numbers of compounds in the earlier stages of research, Phase I and Phase II, there is no increase in Phase III. 'Companies are looking at these drugs after Phase II and asking if they can make money out of them,' says Brown.

> It can cost another $200 million to do Phase III trials and another $500 million in worldwide marketing within the first 18 months. These are billion-dollar decisions. The challenges you face with the clock affect all areas of research and it is a very complicated balancing act to get a smooth pipeline of products. This is why companies are being more opportunistic when they buy in science, such as when BMS paid $2 billion for ImClone. But pharma has always been mad in the prices it will pay. Pfizer bought Warner Lambert for one product, Lipitor, and Pharmacia just for Celebrex.[50]

These billion-dollar decisions affect more than a company's share price. They also determine the range of drugs we are offered in the surgery. Industry wants higher prices and longer periods in which companies can have exclusive rights over data. But what the industry really needs is massive structural change in favour of the smaller companies. Even the Bain report said, 'The blockbuster model that underpinned big pharma's success is now irretrievably broken'. It paints a picture of dinosaurs hamstrung by their own success. 'Organizations of that scale carry considerable inertia, as US Steel, Sears and IBM all discovered. Despite this inertia, the rules of risk and return still apply.'[51]

With smaller and younger companies keen for more of the action, pharma executives face difficult decisions.

> They can't force their companies free from the massive investments in science, selling capacity, plants and organization that used to yield the rare lottery-winning drug. Nor can they dissuade drug industry leaders who believe that incremental changes to the blockbuster approach (alone or with an acquisition) will rekindle the old sparks and restore historic returns, at least for a while.[52]

The blockbuster model had created, the authors said, more than $1 trillion ($1,000 billion) worth of revenues for big pharma in the past decade. 'Given the current economics of drug development, big pharma would need to invest twice as much as it does today to sustain double-digit revenue growth. Instead, big pharma is curbing R&D expenditure to cope with near-term performance pressures,' said the report's authors.

Pharma companies will hold on as long as they can, which is as long as they are allowed to stretch the rules in their favour. It would not be hard (in theory) to stop them profiting so easily at the taxpayers' expense. Where the cancer drugs are concerned, Collier has suggested the Medicines Research Council could perhaps fund the kind of tests the charity Cancer Research UK called for at the UK parliamentary inquiry. 'There is little industry funding for research to determine the subgroups of patients that might benefit from particular therapies,'[53] it said, asking for the knowledge that would enable the latest cancer drugs to be made available only to the patients who would benefit.

From the companies' perspective, says Collier, they can go one of two ways in this respect.

> One is to provide a test and target patients around the world. The company would provide health services with the data as to which patient genotypes would benefit. That would be a very exciting development. The alternative is not to know, and the business is much more efficient, of course, if you are treating ten people rather than one. But governments can't demand such things. One of the threads of the recent inquiry was that the UK government has very limited powers to persuade industry to do anything.[54]

If governments can't ask for, and the industry is unwilling or unable to provide such data voluntarily, there is sense in the people who are paid to represent the public's interests doing their own work to find out how to make the cancer drugs more cost-effective. Griffin remains dubious, however. 'Cancer is thousands of diseases,' he says. 'Many cancers can't be genotyped. Some treatments work much like a car stops if a spanner is thrown in the works. Science doesn't always have the key to know which groups of patients they work in.'[55]

Part 3

Counting the cost

9

The people *vs* pharma

The search for a level playing field in medicine takes place on many levels, the most obvious being economic. And the more commercial environment of the US provides the clearest window as to what ordinary people are up against. The relationship between the public and what is arguably the most important industry to humankind may be toughest in the world's most powerful country, but it is also more open.

With fewer laws in the US restraining what pharma companies can do or say, drugs have a higher profile than anywhere else. They have a more obvious presence in the media, are more expensive and that cost is more likely to be felt in the patients' pockets. Americans not only pay higher prices but also take more drugs and would seem to have a greater acceptance of their role in daily life.

Whether Europeans would want to be jolted out of their state-run healthcare systems is a deeply contested issue in the EU corridors of power, where the industry is subject to two masters, the Commissioner for Enterprise and the Commissioner for Health and Consumer Protection, who rarely, if ever, see eye to eye. With the former working to create a dynamic industry and the latter low-cost healthcare services, there is little middle ground between them.

Laws that protect patients from pharma marketing campaigns, for example, are seen by one side as a way to control demand and keep total costs down. To the other, they are excessive control denying Europeans access to information about drugs from the companies that produce them. The people who support enterprise acknowledge the marketing costs on the public purse and consider it money well spent. But in the 1990s, the decade of blockbuster medicine, the effects of all that relatively unfettered promotional spend were felt by thousands of America's most vulnerable people, its pensioners, leading to a trail of revelations about the true nature of the industry and sowing seeds of discontent throughout its heartland territory.

While the federal US Medicare programme was set up to cater for the healthcare needs of the elderly, it only covered hospital care, not drugs. But during the 1990s, many old people found they were unable to afford their prescription drugs.

The pressure group Families USA had shown the prices of the top 50 drugs prescribed for the elderly had gone up by around 6% in 2002 when the inflation rate was only 1.8%.[1] This wasn't a major hike in itself but doctors were also saying the elderly needed more drugs, as were the ads on the TV. Many prescriptions cost more than $1,000 a year, and some people needed several. Even if they had taken out private policies, there were limits to what they could have because insurance companies were also being squeezed.

The growth in markets for broad-brush medicine during the 1990s was felt most keenly by the elderly, many of whom were having to choose between food and medicine. There were stories of the elderly signing up in droves for special bus tours to Canada or Mexico to benefit from their state-controlled drug prices. People were interviewed to explain how high-dose pills (often costing only fractionally more than the low-doses) could be chopped up into daily portions. Then there was evidence that people were getting drugs via the Internet, benefiting from other countries' cheap prices, thus circumventing the domestic systems that keep US prices high – but also putting them at risk of falling into the traps of growing numbers of counterfeiters.

Buying drugs from anywhere other than the US became a serious political issue. Drugs sold at US prices account for half of global sales and more in terms of profits. Even if those drugs had been manufactured in the US to FDA standards and exported to Canada, say, they could not be legally re-imported, an issue that has been stalled but has not gone away.

Nor is it new. Americans have always paid more than anyone else for their prescription drugs. But it took the protests of a band of well-organized pensioners who could no longer afford what the doctors said they needed for anyone to sit up and take notice. The solution was to placate the discontent rather then deal with the underlying problem.

Politicians, both Republicans and Democrats, had no problem with the idea of paying for pensioners to get their prescription drugs on Medicare. The question was how it was to be funded – via a state-run NHS-type scheme or an extension of the privately run insurance system most Americans were used to and which the industry strongly favoured. Hundreds of billions of dollars were at stake, since not only are the elderly the biggest users of pharma's products by far, but it was thought likely that if state controls even got a foothold in the system, it would automatically lead to lower prices.

Disquiet mounts

While the issue of how to deliver free drugs to US pensioners was being debated, prices began hitting the headlines in another area: the mounting worldwide disquiet about the cost of the life-saving HIV drugs. The vast disparities in wealth between the developed and developing worlds, coupled with the sheer scale of the AIDS pandemic, had led to awkward questions being asked about how the medicines business works and to whose benefit?

What was worse in pharma's eyes, however, was how the issue went on to exacerbate issues rather closer to home. It quickly became apparent that access to prescription drugs was not just a problem in the developing world. Americans didn't like discovering they paid so much more than people in relatively affluent places like Europe, Canada, New Zealand and Australia. And it wasn't just the HIV/AIDS drugs. Jo Ann Emerson, a Republican congresswoman from Missouri declared, 'I will not stand here and see American seniors take a back seat to the pharmaceutical industry. A bottle of tamoxifen, used to fight breast cancer, costs $360 in the US. It costs $60 in Germany.'[2]

The grey campaign was also helped by a general consensus that prices were out of control. Everyone had felt the hikes over the 1990s as insurers tried to cover the mounting costs of healthcare. Premiums were raised and were soon passed on from employers – who have traditionally paid for their staff's health expenses – to employees who found restrictions had been creeping into the deal since they were last sick.

Insurers did what it took to reduce costs. They signed up doctors into health maintenance organizations (HMOs), for example, which operate a bit like a mini-NHS with strict rules about what can and cannot be prescribed. A whole string of class-action lawsuits alleging that HMOs withheld medical services to boost profits expressed some of the mounting anger over healthcare costs in general and drug prices in particular.

Insurers, via HMOs, also started contesting FDA decisions about safe, widely used drugs which they thought patients should pay for themselves in pharmacies rather than have prescribed at the insurers' expense. In May 2001, when Claritin had been successfully stripped of its prescription-only status, the allergy drug was bringing in $2 billion a year, which was a third of the income of the company Schering-Plough, that had the marketing rights.

Moreover, much of this income could be directly attributed to recently introduced liberalization of the laws that control what a drug company can say about prescription drugs to the consumer. One analyst estimated the company had generated $3.50 in extra Claritin sales for every advertising dollar spent.[3] According to the National Institute for Health Care Management (NIHCM), the company spent nearly $100 million advertising the drug to consumers (rather than doctors) that year, generating 15% more sales than the year before, and prompting questions to be asked about the real beneficiaries of pharma advertising.[4]

And it was not only ads for Claritin that consumers responded to. NIHCM, a non-profit group funded partly by health insurers, found that of the $2.25 billion that had been spent advertising prescription drugs that year, more than 95% was concentrated on just 50 drugs. The amounts being spent matched or exceeded advertising spend on all other products. The $160 million Merck spent advertising Vioxx in 2000, for example, was $35 million more than was spent on Pepsi that year; it was equivalent to Dell's advertising spend on its top computers, and only slightly less than the $169 million that General Motors spent on ads for its Saturn model.[5]

Advertising spends had been rising fast as competition for market share in certain blockbuster categories accelerated. In 1997, total spending was under one billion dollars; four years later, in 2001, it had more than doubled to $2.25 billion, with most of that going on TV exposure. The spends rose because they had been shown to work. *Prevention*, a US consumer magazine, found in 1999 that 87% of patients who asked for an advertised drug were prescribed it.[6]

Sales teams also homed in on the same few drugs that earned the big money. A report from the pharma consultancy firm Scott-Levin entitled, 'Physician meeting and event audit' found there were 22,838 physician meetings and events to promote the SSRI-type antidepressants (up 31% over the previous year); 16,650 to promote the statins (up 18%); 13,815 to promote the Cox-2 inhibitors (up 22%); 10,395 on antihistamines (up 25%) and 9,624 (up 71%) on proton pump inhibitors to reduce stomach acid.[7]

People were paying more out of their own pockets as a result of all this frenetic commercial activity, either through higher insurance premiums or because they were being asked to contribute more in so-called co-payments. If they insisted on having the most expensive drugs, in other words, they had to pay for them. These were usually the ones the ads suggested they might benefit from.

Pressure built up in every direction as governors joined in the anti-pharma fervour. Several states started setting up schemes whereby companies were bound to offer rock-bottom prices or risk not having their drugs prescribed at all on state programmes for America's poor and elderly. Drug distributors, meanwhile, said they would rather not do business in those states than disclose information on the kind of discounts they offer.

Trying another tack altogether, the state of Florida experimented with partnership arrangements to offset rising bills, promising to ensure all Pfizer's drugs remained on the preferred list (which means they can be prescribed by doctors without their having to make a special 'prior authorization' request). In exchange, the world's top pharma company would fund disease-management programmes in at least ten major Florida hospitals. It would also hire at least 60 full-time care managers for Medicaid (the state-funded healthcare system) patients with asthma, congestive heart failure, diabetes and hypertension, run a health literacy programme to help low-income residents understand their conditions and treatments – and save the state $33 million over the next two years. The results are hotly disputed, but an early report from the Office of Program Policy Analysis and Government Accountability – a public watchdog that reports directly to the legislature – said the state had more to gain by demanding discounts than asking for a better way to manage drugs.[8]

Meanwhile, litigation escalated. In the early noughties, pharma companies faced a huge number of investigations and lawsuits brought by federal prosecutors, state attorney generals, company whistle-blowers and a host of consumer groups and individuals; and the charges were both criminal and civil. Many of the practices they related to had been going on for years. Charges included defrauding Medicare and Medicaid by billing for inflated prices, or encouraging providers – who can pocket the difference – to do so.

Whistle-blower George Couto, a former Bayer manager, earned himself $34 million (this was a cut of the final settlement) by providing prosecutors with internal documents that showed how his company's scheme had begun in 1995. He said that the largest HMO in the US, Kaiser Permanente, allegedly threatened to stop buying Bayer's antibiotic Cipro because Johnson & Johnson's Floxacin was being offered at a much lower price.

The *New York Times* noted that, because Kaiser was buying $7 million of Cipro a year, Bayer wanted to reduce its price without having to give additional rebates to the state-funded Medicaid program. Under US law, companies are obliged to offer Medicaid the lowest prices, so both companies had reason to concoct a plan that obscured them, thereby defrauding the US taxpayer. *Scrip* reported, 'According to Mr Couto's testimony, Kaiser suggested a solution. Bayer would ship Cipro in the usual way but the words "distributed by Kaiser Foundation Hospitals" would be typed along with Kaiser's national drug code number rather than Bayer's number.'[9]

This was a fairly regular ploy. Bayer agreed to pay $251.6 million in civil damages to settle federal False Claims Liabilities in connection with Cipro and a popular blood pressure drug, Adalat CC. GlaxoSmithKline agreed to pay $87.6 million for repackaging Paxil (Seroxat) in the same way, and Pfizer has paid $49 million for not providing a best price for its bestselling statin, Lipitor. Between 2000 and 2003, it was estimated that eight drug companies paid out a total of $2.2 billion in fines and settlements. Four – TAP Pharmaceuticals, Abbott, AstraZeneca and Bayer – pleaded guilty to criminal charges.[10]

Companies were also pulled up for marketing drugs for unapproved uses, for misleading advertising and for manufacturing irregularities. Angell says:

> In general, companies are only too willing to settle cases rather than risk being convicted of a felony and perhaps barred from Medicare and Medicaid. It may be that the fines, huge though some of them are, are more than offset by the extra income generated by the drug firms' questionable activities, and the whole thing is shrugged off as just one more cost of doing business. And it may be that many of the charges are frivolous – just a matter of greedy plaintiffs' attorneys going for deep pockets or overeager government lawyers trolling for big settlements. But there is no doubt that litigation is increasing, and the industry is, for the first time, beginning to look vulnerable. Over time it adds up, and it can't be good for public relations. Even gnats in great enough numbers can be a real problem.[11]

All this unprecedented pressure on pharma practices and prices has had some effect on sales. The growth of US pharma sales has started to slow down, from 14.5% in 2003 to just 9% in 2004. Americans still spent

$232.7 billion on prescription drugs in the year to September 2004, according to IMS Health.[12] The US share of the global pharma spend is slipping, however, from hovering above the halfway mark to just 45.6% in 2004.[13] Again, this is hardly a major slide but it reverses an upward trend and could go down further if the world's standard-bearer of private medicine found itself defeated by the consumers it purports to serve. If price controls were widely introduced, and Americans stopped paying such high prices, pharma would be in serious trouble.

Friends in high places

Industry's efforts to thwart such threats show the strength of its support from the people who matter, and what US citizens are up against as they try to level the playing field. Direct lobbying action to influence the democratic process is much more upfront in the US than Europe. Peter Rixon, editor of UK-based *The Healthcare Lobbyist*, describes how Washington's revolving-door between public and private life is able to facilitate careers in advocacy that Europeans can only dream about.[14]

A successful career as an advocate for a cause involves a person spending a couple of years in government before moving back into the mainstream, either alone or with a company in the private sector. The policy issues that draw the most funding (occasionally, the most passion), attract the most able players who might then seek another spell in government to build further personal credibility, and so it goes on.

Former Congressman Billy Tauzin, appointed president of pharma's US industry association, the Pharmaceutical Research and Manufacturers of America (PhRMA) in January 2005 at a salary thought to be around the $2 million mark, is a good example. Tauzin had served as chairman of the powerful House Energy and Commerce Committee for eight years, and proven his credentials as one of the chief architects of the law that finally gave US pensioners free access to drugs.

The Medicare drug law, passed at the start of 2003 and operational from 2006, entitles all people over the age of 65 to get their prescription drugs for free at an estimated cost of around $400 billion over ten years. The law has been described as a giveaway to industry on two counts. The first is because it uses the private insurance system, which is more responsive to patient demand for the latest medicines (because insurers have various ways they can pass prices on, unlike the NHS, for example). The second and more significant reason is that there is a specific clause in the law that forbids the Department of Health and Human Services from negotiating drug prices. The US government must pay what pharma charges, in other words, a situation that is unique in the world.

Tauzin was a fairly natural choice to represent pharma interests in these difficult times, and his appointment shows the importance of friends in pharma politics. The latest law is something of a political masterstroke because it gives patients what they want, which is free drugs. It also gives companies what they want, which is high prices plus strong demand for their drugs, which they get since the drugs come free. The only losers are citizens who indirectly pay a much higher drugs bill. In so doing, they also sow the seeds of even higher ones in the future, because the more money there is circulating around the system, the more pressure builds to siphon it off.

Public–private programmes thrive in healthcare. Consider, for example, President George W. Bush's controversial plans to screen the US population for mental health, starting with those still at school. These plans were announced in July 2004 and are gradually being implemented across the nation. Based on the recommendations of the New Freedom Commission on Mental Health, the idea is nothing less than a wholesale transformation of current services that, among other things, wants Americans to appreciate the importance of good mental health as much as they do good physical health. 'The stigma attached to mental illness, which discourages people from seeking care, must be eliminated,' says the Commission's final report.[15]

While some praise the plan's laudable and ambitious goals, others cynically suggest it is fishing for customers to protect the profits of drug companies. The latter reason is that the New Freedom Commission, established by President George W. Bush in April 2002 to look at how mental health services operate, also recommends treatment with the latest and most expensive drugs. 'The panel urges the elimination of the 15–20 year lag between the discovery of effective treatments and their wide use in routine patient care,' the report continues.[16]

Specifically, the Commission aims for integrated care that can screen, identify and respond to problems early. And it cites the Texas Medication Algorithm Project (TMAP) as a model treatment plan. According to the *British Medical Journal*, the Texas project started in 1995 as an alliance of pharma company representatives, the University of Texas, and the mental health and corrections systems of Texas. George W. Bush was state governor at the time and, during his 2000 presidential campaign, boasted of his support for the project and the fact that legislation he passed had expanded Medicaid coverage of psychotropic drugs.[17]

This latest development is an even bigger boon to companies who make antidepressants. Zyprexa, one of the drugs recommended as a first-line treatment in the Texas algorithm, grossed $4.28 billion worldwide in 2003 and is Eli Lilly's top-selling drug. Around 70% of these sales are already paid for by government agencies, such as Medicare and Medicaid, according to Gardiner Harris writing in the *New York Times*.[18]

It is at times like these that one's friends count. Lilly has multiple ties to the Bush administration. The *BMJ* points out that George Bush senior was on Lilly's board of directors and Bush junior appointed Lilly's CEO, Sidney Taurel, to a seat on the Homeland Security Council. Lilly also made $1.6 million in political contributions in 2000, 82% of which went to Bush and the Republican Party.[19]

But the most crushing evidence that the plan had been inspired for financial gain came from another whistle-blower, Allen Jones, who had been an employee of the Pennsylvania Office of the Inspector General, before he was sacked for speaking up. Jones revealed to both the *New York Times* and the *BMJ* that officials with influence over the medication plan in his state had received money and perks from drug companies with a stake in the medication algorithm.

He told the *BMJ* that the same 'political/pharmaceutical alliance' that had generated the Texas project was behind the recommendations of the New Freedom Commission. This, he continued, was

> poised to consolidate the TMAP effort into a comprehensive national policy to treat mental illness with expensive, patented medications of questionable benefit and deadly side effects, and to force private insurers to pick up more of the tab.[20]

Larry D. Sasich of the watchdog group, Public Citizen, said most studies suggest using the older drugs first makes sense.

> There's nothing in the labelling of the newer atypical antipsychotic drugs that suggests they are superior in efficacy to haloperidol [an older 'typical' antipsychotic]. There has to be an enormous amount of unnecessary expenditures for the newer drugs.[21]

Objections to the plan have centred not only on the fact that it uses the most expensive drugs but also that drugs can deny people, especially children, their full emotional experience and therefore risk stunting their development. And do they really need them? According to a report from the US Preventive Services Task Force Report in 2002, evidence on the accuracy and reliability of screening tests in children and adolescents is limited, as it is on the effectiveness of therapy. 'With accuracy, reliability and effectiveness in question, one has to wonder about false positives – how many children will be unnecessarily treated, over-treated, and how many will be harmed?' asked Laura Newman in the *BMJ*.[22]

Other critics have mentioned that other methods of treating mental health are effectively sidelined because public money is spent almost exclusively on drugs. Moreover, with mental illness being so highly subjective, all sorts of civil liberty issues present themselves. Disturbing precedents have already been set in this respect with schoolchildren being prescribed ADD medication against their parents' wishes if teachers feel it is necessary to reduce the effects of their disruptive behaviour on the rest of the class.

George W. Bush's efforts to change medical liability legislation highlight another example of how having friends in high places can pay dividends. This is one of his top congressional priorities for 2005, according to *Scrip*'s Washington editor, Reginald Rhein, and is aimed at reducing medical liability cases, the number of which has skyrocketed in recent years.[23]

In promoting the case for reform, Bush said that medical liability lawsuits, increasing premiums and the defensive practice of medicine cost the federal budget $28 billion a year. While the talk is mainly about capping medical damages against doctors or hospitals, it also includes a clause that bans punitive damages altogether for a manufacturer or distributor of a medical product that complies with FDA standards.

Democrat Senator Byron Dorgan of North Dakota, spoke for citizens rather than industry when he said that the President's plan fits a growing and disturbing pattern.

> This administration has blocked access to lower-priced prescription drugs from other countries. It has disallowed any attempt to negotiate lower prices for drugs purchased by the federal government through Medicare. Now, the president wants to take away every American's right to sue for damages if the drug companies harm them through negligent testing, manufacturing or marketing of their overpriced prescription medicines.[24]

Partnership is the way forward

Those who can afford to influence public opinion believe that the business–government relationship is symbiotic and that the way forward is partnership. 'When I lobby, I try to change government policy in a way that's a win-win for both [Pfizer and the public],' Pfizer CEO Hank McKinnell told Joel Bakan in an interview for his book, *The Corporation*. 'We hope to elect people who have supported policies which are good for the nation.'[25]

The amounts pharma contributed to the 2004 presidential election cycle were not massive considering pharma companies tend to think in billions. Pfizer, for example, gave just under $1.5 million ($1,465,317) and GlaxoSmithKline just under a million ($922,210), according to the Center for Responsive Politics in Washington, and in a two-thirds to George W. Bush and one-third to contender John Kerry split.[26] But these sums are only the high-profile so-called hard dollars. Many more soft dollars are spent influencing public opinion via PR companies and think tanks, or by giving money to patient-support groups that excel at spreading pharma's word. The US National Alliance for the Mentally Ill, a grassroots organization of individuals with brain disorders, and their families, for example, received almost $12 million from 18 drug companies between 1996 and 1999.[27]

All this money influences the democratic process because the people who receive it spread the message pharma wants governments to hear, that people are crying out for their drugs. Says Bakan,

> Democracy requires, at a minimum, some measure of equality of opportunity to participate in the political process. Yet profound inequality is the result when corporations – huge concentrations of shareholder wealth – exercise the same rights as individuals within that process.[28]

People like McKinnell would argue, however, that lobbying *is* the political process and it is all about forging partnerships between the public and private sector. 'Partners should be equals,' Bakan retorts.

> One partner should not wield power over the other, should not regulate the other, should not exert sovereignty over the other. Partners should share the same mission and the same goals. They should work together to solve problems and plan courses of action.
>
> Democracy, on the other hand, is necessarily hierarchical. It requires that the people, through the governments they elect, have sovereignty over corporations, not equality with them; that they have the authority to decide what corporations can, cannot, and must do. If corporations and governments are indeed partners, we should be

> worried about the state of our democracy, for it means that government has effectively abdicated its sovereignty over the corporation.[29]

There may be some comfort to be had from the fact that corporations do try to be good, and to be seen to take their corporate responsibilities seriously. Of course, their definition of good is limited, working to the extent that they and their shareholders can also benefit from their actions. Nevertheless, they do aim to be good partners in regulatory affairs, adhering to the ways of the regulators even when they border on archaic.

A story circulating in manufacturing circles, for example, has it that Pfizer was once manufacturing an antibiotic in its brand new plant in Ringaskiddy, Ireland, where the latest high-tech equipment for checking drug quality had been installed. But, because the plant had not yet got FDA approval for its methods for testing the quality of the processes involved, Pfizer shipped samples of the drug back to the US for testing. The only way to ensure no regulatory hold-ups, in other words, was to use a slower and more cumbersome test 3,500 miles away in Connecticut.[30] Indeed, the bizarreness of this incident prompted the FDA to reflect on its manufacturing rules and standards, opening the door to computerized quality-control methods that other industries had been using for years.

Pharma companies endure a lot of red tape and bureaucracy from the regulators they largely pay for. This makes for a unique and certainly symbiotic relationship, where each side gets to understand, anticipate and compensate for the weaknesses of the other. When one goes down, they both do, to a greater or lesser extent. The nature of the partnership is too oblique for anyone to see what is going on most of the time. It took a really disastrous year in 2004 for the regulators to be forced to account.

This was a year that had seen Vioxx recalled worldwide, the crusade by New York Attorney General Eliot Spitzer for full disclosure of clinical trial data on the antidepressant Seroxat/Paxil, and a shortage of a flu vaccine because of manufacturing irregularities. The regulators had no option but to become stricter and payers tighter if they were not going to lose the public's trust entirely. Viren Mehta, managing partner of Mehta Partners, a global healthcare consultancy, points out that as Medicare prepared to pick up the bill for all US pensioners, policies were being written to remove slack from the system. If passed, they would mean patients paying for more drugs themselves, and the widespread practice of doctors prescribing a drug off-label, which means for a condition for which it has not been officially approved, would be cut down.[31] Both would have the effect of cutting the volume of drugs prescribed.

Criticism of pharma underpinning its marketing with its own 'selective' clinical trials has also led to calls for corrective action. Mehta points out how NICE in the UK has started to sponsor its own counter-studies and the US Centers for Medicare and Medicaid is doing the same for the expensive cancer drugs.

> Other European countries, as well as the EU's Committee for Human Medicinal Products (CHMP) and Japan's Ministry of Health and Welfare, are equally interested. Legislative action may not seem imminent [regulators cannot generally insist companies run studies in the public interest] but this early trend needs to be watched carefully.[32]

Pharma's fundamental problem

Pharma's many problems all stem from one fundamental source, which is that companies need to maintain profit levels with very few new drugs. Nonetheless, pharma is still turning around good growth in revenues and profits for three reasons. First, America has pretty much held its ground as the top market and the source of the disquiet has been stopped with the Medicare laws. Second, new markets are opening up in Asia and elsewhere as countries become more prosperous and can afford more drugs. Third, pharma does have some good new drugs in, for example, cancer.

But no one knows when the innovation drought will end, and most countries except America tend to think along social welfare lines as far as drugs and healthcare are concerned. Citizens who have grown up in state-run systems largely welcome the benefits they bring. The UK NHS, for example, for all its gross and obvious inefficiencies, is still a much-loved institution. When governments try to change how it operates, as they must if only to challenge the inefficiencies, they do so at their political peril and therefore usually with vast amounts of money to show their commitment to its founding principles.

But if treatments are universal and free at the point of service, as the founding principles of the UK's NHS insist, then clearly something has to give if budgets do not keep pace with the demand for medicines at prices the industry wants. Cheap generic drugs are the obvious answer in countries where budgets are stretched to the limit, where the commercial influence on public health is less strong, and where people are generally aware only of what is available, and not of what isn't. This is precisely why governments are doing what they can to persuade doctors to prescribe generically and, if this fails, to allow pharmacists to substitute generic alternatives when the prescriptions come to be dispensed. Indeed, business is already responding to these arguments. The world's sixth largest producer of branded drugs, the Swiss company, Novartis spent £4.4 billion ($7.9 billion) acquiring two major generic producers in February 2005, making it the world's largest manufacturer of generic drugs overnight.[33]

But the EU's refusal to bend its rules so its citizens might pay more for the latest drugs would seem to express the nub of the problem from pharma's global perspective. 'It is within the countries of old Europe, which house 250 million people, that the problems lie,' says pro-industry commentator Philip Brown. 'Here, personal enterprise, self-sufficiency and drive have been squeezed out like juice from an orange, leaving just the pith and the peel.'[34]

These are strong words to describe a situation in which governments are taking what might be described as the only sensible option. In areas where there has not been significant medical advance, why not use drugs that were good a few years ago at a fraction of the price? Apart from anything else, it would mean more money available to treat more people with the genuinely good and innovative medicines.

In the US, where pharma can operate in a far more favourable environment, the current of opinion is anti-Europe, according to Miles White, chairman of PhRMA and CEO of Abbott Laboratories. Consumers, he says, are 'downright angry – and understandably so – about the disparity in prices between the US and other developed countries.'[35]

Yet, at the same time, every single change the US people have tried to foist on pharma in recent years over an unprecedented period of recrimination and inquiry – having to disclose unfavourable clinical data, making it harder to enlist doctors who favour a particular drug, tighter research regulations, lower prices, and so on – has served to level the machinations of a powerful industry with the voice of consumers. And at no point, except when it has been industry-sponsored, has the target of US anger been patients in other countries. It has been directed entirely at how the industry conducts itself and, in particular, how the laws seem to work in the interest of the largest and most powerful companies.

Medical research is not the exclusive preserve of big pharma companies. They may undertake the more expensive job of developing that research into drugs, but the underlying science funded by both private and public money will carry on. If it is good, a way will be found for it to be developed into medicines, if not by pharma then by the hundreds of smaller companies that could do the work, perhaps with state help. A real commitment to bringing more variety and range to the global research effort would not necessarily be impaired by the spending power of biggest players being cut down to size. On the contrary.

The previous chapter showed how smaller companies are already challenging the supremacy of pharma, and in particular, its model of business built around the blockbuster drug. A further challenge comes from ordinary people who have the means, via the Internet, to be on a much more equal footing with their doctors, and from doctors who are responding to these trends by siding, for the first time in their profession's history, more with the patient than the medical establishment.

Professor Joe Collier, former editor of the UK's government-funded *Drug and Therapeutics Bulletin*, reflecting on 40 years of medicine, says:

> There has been an enormous change in culture over the past few years. No question about that. Doctors, certainly the young ones, are totally aware of patient rights and are moving towards the patient being the centre rather than the profession. This is very different to the world I was in as a young man.[36]

It is a new world in many respects. And it is not at all clear how things will settle. The industry lobby holds up the US as a model environment for scientists (which it is), and a model environment for business (which it is). But it is awfully expensive for ordinary Americans to maintain and hard to find many Europeans who are sympathetic once they know the full picture.

The arguments for medical science to be less constrained by the dominance of the pharmaceutical industry are now overwhelming. How ordinary Europeans are expressing them is explored in the next chapter.

10

The European patient

It may be hard for Americans to appreciate just how cocooned Europeans are in free and universal state-funded healthcare systems. In London, Paris or Barcelona the vast majority have no idea what drugs cost, nor any reason to. Neither have they ever had any real choice about how, when or where they are treated. And nor has this mattered much. People may contest medical judgements in exceptional cases, such as when a child's life is at stake but, at the risk of overgeneralization, most try to feel grateful for their healthcare systems because the only alternatives are expensive when set against what is provided by the public for the public for free.

Being so cocooned, their views are easily usurped in a lobbying process that is much less overt than in the US. Dr Andrew Herxheimer, emeritus fellow at the UK Cochrane Centre, explains how patient interest groups that purport to represent the public at European level have in fact been established to support the aims of industry. The International Alliance of Patients' Organizations (IAPO), for example, is registered as a foundation in the Netherlands and funded by Pharmaceutical Partners for Better Healthcare, a consortium of about 30 major companies. And the Global Alliance of Mental Illness Advocacy (GAMIAN) was founded by US pharma company, Bristol-Myers Squibb, and has since developed an autonomous European arm, Gamian Europe. According to Herxheimer:

> The European Commission prefers to hold discussions with these federations rather than patient and consumer groups, apparently because, unlike most voluntary health organisations, they claim to represent patients in many countries. Neither publishes its sources of funds. With other organisations linked to the industry, they successfully lobbied the Commission to propose allowing industry to

> provide direct-to-consumer (DTC) 'information' about prescription medicines.[1]

Moves to allow pharma companies to communicate more directly with potential customers show, perhaps better than any other single issue or incident, how much industry wants the public on side. The value to the public of being so closely aligned with pharma thinking, however, is less clear.

Herxheimer describes, for example, how the UK industry association, the ABPI, saw the idea of overturning the EU's ban on DTC advertising as a critical battle for pharma at the start of the new millennium. He cites *Pharmaceutical Marketing* magazine, which says its action plan was

> to employ ground troops in the form of patient support groups, sympathetic medical opinion and healthcare professionals ... which will lead the debate on the informed patient issue ... This will have the effect of weakening political, ideological and professional defences ... Then the ABPI will follow through with high level precision strikes on specific regulatory enclaves in both Whitehall and Brussels.[2]

An Informed Patient Initiative campaign was started in 1998 as part of this plan, the first phase of which involved a series of focus meetings with patient groupings, where the European industry's version of direct-to-consumer (DTC) advertising was disseminated. This is a much gentler form of what was introduced in the US in 1997, when laws were relaxed to allow advertisements of prescription drugs first in the print media and, by 1999, on television as well. The effect of this relaxation on pharma marketing budgets was electrifying, and the amounts spent on DTC advertising nearly doubled from $844 million in 1997 to $1.5 billion in 1999.[3] It exploded again when television ads were given the go-ahead, with 2002 figures showing that spends have since risen to $2.5 billion.[4]

In the weeks immediately following the 9/11 terrorist attack in 2001, it probably didn't seem odd for an ad in the *New York Times* Magazine to show a worried-looking woman in that city under the headline, 'Millions suffer from chronic anxiety. Millions could be helped by Paxil.' But such ads also show how the line between gratuitous marketing and empowering people is always unclear. Or as researcher Barbara Mintzes asked in the *BMJ*, 'At what point does an understandable response to distressing life events become an indication for drug treatment and a market opportunity?'[5]

The issue shows why the public has good reason to keep some distance in its engagement with pharma. Their aims are not identical. But to cement 'informed patients' as reliable allies in the fight for larger European markets, the ABPI went on to mount an Expert Patient Initiative which highlighted the value of patients and pharma finding ways to work in partnerships that bring mutual benefits to both parties.[6] And indeed, a whole wave of such partnerships can be seen throughout the NHS and other healthcare systems in Europe.

While partnership is always an attractive idea in principle, the downside for public health, always the David to pharma's Goliath, is less obvious. And the central issue is whether drugs are always the best solution. Charles Medawar of Social Audit UK argues that the most dangerous effect of DTC advertising is that it encourages healthy people to think they need medical attention. This leads, he suggests, 'to a new danger to our well-being, that of becoming a nation of healthy hypochondriacs, living gingerly, worrying ourselves half to death.'[7]

The counter-argument could be heard when Dr Jane Henney, a former FDA commissioner, opened a debate on whether DTC advertising was 'patient empowerment or national service burden?' – the title of a UK workshop organized by the Social Market Foundation in 2003. Henney said DTC advertising had worked in the US because it provoked people – a vast number of whom are undermedicated, she stressed – to visit the surgery and initiate discussions with their doctors.[8]

In Europe, only the right to produce factual, quality, non-promotional information on medicines was being sought. But significant resistance from consumer groups questioned industry's claim to be perfectly placed to provide what people really want to know. The UK's Consumers' Association (CA) did its own research on this point and found only 6 in 100 people would trust anything a pharma company said anyway. And in terms of awareness, it found US advertising focused on treatments that attract the highest potential revenues, such as those for allergies, anxiety, baldness, ulcers and cholesterol control. 'Advertising would not raise awareness of a wide range of health conditions and treatments,' the CA said.[9]

All pharma's efforts, on the surface, would seem to have been in vain because, in October 2002, the European parliament voted to retain the ban on DTC. However, it was also a victory for industry because a specific clause in the bill allowed some dismantling of the rules. Controlled DTC promotion in three significantly large disease areas – diabetes,

AIDS and asthma – was allowed for the first time. The reason given was that patient groups had specifically lobbied for it.

Gradual change also helps the payers; most European governments are rightly suspicious of anything that might mean finding more money than they already do for medicines. They don't want pharma having greater freedom to promote its products, if only because the US experience has shown this leads directly to greater demand and higher prices. But they too may be powerless against the commercial arguments. 'There is no doubt that the ultimate aim is direct marketing to patients within 5–10 years,' said Dr George Rae, chairman of the BMA's policy-making division at the time. 'Advertising is about increasing demand and this causes concern.'[10]

MMR and all that

Other signs of the Berlin Wall of healthcare being dismantled come from popular movements that are expressions of a breakdown in trust with the regulator or the medical establishment. One is the low uptake of the triple measles, mumps and rubella (MMR) vaccine, a fact that has been blamed by almost the entire medical establishment on a single study conducted by a single doctor, Dr Andrew Wakefield.

It seems more likely that the seeds of doubt in medical authority had been planted long before Wakefield ever published his paper in the *Lancet* in 1998 that shot to notoriety for suggesting a connection between MMR and childhood autism which could not have been more fiercely contested. Certainly, mass vaccination policy in most countries was developed at a time when no one would have dreamed of questioning the doctor. On the contrary. People knew from living memory what it meant for children to die from a whole range of horrible diseases. Ironically, it is precisely because these policies were so successful that people now live in a reality where the risk–benefit profile they are presented with is very different.

The diseases in question – measles, mumps and rubella – were not considered particularly serious before the vaccines were available, as can be confirmed by any family health guide written before their introduction. Most parents know what it is like to fall sick with them. Mothers may even recall how as girls they had been encouraged to catch rubella by visiting friends who had it, thereby minimizing the chances of falling ill while pregnant and exposing the fetus to a high risk of blindness. Measles, mumps and rubella are precisely the illnesses, in other words, that modern mothers went down with when they were at school and they had lived to tell the tale.

Meanwhile, the steep and mysterious rise in cases of childhood autism around the world is real and it raises the risk side of the equation somewhat. 'The changing balance of the benefit–risk equation is of fundamental importance and has been almost entirely neglected,' says Dr Peter Fletcher, a former principal medical officer for the Department of Health and chief medical assessor to the Committee on the Safety of Medicines. He has since served as an expert witness for some 1,300 families who were claiming compensation from the Department of Health and the vaccine makers.

> The risk element of the naturally occurring infectious diseases was incomparably more serious in the years 1900–1950 than it has been in the following 55 years. This is mainly due to two factors: the dramatic decrease in deprivation in the population and the equally dramatic improvement in public health. This means that serious adverse reactions to immunizations which were quite acceptable at the beginning of the century must now be re-evaluated to take into account these changes.[11]

Whether quietly to cause as little fuss as possible or as an upfront protest, many people have said they don't like a vaccination policy that tells them how their children must take their jabs, particularly when they suspect it has been devised with the convenience of the health service uppermost in mind. This protest has been despite the best medical evidence that says there is no link between MMR and childhood autism.

As a direct result, the first clear signs of a mumps epidemic could be seen sweeping across university campuses in the summer of 2005. 'Nearly a third of 270,000 young people starting courses this autumn have probably not been immunised against the illness,' reported James Meikle, the *Guardian*'s health correspondent.[12] Rates had risen tenfold in a year. In the year to July 2005, there had been 55,093 cases of mumps, against just 5,877 in the same period the previous year. A few years further back and there had been virtually no cases of mumps.

This result had been predicted. Even without entering the minefield of the science that led (rightly or wrongly) to serious doubts about MMR, the government could have provided individual vaccines if the population as a whole was to have a reasonable degree of protection from measles, mumps and rubella. Its reluctance to do so is extraordinary and must be set against the estimated compensation figure of £10–15 billion ($18–28 billion) for which the Department of Health and those companies that haven't been indemnified against the claims would be liable for: thousands of families, each with claims estimated at £3 million ($5.4 million) for lifelong care, if negligence in any part of the licensing process were ever proven.

At present, according to Richard Barr, one of the solicitors representing the families before state-funded legal aid was stopped, it isn't clear which manufacturers' vaccines were used, either the batches or which company made them, nor which strains of both mumps and measles they contained. This means that in the event of a litigation payout, it is not clear who is to blame.[13]

When Jenny Hope, health editor of the *Daily Mail*, was asked by MPs in the House of Commons inquiry into the influence of the pharma industry why journalists refused to let the story die, she said it was because the story itself refused to go away. New evidence is constantly being uncovered and autism rates continue to rise.

In October 2004, US paediatrician Dr F. Edward Yazbak provided another interpretation of the large overseas studies on which the vaccines' safety profile was based. He said the definitive Danish study of more than 500,000 children born between 1991 and 1998 could not rule out a link between MMR and autism because many children went on to get autism after the trial had been concluded. 'The most important age group to look at comprises children aged from five to nine,' he said. 'The number with autism increased from 8.38 per 100,000 before the MMR jab was introduced in 1987, to 77.43 in 2000.'[14]

Even if this rise is not caused by MMR, the fact is autism is rising and no one knows why. Yazbak cites US figures which show that 140,920 children aged 6–21 were diagnosed with autism in 2003, compared with 12,222 in 1993.[15] Erica Goode, a medical journalist with the *New York Times*, cites figures which show cases had tripled from 1987 to 1998, and then doubled from 1998 to 2002.[16] Another study, conducted in Cambridgeshire by Fiona Scott, Simon Baron-Cohen and colleagues from the University of Cambridge, found 196 children aged between 5 and 11 years old with a confirmed autism spectrum disorder – a prevalence of 57 per 100,000.[17] This is more than 14 times the rate of 4 per 100,000 of the 1970s.

Theories abound about how this apparent epidemic has arisen. David Kirby in the US wrote the book *Evidence of Harm* to promote his theory that the culprit is the preservative found in older vaccines, thimerosal, that contains the toxin, mercury. His figures show that reported cases of autism in the 1990s among American children started spiralling, from about 1 in 10,000 in 1987 to a shocking 1 in 166 today.

And Wakefield has more than confirmed the findings of his original study back in 1987, only this time he was wise enough to confine his research to the link between autism and chronic bowel disease and to leave the MMR vaccine out of it.[18] 'He has looked at many, many more case-studies and the results have been published in a respected peer-reviewed journal,' says Fletcher. 'It does seem that what he originally said is almost certainly true.'[19]

But it is only part of a much more intriguing story. Several triggers of autism – toxins, infections, diet, genes, as well as vaccines – have been investigated, but scientists are genuinely mystified because there is no one set of characteristics that holds true for all cases. This is one reason why some have started to suggest the steep rise in incidence has more to do with a deeper understanding of the disease leading to greater recognition of its symptoms. Under this hypothesis, there is no epidemic at all, just a broader definition of autism, particularly at the milder end of the spectrum. And the symptoms have always been vague, ever since the American psychiatrist Leo Kanner first identified the condition in 1943, saying the fundamental feature of autism was the inability of those with the condition 'to relate themselves in the ordinary way to people and situations'.[20]

More recently, British psychologist Simon Baron-Cohen has suggested, somewhat controversially in his book, *The Essential Difference*, that autism is an example of the extreme male brain. What is not in doubt is that a lack of empathy creates a lonely world and a host of related difficulties for the children affected and the families who care for them. Autistic children are 20 times more likely to be excluded from normal schools in the UK, for example.[21]

Since 1980, the diagnostic criteria have been revised five times. And when one considers some of the impossibly vague definitions of conditions that have come under its umbrella, the deeper understanding theory has some credibility. One diagnosis, known as pervasive developmental disorder-not otherwise specified (PDD-NOS), for example, was added to the generally recognized autistic spectrum in 1987. And Asperger's syndrome (sometimes called high-functioning autism) became another official diagnosis in 1994.

What is a government to do?

It is against this background that the UK government must try to persuade people to follow its vaccination policies. It could reassure the public by showing it is looking into the causes of autism, as has been done rather more convincingly in the US. In 2000, the US Congress passed the Children's Health Act, mandating its main research agency, the National Institutes of Health, to fund five centres of excellence into autism research. 'Here was an unprecedented political commitment to expand, intensify, and coordinate research into autism and services for children living with autism,' says Richard Horton, in his book *MMR: Science and Fiction – Exploring a Vaccine Crisis*.[22]

Or the government could have anticipated a steep rise in demand for individual vaccines, particularly against mumps. Instead, it announced the launch of a new five-in-one vaccine for babies in late September 2004. While there is nothing at all to suggest the vaccine for whooping cough, diphtheria, tetanus, polio and a kind of influenza (HiB) is not entirely safe, it suggests a refusal by the authorities to engage with real public concerns. Because such foresight was lacking, thousands of people were left with no choice but to vaccinate their children privately without even the most basic protections in place. The huge demand for single vaccines meant that the rules that ensure they are kept within a specific temperature range throughout their journey from manufacturer to surgery were blatantly broken. If vaccines should fall out of this temperature range, for any of a number of reasons, they are not as effective.

The *Observer* was able to reveal a massive black market in individual vaccines imported from the US. As *Observer* journalist Jo Revill reported:

> Ironically, attempts to bring in the vaccine by the back door are partly fuelled by the government's attempts to encourage the take-up rate for the MMR triple jab, by making it harder and harder for licensed clinics to obtain the single doses they need for their clients.[23]

Sarah Dean is a nurse who believes her son was damaged by MMR. As a consequence of that belief, she set up a vaccination clinic to help mothers have the choices she felt she was denied. Clinics such as hers, those that stick to the rules, were receiving only up to 30 doses a week, according to the *Observer*. Dean is incandescent with rage. 'We have about 18,000 people on our books waiting for immunisation for mumps, either for themselves or their child. At a time when you have outbreaks occurring all around the country, this is not a good situation to be in.'[24]

Meanwhile, an unlicensed clinic operator went on the record to explain how the backdoor route can deliver hundreds of vaccines a week, which can be charged at £130 ($240) a time. 'Between you and me, what we do is use a wholesale importer who backdoors it to us once it is in the UK.' He defended the action by saying, 'All you are doing is trying to get a vaccine which will bring some immunity. But it's as if you're trying to bring in cocaine. It's mad.'[25]

Moving into uncharted territory

Just as some parents refuse to allow their children to be immunized with the MMR vaccine, a more general trend towards non-compliance with doctor's orders can be seen. A joint report by the Royal Pharmaceutical Society of Great Britain and the drug company Merck Sharp & Dohme in 2002 highlighted the fact that eight in ten people were not taking their medicines as directed.[26]

It has been known for some time that a consumerist trend, coupled with less faith in the medical profession, has meant compliance with what doctors say can no longer be taken for granted, even among the seriously ill. The Department of Health responded to this poor record by creating the Medicines Partnership Task Force with a modest annual budget of £1.3 million ($2.4 million). The idea was to promote a shift in the doctor–patient relationship from one of compliance, where patients automatically do what they are told, to one of concordance, where a meeting of minds is encouraged about why a medical intervention may or may not be necessary.

In a sense it was an announcement from the medical profession of an intention to make a conscious effort to be less paternalistic in relating to patients, to listen more and generally take them more seriously. And it came at a time when the UK government had recently embarked on an ambitious ten-year plan to create a patient-led NHS. As the Medicines Partnership got going, handing out grants to measure levels of prevailing ignorance about medicines, it became abundantly clear there was a real need for more understanding about the patients' agenda.

'It often seems to be a case of [patients] feeling a need to maintain the appearance of following the doctor's directions whilst making their own decisions,' a study report from a primary care team in Blackburn and Derwen in the north of England said, after interviewing 260 elderly patients about their drug regimes. 'For many people the prescribing of medicines is something that is done to them and not with them; they see themselves to some extent outside the process.'[27]

The same thing was heard again and again from the mountains of research that has been conducted to support the first serious overhaul the NHS has ever known. Changing an institution like the NHS is expensive. Its budget had grown from £37 billion a year in 1997 to £76 billion in 2005 and is expected to reach £90 billion by the time the plans for a patient-led NHS have been fully rolled out in 2010. Much of this money has been spent creating an infrastructure (such as prices to know what things cost) so that the private sector can pick up the slack when patients start believing they really can choose and the NHS can't cope with the inevitable change in demand.

In medicine, the private sector has always taken a keen interest in anything where its interests could converge with those of the public. And non-compliance is one of them. Medical security firm, International SOS, says it costs pharma $70 billion a year worldwide and that 20% of prescriptions are never filled and half are not taken as prescribed.[28] The Department of Health admits the value of unused medicines returned to pharmacies is more than £100 million ($184 million).[29] And researchers in the Pharmaceutical Journal confirm that it is rising, up 59% over four years, although the rise in prescriptions had only been around 20% in the same period. [30]

Translated, the waste is a disaster in both financial and human terms. There is the oft-cited example of the middle-aged car salesman who was convinced his moderately high blood pressure was caused by stress. He therefore only took his pills when he felt tired or anxious instead of consistently as was required in order for them to work. His blood pressure remained unstable and eight years after his initial diagnosis he suffered a fatal heart attack. Another example, said to apply to 18% of kidney transplant patients, concerns a woman whose new kidney was rejected, not because of a mismatch but because she thought the transplant operation was the end of the problem. She therefore no longer felt a need to take drugs to suppress her immune system. Without the drugs, the body sensed the foreign kidney and rejected it.

As researchers started to look in more detail at why people don't take their drugs, they found that patients and doctors have very different priorities. A survey conducted in 1997, for example, showed the top priority for patients when prescribed a drug is to know its side effects, and the second, to know what the drug actually does. But these top two patient priorities were ranked joint tenth when GPs answered the same questionnaire. The third patient priority, to know any lifestyle changes that might be involved, was also ranked third by GPs. The fourth, how to take the medicine, was ranked second by GPs. And the fifth, what it consists of, was ranked fifteenth by GPs. The top doctor priority, meanwhile, to know the drug's interactions with other medicines, hardly registered at all with patients.[31]

'The goal of the healthcare professional is to treat symptoms or cure disease and for the patient these are but components of a spectrum of other life circumstances,' says Christine Bond, professor of primary care at Aberdeen University. 'So people continue to smoke despite obvious respiratory problems, and others do not take antihypertensive or lipid-lowering treatments because they do not see any immediate benefit to compensate for potentially suffering the side effects of the treatment.'[32]

From compliance to concordance

Suddenly doctors were to be found struggling, probably for the first time in their profession's history, to find convincing reasons why they should be considered of value to patients. According to Collier, trust is the crux of the problem.

> Patients want to be informed but that is not the end of it. There is so much information available and so many subtleties to be understood in how data are collected and so on that it requires quite a trained mind and some time to resolve these things.
>
> Doctors need to get themselves into a position where what they say is believed. They need patients to be able to say, because you're a doctor, I know from your training and thinking that you're working on my behalf. It is an ownership thing. It's like asking if you trust Marks & Spencer, for example, to be working on your behalf. If Marks & Spencer says something is organic, do you trust it? A good relationship with a doctor has that kind of trust.[33]

The idea of concordance between doctor and patient would seem as normal and natural a thing to aspire to as harmonious relations within a family. But it represents a radical departure for medicine, overturning centuries of practice where doctors have always known best and not taken kindly to challenges to their authority.

Professor Marshall Marinker, as chair of a working party leading to the creation of the Medicines Partnership, explains that concordance represents a therapeutic alliance that recognizes two sets of health beliefs, those of the patient and those of the doctor. Marinker goes on to insist that the process of resolving the differences between the two parties does not rely on 'superior' contemporary medical evidence.

> It implies a better understanding than hitherto of the ways in which the patient perceives the appropriateness and usefulness of the doctor's picture of the illness. It implies recognition of the fact that just as all prescribing is an experiment carried out by the doctor, so all medicine taking is an experiment carried out by the patient.[34]

Patients, by doing nothing other than not take their medicines properly, have prompted a serious movement, in other words, to find out where they are coming from. But it must not be forgotten that it is a public–private initiative, where the intention of the stronger partner is not concordance in the sense Marinker is talking about, but to get patients on side so they take their drugs properly. After an initial phase of public funding, the skeleton structures of the Medicines Partnership are expected to be maintained by industry money.

Private initiatives into pharma-inspired concordance already abound. International SOS, for example, is responsible for a 'patient support' programme whereby patients receive regular scheduled calls from trained nurses to remind them to take their therapy. One programme tailored for Roche's obesity drug, Xenical, in Australia resulted in those on the programme staying on treatment for twice as long as non-enrolled patients.[35] How much extra weight they lost is not known. Patients can also receive information via text messaging and mailouts to help them take a drug that, it must be remembered, has been prescribed for their benefit.

Whether described as exercises in concordance or disease management, pharma money is usually to be found. There are also Expert Patient programmes to end the era of the 'passive patient' by educating consumers to manage everyday aspects of chronic illness. The Department of Health launched its own version in 2001 before rolling it out nationwide. The stated aim is to reduce healthcare costs, including the unnecessary consumption of drugs, by encouraging people to get together and share knowledge about their condition.

Again, it sounds great, and again, most of the evidence suggests expert patients take more drugs. A Norwegian study, which taught people with asthma and chronic obstructive pulmonary disease (COPD) the principles of self-management, showed that only a third of patients collected their prescriptions at the start of the exercise. By the end that figure had doubled to 60%.[36] If the drugs work, this is a good result, although one can't help wondering slightly why the other 40% had gone to all the effort of going to the surgery, having a consultation with a doctor, being prescribed a drug, and then choosing not to get it dispensed.

The idea of expert patients and the movement toward concordance in the surgery are intended to raise the confidence of patients as they try to find the best treatments. The danger is that industry influence is now so pervasive within healthcare systems that both initiatives can seem to be working in the opposite direction. Healthcare resources being spent reminding people to take their slimming pills certainly doesn't suggest patient autonomy or empowerment.

Rather, it suggests a cash-strapped health service grateful for any money that doesn't have to come out of its own budgets. Dr Richard Horton told the recent parliamentary inquiry:

> The pharmaceutical industry has been enormously successful at interdigitalising itself in the usual process of healthcare in the UK. It provides equipment, services, buildings, facilities and, of course, hospitality. At almost every level of NHS care provision, the pharmaceutical industry shapes the agenda and the practice of medicine.[37]

Industry influence

Horton is not alone in believing the influence of money in healthcare is fast becoming counterproductive. London GP, Dr Iona Heath, for example, believes initiatives to encourage people to be more compliant disguise the fact that excessive prescribing, driven by commercial interests, is the more pervasive problem. While acknowledging the good intentions behind the setting up of the Medicines Partnership, she points out that its website states that, at any one time, seven in ten of the UK population are taking medicine to treat or prevent ill health. 'This statement is made with no further comment,' she says, 'but how can this level of drug taking be appropriate in a population that, by all objective measures, is healthier than ever before in history?'[38]

She points out that 28% of US hospital admissions of elderly people are caused by a drug-related problem and that substantially more are the result of adverse reactions than of non-compliance.

> Too often a prescribing cascade is set in motion whereby the side effects of one drug produce a new health problem, and so a second drug is prescribed, which in turn produces a new symptom and the need for a third drug. The pathway that leads from osteoarthritis to a non-steriodal anti-inflammatory drug to mild hypertension to a thiazide diuretic and on to diabetes and gout is but one example. The rhetoric of compliance and, more recently, concordance, seems to endorse excessive prescribing uncritically and unethically.[39]

The fundamental problem, she argues, is that medical science has its limitations, which the better informed patient-consumers of today are fully aware of. Every generation of doctors, she says, looks back at the ignorance of its predecessors while overestimating the robustness of its own knowledge. 'Many patients seem wiser and more cautious, apparently fully aware of the evolutionary process whereby today's miracle cure becomes tomorrow's killer. The recent research on the risks of hormone replacement therapy provides only the latest example of the shifting sands of medical research.'

What patients really need, she says, is not more information, but different information. 'There is an urgent need for more honesty about the limitations of medical knowledge. Patients need to be aware of the possibility of both benefits and harms and helped to make decisions based on their own valuation of the various possible outcomes.'

This, she maintains, is unlikely to happen if the crux of the matter is not addressed. That crux is that the patient's version of truth is rarely perceived to be as valid as the doctor's.

> If the dignity and autonomy of each patient is to be genuinely respected, the outcome of the consultation will often conflict with recommended medical guidance. Fundamentally, this is simply another manifestation of that familiar conflict between the utilitarian benefit of the many and the dignity and freedom of the individual, which has persisted throughout history as each successive utopian dream has degenerated into tyranny. The dream of perfect health is the contemporary utopia and comes, as always, accompanied by coercion.[40]

The Di Bella affair

A backlash against coercion was precisely what the Italian health ministry came up against in the extraordinary Di Bella affair of the late 1990s. The coercion, as perceived by the mass of the Italian population, had been to force cancer patients to take drugs that had been shown to work rather than Di Bella's concoction, which famously had not. As bizarre as it sounds, similar scenarios are being played out around the world as consumers increasingly defy government experts. If trust is not re-established in some shape or form, people will continue to take what has not been shown to work, shun what has, and more will begin to wonder what the point of the regulator is.

Professor Luigi Di Bella, the man at the centre of the affair, was an elderly physiologist who claimed to know how to put cancers into remission. The issue concerned how public money is used in healthcare. Specifically, Di Bella said the state should pay for his Multiterapia Di Bella (MDB, a cocktail of drugs and vitamins), just as it did for Glivec, Tamoxifen and all the other prescription anticancers.

Some say the retired doctor was a pawn in one of Italy's political storms. And had he been operating alone, the refusals by the health authorities to fund his treatment may well have gone unnoticed, as they had in the past. But occasionally events act to bring together a number of seemingly unrelated forces to create a whirlwind of such intensity that basic infrastructures become unsettled.

Those forces concerned the press, the political establishment, modern healthcare systems, the choices people are offered, and, most pertinently of all, the authoritarian nature of science in determining those choices. The entire country was caught up for over a year in what the newspaper, *L'Unita*, described as 'a great and tragic illusion'.

The affair pitted the thirteenth child of a clerical worker from the Sicilian village of Linguaglossa against a heartless pharmaceutical industry. It may be significant that it took place only a few years after a major drugs scandal. In 1993, senior officials responsible for approving medicines had been sent to prison, and one committed suicide, for having allowed greed to distort their professional judgement. It had already been demonstrated in the courts, in other words, that the people who are entrusted to protect public health are open to corruption.

And lack of trust goes some way to explaining what went on to become an extraordinary popular uprising against the status quo. It was the people versus the state. And the issue was only resolved when health minister Rosi Bindi met Di Bella on national television in January 1998 and, in front of 9 million people, announced that a series of clinical trials would be staged at the public's expense to settle the matter once and for all. The reason she gave was 'to restore public order'.

With so many people using complementary therapies across the world, the question of proof that raised its head in Italy is instructive. In Italy, the questions were asked from the heart rather than the head. Most people weren't interested in the science; what they saw was a remote medical establishment denying them choice.

Di Bella may also have come to represent for them a kind of humanity that has largely been squeezed out of healthcare as it has become more technical. His whole strategy had been centred around boosting the body's natural defences to strengthen healthy cells, making them more able to fight the disease. There was no complicated science involved, no enzymes being blocked or stimulated. Di Bella was seen as a saviour, in other words, being harassed for shrinking cancers into oblivion. People wanted him to work his miracles. Journalists found case studies. They cheered him on with no thought for how those miracles arose.

Even the Vatican entered the fray, with cardinals saying the treatment should be given free to anyone who could benefit. Such divine endorsement was compounded in December 1997, when a judge in the southern city of Maglie also ruled the cocktail should be funded by the health authority. The emotional strings the case pulled were poignant, involving a two-year-old child fighting for her life against brain cancer. It was a battle that was eventually lost and everyone throughout the land felt for the parents who couldn't afford the growth hormone, somatostatin, thought to be MDB's key ingredient.

Even if they could have afforded it, they wouldn't have found any. Newspapers, milking the story for all it was worth, had published maps of the local pharmacies, urging people to get their supplies in while they could. At this point the medical journal, the *Lancet*, stepped in, saying, 'It is unfortunate that the judiciary has the power to sweep aside carefully constructed prescribing plans on the basis of little clinical opinion.'[41]

Meanwhile, Italian health officials were still requesting clinical evidence to substantiate why some cancers seemed to be loosening their grip. Was it really down to Di Bella's treatment, or was it the conventional therapy most of these patients were also taking? They might also have factored in faith in Di Bella himself, because the affair was very much a story about belief, albeit misplaced.

No one, except perhaps the more serious papers, seemed concerned that the remedy had not been subject to the tests required of any other drug. Nor that the exact composition changed from patient to patient. It was only when MDB had been shown to be, at best, ineffective, that the press started to highlight the connections between Di Bella and the right-wing Alleanza Nazionale party, suggesting the affair had been deliberately created to destabilize the left-leaning government of Romano Prodi. Bindi alleged the Alleanza Nazionale's intention had been to destroy the Italian national health service so the private sector could move in.[42]

Whatever the truth of the allegations, Di Bella's position swiftly began to crumble once confronted with the rules of conventional medicine whereby like must be compared with like. In January 1998, Italian hospitals had been flooded with requests from cancer patients wanting to be included in the trials. By July, many had started to withdraw. Early results from a trial in the Lombardy region showed that out of 333 patients, one had showed a partial response but one-third had no change. Half had local growth of their tumours, and 14% had signs of new cancers. Nausea, vomiting, diarrhoea and vague neurological signs were reported in 23% of patients, some of whom withdrew because of them. The results showed fairly conclusively that the treatments were so hopeless they didn't merit further testing.[43] By Friday 13 November, when Bindi announced the final verdict that MDB was, at best, ineffective, no one was particularly surprised.

Even after such a public humiliation, Di Bella himself never flinched from his position until his death in 2003. The press, however, backpedalled furiously, with the financial daily, *Il Sole-24 Ore*, saying, 'It remains to be explained why, in an advanced society, it is possible to see medicine reduced to a sort of barter system where those who shout loudest are most likely to be right.'[44]

The personal vs the state

Ironically, this is precisely the question that was left hanging as the safety profiles of the Cox-2s and the SSRI antidepressants were being rewritten. But it may not be the most appropriate one. If the Di Bella affair is seen as a protest against an impersonal, mechanistic approach to medicine, then the questions raised are rather different.

If people exercise their right to choice where health is concerned and that involves responding to belief, cherishing hope and thriving on miracles, then whether Di Bella was an out-and-out charlatan, a misguided old fool used for political ends, or a latter-day saint, hardly comes into it. In this consumer light, the significance of the Di Bella affair lies in highlighting the gap between the increasingly popular holistic view of mind and body (where everything is understood to work as one integrated system), and what public health systems can be reasonably expected to endorse.

Specifically, Di Bella signifies a departure from the days when there was only one authority reigning over matters pertaining to health and few thought to question it. Now, even when that rule is maintained, as it was hands-down with Di Bella, it is not necessarily strengthened. This is not because the authority of science is in question; it is because health involves issues that lie beyond the remit of science, and increasingly people want these things acknowledged in their general healthcare.

One way is to go it alone, which is surely not ideal, but distrust is now so pervasive that it is a concrete choice for some. According to journalist Felicity Lawrence,

> At the heart of the rebellion is a refusal to accept the expert's superior ability to judge on their behalf. People are not prepared to accept that exhaustive reviews of the evidence show no link between MMR and autism. They mentally substitute beef and vCJD, or food additives and allergies. They know that epidemiological studies which fail to find correlations are not the same as empirical evidence. Governments have too often given assurances, only to admit a problem later. And even if the risks are small, they know there are alternatives.[45]

As people try out these alternatives in ever-increasing numbers, they challenge the authority governing the healthcare choices the state provides. Where vaccines are concerned, the MMR refuseniks are defying policies that are driven by the economics of mass disease control rather than what serves the health of each child. Where their general health is concerned, the challenges are against marginalizing approaches to health that do not and cannot have corporate backing. Drug therapy itself would be a lot more effective if the public had grounds to be confident the drugs they are prescribed are the best possible treatment for their illness, rather than the most heavily promoted brand from a family of compounds that may all be inappropriate.

That does not means abandoning the doctor altogether, but instead doing everything possible to build up a relationship of trust (changing doctors, if necessary), so that when one is seriously ill and needs the skills of a good doctor, some of the principles of concordance have already been established.

11

Genes, germs and general behaviour

The kind of healthcare we receive is determined, as we have seen, largely by the rules of commerce. Other factors affecting our treatment choices reflect the broader trends in medicine that attract the greatest financial rewards and promote the most glittering careers. These trends show a shifting consensus of opinion as to what causes disease among the three main contenders: genes, germs and general behaviour.

One major shift in medical thinking can be pinpointed to one man in one year. The man was Sir Austin Bradford Hill, professor of medical statistics at London's School of Hygiene and Tropical Medicine, and the year was 1950. This was the end of what is sometimes known as the germ theory of medicine, when Bradford Hill reported on a series of trials he had designed to find a cure for the last major killer of that era, tuberculosis. In that same year, together with his protégé, Sir Richard Doll, he began a study that confirmed smoking as a cause of lung cancer, a feat that was more challenging than it sounds because 90% of the adult male population smoked, making it hard to find suitable control groups of non-smokers.

The latter work was to signal a profound change in how illness is perceived. Once the major killer germs had been beaten and people started to live longer, the focus of medicine naturally turned to the chronic diseases and specifically, the impact of lifestyle and environment. Dr Thomas McKeown, professor of social medicine at Birmingham University, was one of the first to articulate this shift in his influential book of the 1970s, *The Role of Medicine*. This charted how the chronic problem of malnutrition had been solved; how serious threats associated with water and food had been removed from the environment; and how, for the first time, human populations were planning children in keeping with their resources.

> In assessing the contribution of medical measures based on an understanding of the structure and function of the body, it is clearly essential to consider the extent to which the advance in health was due, not to intervention in the working of the machine, but to improvement in the conditions under which it operates.[1]

McKeown's ideas were well received by politicians who, stunned by the rising drugs bill, were keen to push what has since been called the social theory of medicine. This makes a lot of intuitive sense, claiming, in essence, that how we live, what we eat and our cultural environment are the major contributory causes of the chronic diseases of affluence, like heart disease, obesity, ulcers and depression.

Studies soon began linking all aspects of living with disease, and the dazzling post-war achievements of medical science gradually moved from centre stage. Pharma was swift to respond and the chronic diseases of affluence, the things that got studied the most for cultural clues as to their causation, also became the biggest blockbuster markets for drugs.

Making connections

Writing of the year 1980, Dr James le Fanu gives some perspective on this radical departure for medicine.

> Thirty years had elapsed since Sir Austin Bradford Hill had identified tobacco as the cause of lung cancer and now, in hardly any time at all, the other major pieces of the jigsaw had fallen into place. Sir Richard Doll in *The Causes of Cancer* revealed how the Western diet was just as important as tobacco in causing cancer. Professor Samuel Epstein had found that chemical pollutants in the air and water caused a further one in five of all cancers. Sir Douglas Black had rediscovered that poverty was still a major cause of illness in Britain, killing 75,000 people a year – or 200 a day. And it had been proved 'beyond reasonable doubt' that milk and dairy foods were killing thousands a year from heart attacks and an excess of salt was equally implicated in strokes.[2]

By the turn of the century, living had become a dangerous business with few people understanding the principles on which the large population studies that were churning out all these associations between living and disease were based. While no one doubted the overwhelming evidence linking tobacco and lung cancer, and the *Helicobacter* bacterium with peptic ulcers, many scientists despaired at the grounds for many other studies.

Science is much like religion in that it must be practised faithfully to generate knowledge that can be meaningful. But expediency often took the results beyond the boundaries of the simplest reason, finding associations that contradicted other studies. Bradford Hill had not only been meticulous about how trials must be set up to eliminate bias, he was equally strict about how the facts they are designed to elicit should be coherent. He set out a list of criteria, or articles of faith, to ensure facts hang together with everything else that is known to guard against false or meaningless conclusions.

But such orthodoxy gradually gave way and good science became increasingly indistinguishable from bad, particularly in areas that concerned large numbers of people, like food or sex.

> 'What should the public believe?' asked the editor of the *New England Journal of Medicine* in 1994. 'They substitute margarine for butter, only to learn that margarine may be worse for the arteries. They are told to eat oat bran to lower the cholesterol only to learn it is useless. They substitute saccharin for sugar only to hear that some research has found an association with bladder cancer, while others do not.'[3]

Dr James le Fanu insists the social theory is to blame by simultaneously managing to overemphasize the role of illness in people's lives while at the same time trivializing it. 'It generates the myth that the practice of medicine is futile,' he says, 'because the allegedly important factors in health are outside its control.'[4]

What the social theory does, in fact, is take medicine out of a purely professional context. Its value to the orthodox, such as le Fanu, is negligible in terms of stemming the tide of disease, except in the correlation it unearthed between smoking and lung cancer. To others, it has become such a general current of the times, it isn't obvious how medicine fits into the picture at all.

Whatever its merits, it has had a major impact on medicine and shows how skilful pharma is at adapting to the times.

The great cholesterol debate

The great cholesterol debate, which began in the 1930s when the modern epidemic of heart disease first started, explains the background to the popularity the statin class of drugs enjoys today. Le Fanu cites it as an example of the social theory of medicine in action, because the idea of high cholesterol being such a major killer stems from the ideas linking diet and disease in circulation at the time of their invention.

The story starts at the time of the Great Depression, when middle-aged people, men usually, began dying from heart attacks in large numbers. The king's physician Sir Maurice Cassidy noted in 1946 that deaths had risen tenfold in as many years and no one knew why. Moreover, after autopsies were conducted on young American soldiers killed in the Korean War in the 1950s, it was discovered that three-quarters of them – their average age was only 22 – had such pronounced coronary disease it seemed likely that had they survived the war they would certainly have died of a heart attack before they were 50.[5] Against this background, Ancel Keys, then director of the laboratory of physiological hygiene at the University of Minnesota, began his groundbreaking work linking high levels of saturated fat with high cholesterol levels in the blood, furring up the arteries and making people more susceptible to a heart attack. Travelling round the globe he amassed impressive evidence that seemed to suggest the epidemic was a nutritional disorder.

Interestingly, the American Medical Association refused to endorse this theory when it was first presented in 1957 because it couldn't explain the 20-fold rise in cases in the 1940s and 1950s. Besides, it was common knowledge, says le Fanu, that bodily functions are protected by the body's vast network of feedback mechanisms that work to keep things in a state of balance. If people eat less fat, in other words, the body compensates by getting the liver to produce higher levels of cholesterol for its indispensable roles as an integral part of the walls lining our cells and as a precursor of important hormones such as testosterone in males and oestrogen in females.

Keys was not the only scientist who had staked his career on this theory. Within a couple of years he and a lifelong friend, Jeremiah Stamler of Chicago University, had joined the relevant AMA committee and the official verdict was subsequently changed. People were now being advised to change their diet and by the early 1970s, the largest and most expensive scientific experiment ever conceived was launched. It involved more than 60,000 men and cost more than £100 million ($180 million).

By 1982, the results of the Multiple Risk Factor Intervention Trial (MRFIT), which had gone to extraordinary lengths to exhort people to stop smoking and eat less fat, showed this made absolutely no difference. For every 1,000 people who were cajoled to stop eating cakes and pies,

41 people died. For every 1,000 in the control arm, 40 died. A similar World Health Organization (WHO) study finished at roughly the same time with the same striking results.

At around this time, and as mysteriously as the alarming rise in heart disease, the trend started going into steep decline, suggesting the original culprit may well have been some kind of infectious agent. Rather than go with this biological explanation, the role of cholesterol in causing heart disease gained momentum, says le Fanu, with both the drug companies and the dietary protagonists having a mutual interest in salvaging Key's thesis.[6]

In 1984 the first drug to do just that was launched, claiming to reduce the risk of a heart attack by a quarter. This sounds impressive but statistics can be deceptive. The drug, Bristol-Myers Squibb's cholestyramine, had to be sprinkled onto food making it taste ghastly, and two-thirds of those taking it reported side effects of constipation, gas, heartburn and bloating. After seven years of this ordeal, 30 of the 1,900 people taking the drug had suffered a fatal heart attack compared to 38 in the control group. This does correlate with a 25% drop in risk because the difference, eight, is roughly 25% of 38. But it took seven years and an awful lot of effort and expense to 'save' eight lives. Meanwhile, the total number of deaths remained the same in both those taking the drug and the control group. The cost of the drugs back then was £9 million ($16.5 million), which works out at more than a million pounds for each life saved, if indeed it was saved, by the drugs.

This study and others prompted the development of a new class of hypolipaemics, or statins as they are now known. 'Their introduction contributed to a fourfold increase in the world hypolipaemic market from 1986 to 1991, with Merck reporting 1992 sales of $1.3 billion for lovastatin and $650 million for simvastatin,' pharmaceutical journalist Susan Hughes wrote in *Scrip Magazine* in 1993.[7]

Back then, doubts could be heard about the value of bringing cholesterol down too far in people whose hearts were healthy. The *British Medical Journal*, for example, published a meta-analysis (looking at the results of several studies) of the effects of cholesterol-lowering drugs in 1992. It showed that, although coronary heart disease was significantly reduced, total mortality actually increased slightly in the treated groups.[8] There were more deaths, in other words.

Professor Michael Oliver of the Wynn Institute in London also urged caution at the time, telling Hughes:

It is possible that in some sensitive individuals a reduction in cholesterol could be harmful to cell function. Cholesterol is an integral part of the cell membrane, and while in the normal situation cells may be able to adjust to a reduction in blood cholesterol, this may not be the case in all situations. For example, if cells are already compromised by pre-cancerous changes, immune dysfunction or infection, they may not be able to adjust so easily.[9]

The germ factor

Things are constantly astir in the infrastructure of medicine, guiding doctors as to which bodily signs or biomarkers to look out for in the quest to combat disease. The role of infection, however, is an area scientists have argued for years does not get the recognition it deserves because there isn't the money behind it. Some of the reasons for this were seen in our discussion of the length of time it took to get *Helicobacter* recognized as a major cause of ulcers.

Other reasons stem from fairly entrenched ideas about illness (or anything bad for that matter) attacking us from the outside, and the militaristic response it seems to invoke. The great wars on cancer, drugs, poverty and, more recently, terror, confirm this view. But biologist Paul W. Ewald, proponent of what he has termed the germ theory of medicine, believes a new way of thinking is required.

> We need to remember that our expectations are biased by minds that tend to visualize threats as invaders coming from beyond our border. Perhaps the experts are looking in the wrong place. Perhaps the most menacing infectious adversaries are already here.[10]

Ewald reminds us how our bodies are home to millions, if not trillions, of life's tiniest forms, most of which we cohabit with happily and harmoniously. But some manage to foil our immune systems to perpetuate their survival at our expense. He describes, as an example, how the human papillomaviruses operate. Having entered a woman's cervical cells via sex, they can take control, ordering the invaded cell to start responding to instructions from the new boss, instructions that ultimately lead to cervical cancer.

This doesn't happen in all cases, however. In some women who are infected, the virus is unable to get a sufficiently strong foothold to move into the deadly phase of its mission. 'The goal of the papillomavirus is not to create cancer, but to alter allegiances,' says Ewald. 'In the precancerous state, the virus causes the cells to divide at a level that is too high for the good of the body; but that cellular reproduction is good for the virus because it can replicate along with the cells, with little exposure to immune surveillance. The cells are now working for the virus rather than the body, generating a subcommunity with allegiances that conflict with the interests of the larger community [of the body]. The papillomaviruses are difficult to root out because these cells, being the body's own cells, provide the cover of an upstanding citizen.'[11]

That cervical cancer is a sexually transmitted disease (STD) has been known for decades in the medical community, but the virus responsible is not tested for at STD clinics because infection does not always lead to cancer. The public only became generally aware that cervical cancer is caused by an infection when vaccines against the disease became available earlier this decade.

Ewald is convinced the money spent investigating germs is well spent. Compared to the investment in studies seeking genetic causes of disease,

> the most significant returns were generated on the investment in studies of infectious disease. Polio, measles, hepatitis, liver cancer, ulcers, and cervical cancer were all controlled or shown to be controllable during the last half of the twentieth century through the control of infectious agents.[12]

It is easier for non-experts to track the thinking in medicine than to comment on it. As was seen with ulcers, infectious causation was recognized only after a compelling body of evidence had been amassed. Ewald believes the time is fast approaching when there will be compelling evidence for the infectious element to be recognized in many other conditions, including heart disease, Alzheimer's, arthritis, and several cancers besides those of the liver and cervix where causation is already established.

The genetic factor

Brief mention must also be made of the genome, a faster route to kudos in the research community than either germs or human behaviour. And working at such a fundamental level, it is throwing up all sorts of fascinating insights. But for all the research money it attracts, the only thing really being confirmed is just how far the image of DNA as the 'master molecule' is from reality. The universe it opens up is so vast, so new and so inordinately complex it has scientists in awe, knowing they have their work cut out for decades. Even work on the relatively easy areas such as cures for single-gene defects such as Huntington's disease, is proving harder than expected. Genetic breakthroughs in the chronic conditions that could make pharma some real money are even further away and will probably never materialize because the science, in various ways, is leading (if still a long way off) towards drugs that can be tailor-made to requirements.

Researchers involved in tracking the paths of disease and wellness may even relate to Isaac Newton's famous observation when he said, 'I do not know what I may appear to the world, but to myself I seem to have been only a boy playing on the seashore, diverting myself now and then, finding a smoother pebble than ordinary, whilst the great ocean of truth lay all undiscovered before me.'[13]

Even if scientists are not producing drugs that do new things, fundamental changes are happening. Biobanks have sprung up over the past few years in both the public and private sector, for example, to apply the tools that have been created to biological material to find the minute variations in an individual's genetic constitution that lead to disease. What everyone is trying to do, says Stefan Fritsch in *Scrip Magazine*, is identify biomarkers that can predict the onset, prognosis or progression of an illness.[14]

Fritsch also puts such work into some context. 'Although drugs tailored to a particular person's genetic make-up are not yet around the corner, as recent hype has suggested, our knowledge of the underlying causes of disease has increased enormously and continues to grow, thanks to the foundations that have been laid in this worldwide undertaking over the past two decades.'[15]

Biobanks are necessarily large and, as such, draw the public into the infrastructure of medicine in a way that has not been possible before. The UK's Biobank project, for example, was in the process of recruiting its target population of half a million volunteers aged between 45 and 69 at the time of writing. With £57 million ($105 million) in initial funding from the Wellcome Trust, the Medical Research Council, the Department of Health and the Scottish Executive, this public initiative aims to build a major genetic epidemiological resource to meet the needs of medical research for years to come.

In the US, the biobanks tend to be more specific, if only to gender. The Women's Health Initiative, the large-scale studies of which led to changes in the guidelines on hormone replacement therapy, for example, has a population of 170,000 post-menopausal volunteers. Private companies can also make a living analysing large-scale population data, usually in specific disease areas. Their aim is just as Fritsch describes, but is specifically directed as a service to pharma companies to help them be more efficient in their search for new therapies or, more usually, for new enhancements of what is already on the market.

Not everyone's gaze is directed at the next blockbuster, however. Umbrella organizations, such as the international not-for-profit Public Population Project in Genomics (P^{3}G), aim to combine the data from all the various biobanks around the world; its stated goals are to understand the interaction between genes, the environment, lifestyle and disease, and to create an engine for the transfer of this knowledge to healthcare systems.[16]

If people are dubious about this sort of knowledge, it is often because they know they have no control over where it goes and how it is used. But issues to do with consent – tight enough to protect individual rights and loose enough to keep samples usable for years – are being worked through and the work does at least promise genuinely new insight into how disease is formed; even what wellness looks like.

If anything, the bigger picture should put greater pressure on pharma companies to change their blockbuster approach because it just doesn't work at this level of detail. If medicine's infrastructure is seen as all the activity going on beneath the surface of that ocean of truth Newton described, then pharma will find it a lot harder to create the waves of conviction that led to so many blockbuster drugs over the past couple of decades. This is to do with the fact that the waters themselves have changed with the new knowledge. They are becoming clearer.

The human factor

If people are disillusioned with conventional medicine, either because it doesn't work for them or because they don't like the ideas behind it, there is very little they can do other than move over silently to the complementary schools of thought that are generally to be found in the shallower and calmer waters. Worldwide, an estimated $60 billion a year is now spent on a vast range of largely unregulated treatments, and levels are rising.[17] In many countries, it is the fastest growing healthcare sector. Spending doubled in the US in just a decade and it is said Americans would prefer to turn first to an alternative therapist rather than a family doctor.[18] In the UK, three out of four people told a *Times* Body & Soul newspaper survey that they would like such treatments made available on the NHS.[19]

For years, complementary and alternative medicine (CAM) has been treated a bit like women's football or vegetarian sausages: fine, but hardly the real thing. But work exploring the new science, which seriously is the real thing, is making people think again. According to a recent *New Scientist* editorial:

> The more scientists study CAM, the more surprises and challenges it throws up. It is forcing researchers to rethink some cherished ideas about medicine, from what makes an ideal drug and the design of clinical trials to the underlying causes of disease.[20]

CAM embraces many different practices but they all tend to share the same broad holistic perspective. In essence, this says that a healthy body is a system in harmony with itself and with its surroundings. Moreover, diseases can be created by a fault that is distributed over the whole body rather than in one specific part.

The secrets contained in our genome endorse the holistic view in a theoretical and empirical sense, if not yet a practical one. Michael Hyland, professor of health psychology at Plymouth University, points out that complexity theory shows that the properties of some complex systems – networks, in particular – cannot be attributed to individual components but emerge from the whole system. 'So why shouldn't disease emerge from the body in a similar way?' he asks. 'If so, conventional medicine will never be enough to cure all our ills. And the assumptions of CAM may not be as unscientific as they seem.'[21]

That our bodies are composed of vast series of networks is supported by empirical fact. Networks are systems that do lots of things simultaneously, and the brain is only the most obvious example. Its ability to think, compose sentences, recall memories, absorb knowledge, make sense of it, and so on, all at the same time, is both remarkable and unremarkable at the same time. The hormone system has equally impressive functionality. Vivienne Parry's book *The Truth About Hormones* describes them as agents that control our growth, our metabolism, weight, water-balance, body clock, fertility, muscle bulk, mood, speed of ageing, whether we want sex or not (and whether we enjoy it) and even who we fall in love with. All these fabulously complex systems or networks, are governed by communication systems scientists have only recently begun to explore.

Many modern syndromes, such as chronic fatigue or irritable bowels, would seem to support a network approach to disease because they can produce a whole range of symptoms that are either not detected by existing methods or not recognized. 'Pathologies like this are errors in the relationship between parts throughout the system, rather than an error in any one part,' says Hyland, distinguishing them from illnesses like flu that generate consistent symptoms which can be measured to form the basis of a conventional diagnosis.[22]

The errors that give rise to network pathologies, he suggests, stem from the body self-organizing in response to some disturbance. The next bit is harder to follow. Hyland's hypothesis is that the entire extended network of the body has evolved the capacity to learn and to become more complex, forming an 'intelligent body'. When confronted with some disturbance, it can become confused, ending up worse at self-regulation than before.[23]

Network pathologies, says Hyland, suggest 'a failure of self-regulation, in which some parameter of a control system has been set wrong.'[24] Asthma, in which the airways become inflamed because the immune system is overactive, is a classic example of a disease that might have a network cause. Indeed, all the so-called autoimmune diseases, such as arthritis, which are caused because the immune system has broken down in some way, might fall into this category.

This, of course, is what holistic practitioners have been saying for years, seeing as they do patients who have been unable to find drugs that work. Quoting Hyland again:

> Inhaled steroids suppress the inflammation caused by asthma, but if you stop the steroids the inflammation returns. On the other hand, treatment by a complementary practitioner can – for whatever reason – create much longer-term changes; it tends to cure rather than simply suppress, suggesting that such treatments work at a network level. They don't 'make' a cure. Instead they disturb the system, giving it a new opportunity to settle down in a new position. Where it settles down depends on other contextual factors inputting to the network.[25]

If patients trust their practitioner they are also more likely to follow advice to do basic things like eat well, take regular exercise and sleep. These positive contextual factors all contribute to the good results seen by the more successful complementary therapists.

A patient-led revolution

As people walk away from what is on offer in the surgery in large numbers, questions arise about the basis on which healthcare systems are founded. And the sticking point is the problem of proving what works and what doesn't regardless of people's culture, their genetic constitution, how they choose to live, how much they want to get better, their trust in their doctor, or any of a million other variables anyone brings to the equation. If medicines are to be paid for out of a collective purse, the not unreasonable line of thinking goes, a collective benefit must be shown.

In no other area in which science has transformed our lives, is its authority subject to such variance in how it is applied in daily life. Information technology, for example, requires people to adapt to the protocols of the computer if they want the benefits, which are pretty standard. But they don't have to believe in either the Dell dealer or the underlying technology for it to work. With medicine, people do have to buy in at some level to the promise of what it purports to do, and the effects are far from standard. A couple of glasses of wine, as we well know, can send some of us under the table and have virtually no effect on others. The time of day one drinks or the amount of food in one's body also makes a difference.

This human factor that makes medicine unique is also the very reason why, to the orthodox mind, it is critical that it be eliminated in the testing of medicines. This is how medical science derives its authority. The self-interest of the patient in getting well is removed along with that of the study sponsors in obtaining the result they want. The idea is to prove what works and what doesn't, regardless of any influence the patient, doctor or drug company might bring to bear on the course of the trial.

Such a method not only suits drugs, it creates them, elbowing out anything that cannot pass the industry gold standard, the randomized controlled trial. It sets the parameters for the discourse of post-war medicine, above what doctors observe in their clinics and certainly above how patients themselves perceive the effects of drugs. Scientists, doctors, regulators, the people who pay for medicine, and those who take them, want measurable facts on which to base their decisions. The randomized controlled trial is without doubt the best way of providing such facts.

The trouble is it is seriously limited in the facts it can provide because it can only test one thing at a time. Moreover, the sheer million-dollar cost of large-scale trials means they usually respond to questions pharma wants answering, which are not necessarily the same as those of the public. This state of affairs, which has always been a source of deep frustration to those on the fringes of medicine, reached fever pitch when the EU Food Supplements Directive was threatening to sweep supplements off the shelves.

The idea was to bring safe maximum limits into line across nation states but, as Rose Shepherd suggested in a passionate piece she wrote for the *Observer Magazine*, the move hijacked food supplements, forcing them to be seen as medicines. The harm this was supposed to do was not nearly as well articulated as the sheer indignation that anyone could even think of messing with the one thing people feel they have some control over in maintaining their health, their diet and the vitamins they take to supplement it.

> In the 21st century we live under siege. There are concerns about pesticides, herbicides, antibiotics, genetically-modified food, mobile phones, microwaves, amalgam fillings, falling sperm counts, mad cows, MMR – even milk. Farmed salmon is a Trojan Horse for carcinogens. Obesity and diabetes are on the march. There is a mass of documentation on all this. So what is the European Commission's big idea? 'Let's clamp down on vitamins and minerals.' It would be funny if it weren't so tragic. While the EU has been busy drafting legislation, we seem to have been sleepwalking into a situation where chemists and health stores will be purged of hundreds of nutritional supplements.[26]

Protection or control?

Nutrition is an interesting area of medicine because it has seemingly bounded its way into the surgery via the back door. It is hardly fringe, but nor is it entirely conventional, having worked its way up the ranks of medical orthodoxy on the strength of growing evidence and a number of high-ranking champions who spread its word in the normal course of their work. In the UK, such enthusiasts include Professor André Tylee, chairman of the National Institute for Mental Health, who is responsible for educating GPs in the treatment of mental health.

He has no shortage of evidence about the value of a good diet. Malcom Peet, an NHS psychiatric consultant, for example, recently led separate studies with schizophrenics and depressives who were failing to respond to drugs. 'Both studies concluded that the fish oil EPA, is effective,' wrote Lucy Mayhew in the *Guardian*. 'In 2005, Dr Basant Puri, a consultant psychiatrist at Imperial College School of Medicine, published an entire book dedicated to explaining why EPA is so good at treating depression.'[27] Meanwhile, Dr Alex Richardson, a senior research fellow at Oxford University and also director of the charity, Food and Behaviour Research, has published work showing remarkable turnarounds in concentration, attention and disruptive behaviour after combining EPA with omega-6 to treat dyslexics and ADD sufferers. While pointing to the rising prevalence of childhood behavioural problems, where drug treatments are not working, Richardson is also keen to stress that nutrition cannot work in isolation. 'You can't carry a single nutritional supplement around as a talisman for superhealth,' he says, 'because usually specific vitamins, minerals or enzymes are necessary to ensure the key nutrient is absorbed.'[28]

Because these areas are so complex, ordinary people would benefit if their doctors were able not only to help them interpret the facts as they are known, but also to consider using some of the evidence of using food in preference to drugs. While 40% of patients who walk into doctors' surgeries are said to be suffering from a mental health problem, two-thirds of GPs have had no specific nutritional mental health training and therefore do not routinely consider what their patients are eating. Tylee is so passionate about the benefits of nutritional therapy in mental health he wants it to become the first line of treatment doctors use when dealing with mental illness.

His reasons become more compelling when one visits any Internet chat room on a mainstream behavioural problem such as ADD or depression. There, one can see from the correspondence the horrendous and circular dosing schedules of mind-altering drugs that many young people are ensnared in. And worse, as you enter the private world of that particular behavioural condition, you pick up a conviction that this is normal, that you are trespassing on the private ground of some exclusive club where members juggle the consumption of two, three, sometimes four, different drugs a day. They discuss doses, they share experiences of taking one product to control anxiety and another to improve attention, they report consultations with doctors who have dared to suggest they take a more methodical approach to working out what works best with what at what doses and at what times of the day.

Against this background, James MacLean's escape from the world of pharmacology is refreshing. It came through paying more attention to his diet. Having developed manic depression in his second year at university, he was put on antipsychotic and antidepressive medication that singularly didn't work. He put on five stone in weight, which made him more depressed, and eventually he left university without getting a degree, compounding his problems further. When he started to believe the radio was talking to him, he sought further help. 'Within the space of ten days I was sectioned, then released, then detained again three times,' he told Lucy Mayhew, writing for the *Guardian*.[29]

His sister-in-law suggested a nutritionist after his latest release from mental hospital. After an Internet search yielded a quack who wanted $10,000 for the first consultation, eventually an establishment they could trust was found and they followed instructions. Tests directed James to a new diet that included a comprehensive range of supplements, including high doses of niacin and essential fats. 'The difference was startling,' he said. 'I feel sharper than before and I'm now super-motivated. I have lost three stone in the last two months and I feel whole again.'[30] He has also reapplied to read sports science at university and has dreams to play rugby professionally.

Even if James relapses, and his talk of being supermotivated turns out to be just the manic phase of a cycle he has not yet beaten, he has other tools to help him in what could be, and often is, a life-long battle against depression. His experience, nevertheless, shows drugs are not the only answer.

When food works better than medicine

Depression is by no means the only area where medicine is being challenged by food. So it was not entirely surprising to find nutritionists, and their legions of followers, taking such exception when the EU decided it wanted to re-classify supplements as 'medicine', thereby insisting they abide by the rules surrounding medicine, which are much stricter than those surrounding food.

But stricter rules could actually help the public if they legitimized studies to sort out the value of food and its various constituent ingredients once and for all. But it is by no means certain this will happen. What they will do is tighten up a situation where health supplements are sold, in the UK at least, in open defiance of labelling laws which were enacted to control what can and cannot be said about health products.

If you go into any UK health store, you will notice many, if not most, products are labelled with no more than their name. People have no need of labels, in other words, because the alleged benefits have passed into conventional wisdom from a mixture of anecdotal evidence or from what people have read in magazines, where there are virtually no rules about what can be said about a health product.

At a time when medicine is capable of changing lines of kinship, switching hearts and designing babies, it seems extraordinary people can be so confused about something as basic as the food they eat. But that is the case, and it is precisely why rules are being introduced and why those rules are so hotly contested. Everyone wants certainty. Its just that the problems run a lot deeper, because food, being composed of multiple ingredients, doesn't lend itself well to the conventional methods of science. The randomized controlled trial, for example, works best testing one thing at a time. And although perfectly respectable studies can be, and are, designed to get over these problems, the most cursory look at research into the components of food shows how fiendishly difficult it is.

First, it is hard to be precise about what one is testing. Mark Peplow, writing in the excellent but now defunct UK newsletter, *Medicine Today*, explains that vitamin E, for example, comes in two different forms, tocopherol and tocotrienol, each of which has four sub-divisions named alpha, beta, gamma and delta. And even though alpha-tocopherol is the most important where nutrition is concerned, and is therefore the form that has been studied most extensively, this in itself comes in eight forms, called stereoisomers, which are all processed by the body in different ways.[31]

Second, since there is no obvious way to patent natural ingredients, quality trials are thin on the ground and arguments between experts commonplace, particularly over safety limits. In many countries these are limited to three times the recommended daily amounts (RDA), and are also fiercely disputed. Patrick Holford, founder of the UK's Institute of Optimum Nutrition (ION) and author of the bestselling *Optimum Nutrition Bible*, has dubbed them the 'bog standard' rather than the gold standard. He writes:

> I call them the Ridiculous Dietary Arbitraries. The RDA is not a scientifically robust score for a nutrient. It's the level that prevents over deficiency, and if you take the case of vitamin C, it started at 30mg, then went to 45mg, then 60mg, while in the US it's 85mg. Now, 30mg does prevent scurvy, but scientists on the panels who decide RDAs are gradually thinking that more might be better. We [the ION] work from what is arguably the most scientific position, which is to ask, 'What is the optimal intake of a nutrient?' What level of, say, vitamin C confers maximum protection against infections? And we know that is around 1,000mg.[32]

In the *Daily Mail*, meanwhile, in a box accompanying a story by another expert, Catherine Collins, the chief dietician at St George's Hospital, London, the RDA for vitamin C was said to be 40mg with a maximum safe daily intake of 1,000mg. Large amounts, it said, can bring on stomach pains, diarrhoea and flatulence, which stop as soon as you stop taking the supplements.[33]

People are all the more confused if they know the work on vitamin C and cancer by Dr Linus Pauling, a Nobel Prize winner in chemistry in 1954 and for his contributions to peace in 1962, as well as a pioneer in what he called the orthomolecular approach to illness. His book *Cancer and Vitamin* C, co-authored by Dr Ewan Cameron and published in 1979, is an example of this as it cites case study after case study of people whose lives had been extended by years rather than months simply with vitamin C.

> It seems abundantly clear that ascorbic acid (vitamin C) is directly involved in many of the natural mechanisms that protect an individual against cancer. Therefore, as a matter of principle, no matter what form of established cancer treatment is employed, active steps should be taken to ensure that patient's ascorbate reserves are constantly kept high in order to allow his protective immune system to function always at maximum efficiency.[34]

As for the guidelines, Pauling says, 'the officially recommended dietary intake of about 45mg of vitamin C per day is so much less than the optimum as to constitute in itself a significant cause of cancer ... For most people a daily intake between 1,000 and 10,000mg may lead to the best of health.'[35]

Pauling's thinking not only seems to lend some credence of the germ theory of medicine because it suggests vitamin C works against cancer-forming disease agents. But it also shows how greater certainty about the benefits of health supplements would serve the public well. It is not only vitamin E or C that causes confusion; these are just two particular windows through which one can observe the general chaos.

Medical authority, not feeling it has to prove itself to anyone, has kept a respectable distance from anything that cannot obviously pass the gold standard; it hasn't got involved. Because vitamin C is old, obvious and natural, the precise opposites of everything needed for a patent, pharma doesn't get involved. Its value in fighting infections and as a protection against cancer is of no interest to anyone except the public. The NHS occasionally conducts studies in the public interest, such as the one in 2004 confirming the cost of the Alzheimer's drug, Aricept, to be too expensive. But vitamin C has no champion other than nutritionists and their followers, who argue among themselves and have neither the money nor the presence to get any real authority in a healthcare business so dominated by the large pharma firms.

When therapy works better than medicine

If conventional science does not lend itself well to studying food, such an obvious factor in our health, it is equally at odds with most complementary therapies and indeed, anything that has a human element, another fairly obvious factor in healing. According to Toby Murcott, author of *The Whole Story: Alternative Medicine on Trial*:

> Randomised controlled trials are poor at assessing long-term interventions. They are poor at evaluating treatments that rely on the therapist–patient relationship. They are unable to pick up rare events or easily evaluate treatments for rare conditions. It is very difficult to design them for complex interventions and for individualised treatments. These limitations are known and accepted by the clinical researchers who use them and the data that come from them.[36]

Nevertheless, they go some way to explaining the lack of choices patients are offered in the surgery. Drugs are as good as it gets for most of us most of the time, because the people who pay for medicines prefer, usually for entirely pragmatic reasons, to fund drug-based programmes for depression, for example, rather than anything else. It is not that that it has been shown that drugs provide better value for money than diet, cognitive behavioural therapy, or any other of the non-pharmaceutical options that are springing up. On the contrary. It is simply that the latter are notoriously hard to assess because patient input, and the quality of the relationship with the therapist, are so critical to the outcome.

CAM therapists must find other ways, therefore, of demonstrating the value of their skills, so reasonable citizens can be happy to pay for them. Once again, things are far from equal. We have seen the enormous power at the disposal of the large pharmaceutical companies to perpetuate a model of medicine that, from almost every angle, seems to have societies caught up in a cycle of diminishing returns.

Where CAM is concerned the inequalities have as much to do with how illness and treatment are perceived as how they are measured. Dr George Lewith, a British GP, acupuncturist and Westminster University professor, points out that complementary medicine is a patient-led revolution.

> Yet studies tend to ignore patients' perceptions of a treatment. The old randomised controlled trials take the patient out of the equation and are indicative of doctors controlling the whole process. We need to start from a position of equitableness between doctors and patients, and report with equal force the doctors' and patients' perception. I don't think you should be doing clinical trials in CAM without knowing why people are seeking CAM in the first place. Is there any point, for example, in testing whether homoeopathy reduces inflammation in arthritic conditions, if what really appeals to people about the treatment is pain relief without side effects?[37]

The results can be disputed even when conventional questions are asked. In one randomized controlled trial, designed to test whether acupuncture helped people with persistent neck pain, patient views were ignored to the point of rubbishing what CAM researchers considered to be a respectable result. Published in the *Annals of Internal Medicine* in December 2004, the study showed a 12% greater improvement in the group who received real acupuncture than the one that got dummy jabs. Everyone agreed the results were statistically significant (i.e., acupuncture works for persistent neck pain), but doctors said this wasn't clinically significant because it wasn't making enough difference to patients. CAM researchers disagreed, and the differences were impossible to resolve because each used their own yardsticks, highlighting the extent of the problems involved in trying to validate such treatments to create a more level playing field in medicine.

Lewith insists he is not an unthinking advocate for CAM. 'I am trying to be a good scientist,' he told Simon Crompton in *The Times*, who went on to say, 'but it riles him that many who claim to be good scientists are happy to overlook the fact that there are bronchodilators for asthma on the market that work only 8% better than a placebo. But when it comes to acupuncture, they will say that a 10–15% improvement over placebo isn't good enough.'[38]

Alternative treatments challenge the evidence required by medicine in other ways. CAM studies can show high levels (80–90%) of satisfaction even if there is no improvement in the condition. A UK survey of cancer patients, for example, found such high ratings due to patients feeling emotionally stronger, less anxious and more hopeful about the future – and this was even if the cancer remained unchanged.[39]

Such evidence is not acknowledged by the people who pay for medicines, perhaps rightly, since the bottom line has always been that a treatment must show an improvement in the condition, however marginal. But even if cancer patients are offered the best drugs science can offer and even if they are blessed with the right genotype to benefit from them, they don't hold out for ever.

Apart from antibiotics for acute infections, all drugs for serious illness fail eventually, however brilliant the scientific input. A friend of mine who had just six months, from diagnosis to death from cancer, to come to terms with what was happening to her and her family, would have welcomed any extra time drugs might buy. But what was most important to her and her family were precisely the values highlighted in the CAM study; values that are hardly surprising to healthcare professionals who deal with cancer every day but which are not reflected within current healthcare set-ups that, as Lewith says, write the patient's views almost entirely out of the equation.

Conventional medicine is, of course, simply the currently acceptable medicine, based as it is on a particular idea about experimental proof – involving a specific set of theories of knowledge. If those ideas are to be successfully challenged, leading to drugs becoming just one of several choices offered in the surgery, then new yardsticks must be found that go beyond the current narrow biomedical boundaries.

Murcott looks at how other disciplines, such as anthropology, may have the tools to examine some of the concepts that are implicit in CAM. Its theory of knowledge includes various definitions as to what counts as evidence and may be able to deal with ideas such as holism, the interaction between practitioner and client, and the importance of putting experience into some kind of cultural context to give it meaning. As such, it might represent a way of, if not reconciling the vast divide between heart and mind in contemporary healthcare, then at least providing a broader framework in which to discuss the issues involved.

The key issue is, of course, the placebo effect, a person's inherent ability to heal, which works irrespective of whether a patient is having needles stuck in them, taking the latest health supplement or swallowing the latest pain medication.

12

Patients take the lead

It is ironic that the areas of medicine where the placebo effect has been shown to be most powerful – pain and depression – are precisely the areas at the centre of the recent regulatory storms. And the irony shows succinctly how ultimately self-defeating healthcare systems can be if trust is allowed to slip away.

The placebo effect works on trust. Vioxx and the SSRIs present a picture of the medicines business that had the effect of destroying that trust. Even though family doctors were as ignorant as anyone else of the true safety profile of both classes of drug, they are damned by association in the same way dubious practices in the food chain can lead to a distrust of supermarkets. Pharma is a false friend to doctors when its marketing practices can be shown to adversely affect the quality of their relationships with patients.

But this line of causation is disputed. The UK government's response to the parliamentary health committee's report on the industry insists that marketing practices are not excessive. It points out that almost 78% of all UK prescribing is generic and that 'clinicians are responsible people who have undergone years of training and make critical decisions about the health of their patients each day.'[1]

Its only concession was to ask the industry to tighten up its codes of conduct. The Prescription Medicines Code of Practice Authority was established in 1993 as a forum for complaints from the public (in practice, it is usually doctors) about how companies behave. The ABPI acts as both judge and jury, so even though the government might ask industry to take on the MPs' suggestions – specifically, that there should be limits on the level of promotion to doctors – it is unlikely to send out any ringing signals that anything is wrong.

There is another reason why patients don't trust their doctors as their parents or grandparents did. This has to do with the fact that medicine's increasingly ambiguous role in society is part of a more general crisis within the scientific community. A report from the UK House of Lords Select Committee on Science and Technology, published in February 2000, concluded that society's relationship with science had entered a critical phase. Having been briefed to look at how science is reported in the press, the committee found interest in the subject to be high, but trust in what scientists actually said low. Nine in ten people said they were interested in new medical discoveries, for example, compared with 66% who were interested in sport. But confidence had been 'rocked' by certainties that turned out to be ill-advised – for example, that mad cow disease couldn't affect humans. In one survey the Lords considered in evidence, only 5 in every 100 people said they had confidence in government scientists. 'In modern democratic conditions,' they concluded, 'science like any other player in the public arena ignores public attitudes and values at its peril.'[2]

Public trust has been affected not only by government statements that were too optimistic about limitations to knowledge, but also by acrimonious disputes such as those surrounding MMR. The lack of any convincing body that can mediate between the opposing parties makes it impossible for the public to glean any sense of objectivity or fairness in resolving scientific conflicts. Trust isn't broken as such; it just finds other things to attach itself to.

The principle always to 'hear the other side', for example, is singularly lacking. 'Adjudication between conflicting claims demands that society has the right institutions in place to do so,' says *Lancet* editor, Richard Horton, as he calls for a National Agency for Science and Health (NASH) to be established so differing and unpopular views can always be heard, discussed and challenged and, perhaps more importantly, be seen to be heard, discussed and challenged. 'This should be society's overriding concern,' he continues. 'We are living through a civic crisis of rationality, one that nobody seems willing or able to address, but one that the dispute over the MMR vaccine all too readily underlines.'[3]

'The new agency would play a substantial part in strengthening our democracy, in reviving civic rationality, in creating the space to resolve conflicts over evidence about risks, in countering pervasive and unjustified social fears, in providing the necessary and just procedural arrangements for doing so, and in answering questions about the nature of rational debate.'[4]

But sweeping in a new top layer of decision makers is no guarantee they will be trusted any more than the current incumbents. Nor is it clear how the central problem – how to know how the public think and what risks they are prepared to accept – will be addressed. At least in medicine, there is a forum in the doctor–patient relationship for discussing individual risks. The debates on fluoride in the water supply, on the other hand, along with genetically modified food, animal experimentation, stem-cell research, global warming, and anything else that affects us collectively, are still largely conducted by people the general public has very little to do with.

Doctors and patients

The doctor–patient relationship may be grossly imperfect in healthcare systems that neglect the time required to develop it, but it is arguably the most underrated resource there is for creating robust public health and reducing levels of anxiety. And if the crisis in medicine is seen in terms of how pharma's commercial grip over healthcare affects the reputation of family doctors, it provides a clear route out – via the one side of the pharma–doctor–patient triangle that pharma has no place in.

And the momentum building up from the compliance-to-concordance initiative is just one of a veritable orchestra of signals suggesting now is a perfect time to start. The move to concordance entails doctors struggling to hear where the public are coming from. And that rests on a whole plethora of policies encouraging doctors to think about the technicalities of patient treatment (how long they should have to wait to be seen, where they want to be treated, what they should have done, and so on).

Doctors are on our side. They may have all sorts of other agendas going on but they need patients to justify their existence, just like patients need doctors when they are genuinely ill. Both, for different reasons, benefit from the drugs provided by pharma. But not in the same way as doctors and patients need each other.

This is one reason why doctors in the US are trying to demonstrate how their relationship with patients can be crucial to recovery. At the time of writing, various publicly funded trials were running their course to gather the ammunition for arguments that doctors should be able to spend more time with their patients. But even before the results come through, the setting up of the trials themselves shows the art of medicine to be a delicate business.

Ted Kaptchuk, who heads a placebo working group at Harvard Medical School, is leading one such trial involving a drug that treats an intractable, common stomach disorder. Half the patients are treated with the drug by a doctor who is positive about the medicine and who patiently listens to their account of how the symptoms manifest. The others are treated by a doctor who gives a fairly matter-of-fact presentation of the medicine before leaving the room. The idea is to demonstrate the worth not of drugs, but of doctors. 'We have these great, powerful, ever-more-effective medicines,' says Kaptchuk. 'But we believe that the loss of the art of medicine makes these medicines less effective than they can be.'[5]

But if the trials do deliver positive results, a paradox is presented. It tells us, on the one hand, that what people want, the clear and unadulterated truth, doesn't necessarily optimize clinical outcomes. On the other, we also know that patients need to feel they have been given all the relevant information by their doctors to make an informed choice. This paradox can only be resolved within the framework of the individual doctor–patient relationship, with people setting their own parameters about the degree of involvement they want in their healthcare.

It also illustrates how the medicines business is not remotely straightforward and why the business of health and the business of pharma must never be confused. In the business of health, patients must do whatever they can to create good relationships with doctors, just as the professionals must carry on trying to open up to patients by listening to their concerns about their condition and the treatments they are offered.

The business of pharma

The business of pharma, meanwhile, is a commercial enterprise that has been able to build up massive power bases that have a virtual stranglehold on how health is both seen and delivered. Pharma's products may be brilliant or they may be hopeless. The important thing if the business of health is not to be impaired is that the public can be confident they are getting the most appropriate form of treatment, and that their doctors are drawing on the full range of scientific ingenuity and knowledge that exists.

That confidence is not there at present. Proposals to restore it came from Dr Marcia Angell in her book, *The Truth About the Drug Companies*, before either Vioxx had been withdrawn or the news broke that the safety risks of the SSRIs had been withheld from the public. As a doctor and an academic, she compiled a list of changes she considered should be implemented to redress the balance of power away from commercial imperatives and in favour of public health.[6]

- New drugs should always be compared not just with placebos but with old drugs for the same conditions.
- Regulatory bodies need to be strengthened as independent agencies, so instead of facilitating drug development, they return to regulating it.
- Drug companies should no longer be permitted to control the clinical testing of their own drugs. To ensure clinical trials serve a genuine medical need and are properly designed, conducted and reported, Angell proposed that an Institute for Prescription Drug Trials be established to administer the clinical trials of prescription drugs.
- The laws should be tightened so the period of exclusivity in which monopoly prices can be charged is shortened and made less flexible.
- Drug companies should be excluded from offering medical education.
- Direct-to-consumer advertising of prescription drugs should be banned.
- Pharma's books should be open to the public because of the preferential tax breaks research attracts and the importance of its products to public health.
- Drug pricing should not only be transparent but reasonable and as uniform as possible for all purchasers.

She is the first to admit it is little more than a wish list. And despite moves being swiftly taken in the wake of the Vioxx withdrawal – on both sides of the Atlantic – to restore public faith in medicines, none of Angell's specific proposals have seen the light of day. Those that have got close, such as industry's proposals for full disclosure of all clinical trial results, came about not as a concession to public fears, as one might like to believe, but after the industry was forced to go in that direction.

The idea of a public register of clinical trial results came about in the UK, for example, only after GlaxoSmithKline had agreed to set up a public register of its own trials. This was part of a legal settlement in August 2004, in which the New York attorney general alleged that negative trial results about the suicide risks of Paxil/Seroxat in children had been concealed. It is not yet clear how such a register will be overseen.

Other moves to shore up public confidence included promises to eliminate conflicts of interest, more impartial information about the risks of drugs, and better communication generally with the public. It remains to be seen how regulatory agencies are to communicate effectively with the public when there is no trust, and when all opportunities to grapple with the issues that work against trust were patently neglected in the government's response to its parliamentary inquiry. One was a recommendation that responsibility for representing pharma's interests be moved from the Department of Health to the Department of Trade and Industry. This, the MPs said, would end the farcical situation where the same ministers must act as both the major purchaser of the industry and its primary sponsor.

'The relationship between patients, Government, the NHS, industry and other stakeholders is an intricate one,' the government said in response. 'Having one department lead helps to balance these interests, while separation could bring an unhelpful tension between health priorities, and economic drivers.'[7]

Some might argue that tension is precisely what is needed between health priorities and economic drivers, and that the only route to restoring trust in medicine lies within those very conflicts. That only by battling them out more thoroughly than has been possible in these pages, in other words, can people see for themselves that an overwhelming dependence on the pharma industry cannot be in any reasonable person's best long-term health or financial interests.

Any hope for real change vanished when the second opportunity was also lost. This was a call for an independent review of the UK's regulatory body, the Medicines and Healthcare Products Regulatory Agency (MHRA). What the MPs wanted to know was whether this key body in the medicines business uses processes for decision making that reflect patients' health needs and society's expectations. To that end, it specifically asked that the review seek ways to make the regulator more independent of both government and industry.

This could have been a spectacular and rare chance to consider a new kind of regulatory framework that could at least consider the suggestions Angell proposed to get the US public a better deal from the pharma industry. In the UK, the voices calling for change came from the highest authority in the land after the Queen, Parliament, but the response from the government in charge could hardly have been more complacent.

Parliament consists of our elected representatives. The recommendations of its health committee speak on behalf of the public. It is the government, supported by the civil service, that is resisting change. In the official response, the Secretary of State for Health suggested that while some tweaking may be necessary, things are largely fine. 'The current practices that govern how the Government relates to the pharmaceutical industry, and the commitments given in response to the Committee's recommendations can reassure patients that this Government is working to provide the innovative and safe medicines that they have the right to expect.'[8]

The MPs who were so critical of the MHRA were also keen to point out that the UK industry is in many ways outstanding. 'It conducts much excellent research, produces products which make a vital contribution to the health of the nation and is of great economic importance.'[9] Nevertheless, their concerns were more about 'the volume, extent and intensity of the industry's influence'. These, they said, impacted not only on clinical medicine and research but also on patients, regulators, the media, civil servants and politicians. 'In some circumstances, one particular item of influence may be of relatively little importance. Only when it is viewed as part of a larger package of influences is the true effect of the companies' activity recognised and the potential for distortion seen.'[10]

Enter the healthcare consumer

One of the core problems seems to be that the regulation of the industry was established at a time when the public trusted medical authority and indeed, was deferential to it. Generally, people did what their doctors said. Moreover, as was seen in the opening chapters, the drugs developed in the golden post-war era not only did new things but were relatively cheap. A situation where medicines could do more harm than good was not even entertained, nor was it thought necessary to create channels for the public to get involved in how they are developed and regulated. They weren't thought to be interested, and there was always the problem of the science. Besides, there was greater trust in family doctors to make decisions on their behalf.

Such attitudes seem to belong to another lifetime. Now, everyone wants the public involved because it is in no one's interests for medicines, arguably one of society's most important endeavours, not to have the trust of the people they are designed to help. Regulatory bodies around the world have started inviting members of the public on to their committees to represent the public and are providing them with training to deal with the issues involved.

Nevertheless, this route will always be limited by the fact that the forums for discussion are so entrenched in established thinking. Any fresh ideas are more likely to come from another, entirely different, route towards change. This is one being promoted by the UK government, the pharma industry and the medical profession – all for their own separate reasons.

It is the idea of the autonomous patient, the person who thinks for him or herself. The pharma industry endorses this idea because it believes such people are less likely to listen to the tempering influence of the doctor, thereby enabling pharma to sell more drugs. Governments, meanwhile, believe patient autonomy means people will take greater responsibility for their health thereby using fewer drugs. And doctors are being encouraged to change the habits of a lifetime and start listening more closely to what patients say under the compliance-to-concordance initiative.

The dynamics between pharma, government and the medical establishment have traditionally kept patients passive and compliant. Now, they are all in favour of people playing a greater role in maintaining their health. If this sounds like a victory for the patient, it is not yet clear how they will emerge from all this attention, because it is new territory and very much a symptom of a health-obsessed consumer society.

Health has not always been the commodity to be bought and sold that it is today. Pulitzer Prize winner, Professor René Dubos, for example, saw it as a measure of the totality of one's life, not something to be attained by eradicating unpleasant symptoms or early warning systems that suggest something may be awry at a deeper level. 'While it may be comforting to imagine a life free of stresses and strains in a carefree world, this will remain an ideal dream,' he said in his book, *Mirage of Health*. 'Man has elected to fight, not necessarily for himself but for a process of emotional, intellectual and ethical growth that goes on forever. To grow in the midst of dangers is the fate of the human race, because it is the law of the spirit.'

Such ideas resound in the contemporary interest in complementary medicine as people try to make sense of what their bodies are telling them. But they don't sell drugs. They are rarely to be found in the mainstream. Serious commercial players don't say the symptoms they promise to eliminate have a function or will go away naturally. That would be like a car manufacturer promoting the idea of walking or taking the bus.

Over the past couple of decades, pharma has been the major beneficiary of social change towards consumerism in healthcare. It is no coincidence that the rising pharmaceutical spend on the big broad-spectrum conditions has been in parallel with an obsession about health. And, of course, it has been helped enormously by the revolutionary new dimension to health made possible by the Internet. The quest for good health could suddenly find expression in infinitely more ways as the commercialization of the prize you can be sure everyone wants, longevity and health, gathered momentum.

The consumer is king

Scenarios where the consumer is king are painted in endless different formats, reflecting the extent to which pharma companies are pushing for a more direct relationship with the public. They may have the regulators on their back, the science against them, patents expiring, the investment community turning their backs, everyone screaming for lower prices. The one and only thing they do have going for them is the *zeitgeist*. It doesn't exactly swim against the cultural tide to convince people it is more of a crime to suffer in silence from a condition than to take something that can sort it instantly.

But people don't necessarily suffer in silence. They make their own sense of what is happening to them; they may even do great things because of what is happening to them. Nevertheless, these efforts, often made without a doctor they trust at their side, pale against the effects of a consumer society that will always promote the easy, most convenient, route because that is how people make money. More importantly, convenience in health is driven in the same way it is in food and for the same reasons: to fit in with busy lives. One difference with health, however, is that as people age and their bodies naturally deteriorate, it is not only for convenience that medicines are sought.

Youth, as George Bernard Shaw once wisely said, is wasted on the young. And if it can be rekindled, in any shape or form, it is welcomed. 'We have botulinum toxin for the treatment of wrinkles; minoxidil for male pattern baldness; tooth whitening treatments; hormone replacement therapy,' says Shah Ebrahim, professor of epidemiology of ageing at Bristol University. 'Hollywood and the media may promote positive images of older people, but it would be surprising if society's stereotypes of beauty were to be reoriented towards images of old age. So demands for medical fixes for ageing are likely to grow.'[11]

But while the boundaries between clinical and social medicine converge, Ebrahim goes on to point out that 'medicalisation of the two commonest social scourges of old age – poverty and loneliness – has not occurred.'[12] These limits to medicine provide another reflection of the human factor that is so ruthlessly dismissed throughout its development.

Medicines are not created for people who cannot afford them, nor are they designed to promote good relationships with other human beings. If anything, it is the contrary: to obviate the need for good supportive relationships or to compensate for loneliness.

Nevertheless, a society that promotes impossible lifestyles, based around fabulously beautiful and wealthy A-list celebrities, is bound to need help because the truth is it's hard work keeping up. The things that help – smoking, drinking, overeating, doing recreational drugs, watching TV – don't make us healthy. Coupled with pharma's real need for blockbuster revenues, the inevitable result is what we see: a pattern of demand for drugs that seems to know no limit.

When more lanes are built to relieve traffic congestion, and more jams result, the explanation in traffic control circles is that people have this huge pent-up desire to use their cars as much as possible. More roads simply mean they drive more. Similarly, when more money is available for drugs, demand soon grows to stretch the budgets to new limits.

In many ways, the escalation in drug taking is out of anyone's control. 'The narcissistic character of the contemporary cult of health reflects the anxieties of an increasingly atomised society,' argues Dr Michael Fitzpatrick, a London GP, in his book *The Tyranny of Health: Doctors and the Regulation of Lifestyle*. And an obsession with illness is the perfect means to raise the profile of medicine. By selling the illness, you naturally push up sales of the treatment, sometimes very significantly, especially when the consumer can be persuaded to ask for it by name, as happens in the US. Moreover, with patients, doctors and pharma locked in a mutually dependent and ultra-morbid ménage à trois, there seems to be little prospect of escape, except via a solid doctor–patient relationship.

The medicalization of society

It may not exist, this utopian bond of trust in which both doctor and patient find in the other a sense of humanity that enriches them equally. But the lavish attentions of the pharma industry don't help. At the very least, this bond has to be strong enough to withstand pharma's influence over both parties. And it doesn't help that both have interests that genuinely overlap with pharma's. 'Patients and their professional advocacy groups can gain moral and financial benefit from having their condition defined as a disease,' points out Dr Richard Smith, editing a special edition of the *BMJ* devoted to the medicalization of society. 'Doctors, particularly some specialists, may welcome the boost to status, influence and income that comes when new territory is defined as medical. Global pharmaceutical companies have a clear interest in medicalizing life's problems, and there is now a pill for every ill.'[13]

From pharma's perspective, doctors are helpful but not strictly necessary, as they were in the past. In the early days of e-health, for example, the hype was almost deafening about how the healthcare consumer would shift power in the surgery overnight to put the patient, rather than the doctor, in control. 'The forces of consumerism, information management, technology and science, facilitated by the e-environment, all focus on one thing, the individual,' consultant Patricia Pesanello told a pharma conference in 2000.

> We suggest that these forces also point to a new healthcare vision, one that focuses on individualised health management, which in an e-environment is informed, interactive, immediate, and integrated. Put another way, healthcare will be delivered in an automated context, making full use of electronic medical records, personalised treatment protocols, and ultimately, personal medicines.[14]

It all sounded fantastic but, of course, couldn't get round the fact that most people appreciate a doctor and a bit of care and attention, especially when ill. As author Madeline Bunting observed, 'The central tenet of consumerism is choice; when you're ill, you don't have the strength to make complicated choices. You want a relationship of trust and mutual respect in which someone very experienced and knowledgeable helps to make you better.'[15]

Nevertheless, the idea of having a greater say in health decisions is compelling. The Internet has made this possible. By enabling medical knowledge to be distributed in a more egalitarian manner, it instantly transformed the relationship one could have with one's doctor. Through chat rooms, for example, users could not only conduct their own research on clinical evidence but also hear other people's experience of treatments.

Meanwhile, from a commercial point of view, the Internet provides connectivity and delivers communities patients can visit to discuss their condition with fellow sufferers. If they need professional help they are usually obliged to register, thereby answering questions about their condition and, importantly, how it is being treated. Sites exist simply to gather and trade this kind of information, such is the currency hard health data can command.

Empowered healthcare consumers were expected to change the whole thrust of the medicines business because they would be the ones to decide whether or not they wanted, not needed, medication. The doctor would merely process the request, pushing the onus on to the insurance plan (in the US) and the state-run systems (everywhere else) to say what can and cannot be provided from collective funds.

Only then did it become apparent the consumer is both king and not king at the same time: king to the extent that consumers set up the dynamic to create a much larger healthcare market; and not king in that they remain patients needing the go-ahead from a doctor before the NHS (or any other healthcare plan they are signed up with) sanctions their preferred treatment.

Moreover, being king did not mean they could do as they liked. New schemes to save healthcare providers money didn't always have the desired effect. Targeting people with conditions such as HIV/AIDS, diabetes and heart disease, the Internet made it possible for these traditional high-maintenance groups to be managed remotely. Diabetes programmes, for example, may require them to log on to a site, enter their glucose levels and answer questions about diabetic problems such as dizziness and shaking. The proprietary site checks the levels are within an acceptable range, something one might have thought an empowered healthcare consumer could be trusted to do on their own.

Meanwhile, it was thought self-diagnosis would increasingly become the norm, leading over time to almost as many conditions as there are facets of human expression. Medicine without doctors soon seemed like an illusion because treating someone as king and having them act like one are two completely different things. When consumers really are king they ask questions, shop around and, in so doing, ensure bad products and practitioners go to the wall. In medicine, all they can do is change doctor – and that can be hard – or visit a complementary therapist. They are neither scientists nor doctors; just ordinary people wanting to perform better in a harsh world where youth and health hold the trump cards.

Moreover, most people have little experience of what they are buying, or of judging the effects. It's not like buying a car. The Internet may be helpful for finding out about a condition, but in terms of what to do next, it suffers from an increasingly shark-infested feel with a plethora of commercially driven sites, despite the fact excellent non-commercial sites do now exist.

If patients really were king, they would query the terms of reference of studies that suggest 80% of people can expect to suffer depression at some time in their lives, or that 43% of women suffer an unhealthy response when having sex. Instead, as with the effect of pharma marketing on doctors, there is a sort of drip effect. Even if people genuinely try to ignore such commercially inspired drivel, some of it gets through.

Pushing back the tide

As we have seen, everything in the medicines business creeps forward in the best interests of commerce and when it gets too far out of kilter with the public interest, is pulled back in line. Professor Eric Topol risked his reputation to alert the public when evidence about Vioxx had become overwhelming. Professor Martin Bobrow and others spoke up when the patent laws were trivializing medicine and life to the extent of trying to lay claim to owning slices of it.

Pharma journalist Ray Moynihan may have felt pharma's marketing practices had inched too far out of line when a study in the *Journal of the American Medical Association* showed that 43% of women suffered from female sexual dysfunction (FSD). When he located the original study, he found the authors had close links to Pfizer, which was testing Viagra in women at the time. He also found 1,500 women, between the ages of 18 and 59, had been asked if they had experienced any of seven problems for two months or more over the previous year. One was a lack of desire for sex and another anxiety about sexual performance. No questions were asked about the length of their relationships, a major factor in many people's sex lives, nor about what else the women did, how many children they were looking after, and so on.

The results of that study were widely quoted in the press and driven by pharma marketing teams that, as we have seen, bring illnesses out of the closet by making them real and normal, by explaining the chemistry behind them, and finally, offering a pill. It doesn't matter whether the issue is high cholesterol levels, a low sex drive or an overactive or underactive thyroid, the method is the same. When there's a mass-market drug to sell, the problem is medical and the solution is pharmaceutical. Anything that complicates this model is rarely given much prominence.

It is an unfair market because the public do not see the billion-dollar revenues riding on people's perceptions that something is broken and needs to be fixed. Nor is it easy for them to find out about them. As consumers wanting help with their sex lives, their only stipulation is that it should be safe – and work. In this way, medicine enters the most intimate areas of our lives despite evidence that our bodies respond in ways we so want them to without drugs. Pfizer, for example, did everything it could to show Viagra could work in women. It carried out several large-scale trials in women with apparent FSD only to find the women on Viagra responded but those on placebo responded more.

The placebo effect can be put down to women's understandable desire in contemporary culture to have a strong sexual response. Doctors such as Leonore Tiefler, clinical associate of psychiatry at New York University, protested at having their territory infiltrated in this way. Tiefler went on to compare sex with dancing to make her point that not everything has a medical cause:

> If you break an ankle while you're dancing you go to a doctor. But your doctor does not take a dance history and would not advise you whether your dancing is normal. The medical model is about defining what's healthy and what's sick – but sex is not like that.[16]

Healthcare consumerism broadens the boundaries, however. And while Pfizer's trials failed, much development has been stimulated by this large and apparently unmet need. When Procter & Gamble (P&G) was in the final stages of testing its testosterone patch for women in May 2004, Mary Johnson, a P&G spokeswoman, told the *Wall Street Journal*, 'This isn't about oversexing women. This is about restoring something they have lost.'[17] Such drugs may do very well, if only as vehicles for the placebo response, but the issues surrounding them also show the cultural factors at work and why the information war about the nature of health is made very much easier for pharma if you are addressing people who will always want what they have lost, particularly if it is related to youth, and even more so if it is to do with sex.

And that would be all very well but for the fact that big pharma has the overwhelming advantage because it has more money to spend and more to gain than anyone else from messages that medicines are better than any of the alternatives – even tried and tested ones, like bunches of flowers and other tokens of affection and appreciation that women have been crying out for for years. Without wishing to trivialize the experience of even one woman who really has lost the testosterone P&G can restore, there are hundreds of others for whom the flower option would work out a lot cheaper in the long run.

Governments and the public

Governments in most developed countries pick up the drugs bill. And if there is one argument in favour of socialized medicine, it is that it creates some real dynamic within the system to curb unnecessary drug spend. With more than half of all visits to surgeries and hospital out-patient departments in the UK (arguably more in the US) said to have no good medical reason, it can be helpful to have some restrictions placed on a rampant collective anxiety about health.

A report released by the British Medical Association in August 2005 confirmed the downside of ruling out every health fear by checking it out privately. Whole-body scanning tests may be unnecessary and even downright dangerous, it said, adding that the radiation from computed tomography is 100 times stronger than from a normal X-ray. Moreover, quality control of many of the tests and follow-up is poor, and there is always the risk of reporting a disease that is not present. Even if the tests are clear, the anxiety doesn't necessarily go away.

Recognizing such intensely fraught consumerist times, and faced with an out-of-control drugs bill, the UK government hit upon the idea of exhorting people to choose health by living healthily. This no-brainer seems indicative of the paucity of thinking in public health circles. Says Rosalind Raine, a clinical scientist at the London School of Hygiene and Tropical Medicine's Department of Public Health:

> It is well established that information alone does not entice people to change behaviour. Nor will the provision of fruit for your lunch box alter eating habits so long as healthy eating is perceived to be posh. Improving public health is about changing behaviour. We need an in-depth understanding of the personal values, beliefs, preferences, and aspirations that drive behaviours in different social groups. Only then can we begin to design interventions to modify deep-seated cultural norms and to challenge ingrained ambivalence.[18]

This public health function, to be obsessively concerned with how to change behaviour so people don't need drugs, must also be set against the marketing machines of companies that do everything they can to ensure people do need drugs. And one can't help concluding that this failure to confront the practices of the pharmaceutical industry more effectively where they don't promote public health is precisely what draws industry and governments ever closer together.

As partners in various initiatives, they can encourage patients to take greater responsibility for their health, empower them with confidence to manage their conditions, promote messages about how to live healthily, train doctors to listen to what patients have to say. What this inherently flawed partnership can't do is significantly change the commercial forces that have become so central to healthcare systems around the world. This is especially true, of course, if governments also have a role to sponsor the industry, which is the case in the UK and US, and elsewhere to a greater or lesser degree.

Indeed, the response of the UK government to the unprecedented criticism by its MPs of how it governs pharma was largely to reiterate its confidence in how bonds between the public and private sector in health are getting closer. The Pharmaceutical Industry Competitiveness Task Force, for example, which was established in 1999 to align thinking between industry and government, has resulted in the establishment of a Ministerial Industry Strategy Group to formulate long-term leadership strategy for medicines, each strand of which can be seen to cement pharma even more deeply into the infrastructure of public healthcare.[19]

The other thing this massive public–private endeavour cannot do is stop the consumer tide that has started to challenge its experts. When the UK government decided to take the low-dose statin, Zocor Heart-Pro, off the prescription list, it effectively passed the cost of around £13 ($23) a month to people with a low risk of heart disease. If they want it, they must pay, in other words. Nothing wrong with that, but its guidance does not present an uncontested picture of the facts. The Department of Health encourages all men over the age of 55 to take Zocor for life. If they have any risk factors for heart disease, they should start at 45. Women, meanwhile, should start at 55 if they have at least one risk factor. The guidance is reinforced by pharmacists telling them that, in trials those taking Zocor can reduce their risk of a heart attack by 25–30%.

When 7 million potential customers are asked to pay, reasonable questions arise about what they are paying for. The WOSCOP (West of Scotland Coronary Prevention) study, conducted on healthy people, shows what this kind of marginal benefit means in practice. Of 10,000 patients treated with a statin over five years, the study showed that 9,755 would receive no benefit, says Nick Freemantle, professor of clinical epidemiology and biostatistics at Birmingham University. Moreover, he adds, a policy of pushing people to take statins when they are at low risk of heart disease encourages them to believe they are ill when they are not.[20]

What about the doctors?

Doctors like Professor Freemantle and others cited in this book may be invaluable in highlighting the other side of the pharma story in their medical journals. But doctors have problems of their own adapting to autonomous patients and policies that aim to ensure their views are central to consultations. And as the second line of defence against an industry that would have as many people as possible on medication, they too are being judged as failing. 'Prescribers must take their share of the blame for the problems that have resulted from the prescribing of the SSRI antidepressants and Cox-2 inhibitors,' said the report of the UK's parliamentary inquiry into the pharma industry.[21]

Family doctors are lowly players in the medical hierarchy and rarely attract the big money that is open to consultants for industry work. In the US, the top doctors can earn up to $20,000 for a single public speaking engagement; for consultancy work, usually less than $10,000 a year but it can be much more; a place on an advisory board which brings about these other perks; and equity holdings that can be worth up to $1 million.[22]

Family doctors, in contrast, get things like free biros and lunches when they are visited by drug reps. And younger doctors, it seems, want the trust of their patients enough to go against these accepted practices, with various organizations calling for an end to gift giving, free lunches, sponsored education and paid speaking. 'Our quarrel is not with the pharmaceutical industry,' says the New York based No Free Lunch campaign, 'but with pharmaceutical promotion. The time has come to eliminate its influence from our practices.'

Moves to shift the model for surgery decision making from compliance to concordance show that patients also have work to do. Dr Patrick Pietroni, head of an NHS regional education support unit, points out:

> The fundamental shift required in moving from an 'expert doctor' centred model to one focused on patients' needs is a long way away. Patients may indeed be wanting to have a say in their care, but the ensuing conversation is often more like a shouting match than an orderly discussion where each side respects the skills, needs, and status of the other.[23]

Doctors, money and healthcare

A central strand of this book has been that the massive influence of pharma money on doctors, patients and healthcare systems generally can work against public health. I have tried to show how market forces in medicine are responsible for the kind of healthcare we receive, in both a good and a bad sense, and how commerce also works to constantly extend the boundaries of illness.

It is not pharma money that is bad in all this. It is money *per se*, says Dr Michael Greenberg, a dermatologist in Elk Grove Village, Illinois, and former columnist for the American Medical Association publication, *American Medical News*. He says it took a major emotional crisis before he was able to see how excessive amounts of money circulating in medicine had deeply tainted his original reasons for entering the profession, making him ill as a result. The actual crisis was precipitated by the threat that came from another dermatologist entering his patch. Having enjoyed more than 20 years of financial success that he said he never truly believed he deserved, the idea of competition caused him to lose perspective and he became convinced he would lose everything. He began working round the clock for months without a break, forcing him to become a patient himself.

> I don't know about in the UK, but in the US it is easy to see patients as liabilities because you have to see so many in a day. Everything is about the bottom line. Patients have to be moved through quickly to make more money.
>
> It was only when I became ill myself that I could see how I had become focused on the money, rather than the patients. And that was not making me happy. Now the whole focus of my practice is based around two rules: one is that no one is ever rushed. And the second is that no one is ever turned away for lack of money. My practice is swamped with people and I still can't believe how much money I make. Most important of all, however, is that I enjoy my work again.[24]

Greenberg's experience may be unusual, but his change of heart has made him perceptive about how the doctor–patient relationship might be strengthened. 'The first thing patients need to do is realize that the MD after our names does not stand for minor deity,' he says. 'Patients have to take us off the pedestal they have put us on and talk to us as they might a family member. It is patients who will humanize medicine but they have to start telling us when we are behaving badly, for example, and realize there are things that can't be fixed by medicine.'

The effort to build up a relationship of trust with a doctor is paid back over the years and is transferable to other doctors because the cause, like the placebo effect, rests with the patient. Of course, in an area as intimate as medicine, there can be no template as to the exact nature of the relationship, because the style and manner of one doctor can suit some people and be offensive to others. The important thing is to find someone you think you may be able to trust. Even small things, like trying always to see that same doctor, can make a huge difference. And if that doctor is persistently dismissive of your concerns, then you should feel government, or health insurance, policy supports you in your decision to find a new doctor. If anything meaningful is to be taken from the recent shocks to the regulatory system, it could be that people recognize doctors as the best chance they have in a world where all the powers that be seem to unashamedly push the pharmacological route. This doesn't mean not using complementary therapists, just recognizing that conventional family doctors have the advantages of continuity, of having to follow strict ethical codes of behaviour, of acting as gatekeepers to secondary care when the need arises, of having no intrinsic reason to dupe or deceive you, and who are paid to be on your side.

Even though doctors and patients may seem to be as distant from each other as Mars is from Venus, they are locked in a partnership that goes infinitely deeper than anything the pharmaceutical industry can ever hope to achieve. Doctors have to believe in the medicines they prescribe but patients only have to believe in the doctors. In truth, they don't even have to believe in their doctors; but they do have to believe in something. To illustrate this point, US journalist Norman Cousins recalls watching cellist Pablo Casals come alive physically while playing Bach just a few weeks before the great man's ninetieth birthday. He wrote:

> Judging from his difficulty in walking and from the way he held his arms, I guessed he was suffering from rheumatoid arthritis. His emphysema was evident in his labored breathing. He came into the living room on [his wife] Marta's arm. He was badly stooped. His head was pitched forward and he walked with a shuffle. His hands were swollen and his fingers were clenched.
>
> Even before going to the breakfast table, Don Pablo went to the piano – which, I learned, was a daily ritual. He arranged himself with some difficulty on the piano bench, then with discernible effort raised his swollen and clenched fingers above the keyboard.
>
> I was not prepared for the miracle that was about to happen. The fingers slowly unlocked and reached toward the keys like the buds of a plant toward the sunlight. His back straightened. He seemed to breathe more freely. Now his fingers settled on the keys. Then came

> the opening bars of Bach's *Wohltemperierte Klavier*, played with great sensitivity and control. He hummed as he played, then said that Bach spoke to him here – and he placed his hand over his heart.
>
> Then he plunged into a Brahms concerto and his fingers, now agile and powerful, raced across the keyboard with dazzling speed. His entire body seemed fused with the music; it was no longer stiff and shrunken but supple and graceful and completely freed of its arthritic coils.[25]

Later that evening, Cousins observed the miracle again, this time as Casals played the cello. 'His fingers, hands and arms were in sublime coordination as they responded to the demands of his brain for the controlled beauty of movement and tone. Any cellist 30 years his junior would have been proud to have such extraordinary physical command.'[26]

Medicines may be more convenient than becoming a musical legend but Casals demonstrates how the placebo works in many ways. 'He was caught up in his own creativity,' says Cousins, 'in his own desire to accomplish a specific purpose, and the effect was both genuine and observable.'

Everyone must die eventually. The point is surely how well we live. Which is why, as far as the medicines business is concerned, the compliance-to-concordance initiative could be the only hope it has of ever being jolted sufficiently to insist public health is considered separately from the commercial needs of pharma. It's a long shot, admittedly. But the strength of the doctor–patient relationship is that it embraces ordinary people. Nothing else does. If there are regulatory failings further up the chain of command, as there have been with Vioxx and the SSRIs, doctors are the ones to break the news. Their job is to be on our side. Everyone in healthcare wants the patient to speak up. Even the NHS is doing everything it can to get patients to start expressing a preference, if only for one hospital rather than another.

Meanwhile, pharma also wants the patient to speak up, to become more involved in the medicines they take and, at the very least, to remember to take them. That choice is ours, whatever doctors tell us: what to measure to be healthy, or what to eat, or what drugs to take. The exercise in concordance is where we can express that choice. It may be only a start, but everything has to start somewhere, and what else can anyone do in the face of such a powerful industry as pharma?

Appendix

The Pharmaceutical Price Regulation Scheme

The Pharmaceutical Price Regulation Scheme (PPRS) is a mechanism for determining how much money drug companies can make through the sales of their medicines to the NHS. It applies only to companies supplying licensed brand-name products and is restricted further to those with annual NHS sales of more than £25 million. The 44 companies currently involved at this level account for 94% of the total NHS spend on brand-name products.

Paragraphs 113–120 of the report outlining the conclusions of the 2004 parliamentary inquiry into the pharmaceutical industry explain that each year, through the scheme, companies are set a level of return on capital (ROC). This is what they can earn through sales to the NHS. Once this profit target has been agreed, it is for the company to adjust the prices of its portfolio to reach it. Margins of tolerance (MOTs) are built in so that companies reimburse the NHS when their returns are more than 140% of the target. Similarly, price rises are permitted only when returns are less than 40% of this figure. Increasing the prices of established drugs is not encouraged, so companies generally aim to reach their ROC targets by charging high prices for their drugs at the time of launch or by broadening their sales base.

To set this permissible profit level, a company submits details of its business in an annual financial return, one section of which seeks information on fixed assets (which include the historic cost of the company's UK sites, land, buildings, plant and machinery). The profit companies are allowed is 21% of the fixed asset figure. With MOTs, this can rise to 29.4%.

On top of this, companies can offset considerable research and marketing expenses. For R&D, the allowance is 28% of the company's sales to the NHS. For drug promotion, the figure is 4% of sales, plus another 4% for providing information about their drugs. By determining company profit margins allowed against the sale of medicines to the NHS, and by incorporating into these margins allowances for R&D, innovation, drug promotion and the provision of information, the PPRS is generally recognized as the key instrument by which the Department of Health acts as sponsor of the UK-based industry.

Notes

1 *The cost of convenience*

1. 'Global pharma sales up by 9% to $492 billion in 2003.' *Scrip World Pharmaceutical News*. 24 March 2004.
2. 'AstraZeneca set to promote Crestor launch.' Geoff Dyer. *Financial Times*. 24 October 2003.
3. 'Global pharma sales up by 9% to $492 billion in 2003.' *Scrip World Pharmaceutical News*. 24 March 2004.
4. Banc of America Securities Equity Research on Shire Pharmaceuticals. 6 March 2003.
5. 'Why depression still mystifies us.' J. Raymond Depaulo. *Cerebrum* 2.1. Winter 2000, p. 47.
6. 'The first of 3,000 issues of Scrip.' *Scrip World Pharmaceutical News*. 29 October 2004.
7. 'Does lack of launches spell end of expansion?' Ian Lloyd. *Scrip Magazine*. February 2005, p. 24.
8. *The Rise and Fall of Modern Medicine*. James le Fanu. London: Abacus, 2001, p. 216.
9. Le Fanu, *The Rise and Fall of Modern Medicine*, p. 208.
10. Le Fanu, *The Rise and Fall of Modern Medicine*, p. 209.
11. 'Destiny and the Genes.' P.G.H. Gell. *The Encyclopaedia of Medical Ignorance*. Eds R. Duncan and M. Weston-Smith. Kinglinton: Pergamon, 1984.
12. *The Truth About the Drug Companies*. Marcia Angell. New York: Random House, 2004, p. 11.
13. 'The Fortune 500.' *Fortune*. 15 April 2002, pp. 11–12.
14. '2002 Drug industry profits: hefty pharmaceutical company margins dwarf other industries.' Public Citizen Congress Watch, June 2003. www.citizen.org/documents/Pharma_Report.pdf.

15. 'Growth, in moderation.' Graham Lewis, Selena Class and Eva Edery, *Scrip Magazine*. February 2005, p. 29.
16. *OECD Health Data 2004*, 3rd edition.
17. 'Therapeutic class wars: drug promotion in a competitive marketplace.' David A. Kessler, Janet L. Rose, Robert J. Temple, Renie Shapiro and Joseph P. Griffin. *New England Journal of Medicine*. 17 November 1994, pp. 1350–53.
18. 'FDA's counsel accused of being too close to drug industry.' Jeanne Lenzer. *British Medical Journal*. 24 July 2004. 2004;329:189.
19. *The Influence of the Pharmaceutical Industry*. Report of the House of Commons Health Committee. 5 April 2005, p. 3.
20. *The Influence of the Pharmaceutical Industry*, p. 4.
21. *The Influence of the Pharmaceutical Industry*, p. 3.
22. *The Influence of the Pharmaceutical Industry*, p. 4.
23. 'Feeling confident in the countdown to patent expiry.' Karen Beynon. *Scrip Magazine*. January 2000, p. 32.
24. '*Lancet* attack too bitter a pill for AZ to swallow.' Geoff Dyer. *Financial Times*. 24 October 2003.
25. *The Influence of the Pharmaceutical Industry*, p. 6.
26. 'FDA is incapable of protecting FDA against another Vioxx.' Jeanne Lenzer. *British Medical Journal*. 27 November 2004. 2004:329:1253.
27. 'No smoking gun at Vioxx hearing.' *Scrip World Pharmaceutical News*. 24 November 2004, p. 16.
28. 'Concerns raised over Cox-2 panellists' industry ties.' *Scrip World Pharmaceutical News*. 4 March 2005, p. 12.
29. 'It's a tough one ...' James Meek. *Guardian* G2. 2 May 2005.
30. 'The White Paper on public health.' Rosalind Raine, MRC clinical scientist, Dept of Public Health, London School of Hygiene and Tropical Medicine. *British Medical Journal*. 27 November 2004. 2004:329:1247–8.
31. *Limits to Medicine*. Ivan Illich. Harmondsworth: Penguin Books, 1988, p. 129.
32. 'Patients' ambivalence about taking antidepressants: a qualitative study.' Janet Grime. *Pharmaceutical Journal*. 11 October 2003.
33. *A Long Walk Home*. Rachel Clark. Oxford: Radcliffe, 2002, p. 1.
34. *The Influence of the Pharmaceutical Industry*, p. 4.
35. *On Being Human*. Daisaku Ikeda, Rene Simard and Guy Bourgeault. Santa Monica, CA: Middleway, 2003, p. 14.
36. Le Fanu, *The Rise and Fall of Modern Medicine*, p. 383.
37. 'Anarchy with a smile: an interview with Rebecca Solnit.' Stuart Jeffries. *Guardian*. 31 May 2005.

2 *The company of giants*

1. 'Takeda takes top profit slot.' Peter Charlish. *Scrip Magazine*. February 2005, p. 35.
2. *The $800 Million Pill*. Merrill Goozner. Berkeley: University of California Press, 2004, p. 218.
3. *Plague Time: The New Germ Theory of Disease*. Paul W. Ewald. New York: Anchor Books, 2002, p. 99.
4. Ewald, *Plague Time*, p. 102.
5. Ewald, *Plague Time*, p. 5.
6. 'Growth, in moderation.' Graham Lewis, Selena Class and Eva Edery. *Scrip Magazine*. February 2005, p. 29.
7. 'Blockbusters then, now and later.' *In Vivo: The Business and Medicine Report*. June 2003.
8. 'Blockbusters then, now and later.' *In Vivo: The Business and Medicine Report*. June 2003.
9. 'Dominated by the urge to merge.' Karen Beynon. *Scrip Magazine*. January 1999.
10. 'Has big pharma lost the plot?' Philip Brown. *Scrip Magazine*. January 2001, p. 3.
11. Charlish, 'Takeda takes top profit slot,' p. 35.
12. 'Managing the innovation gap with M&As.' Robin Davison. *Scrip Magazine*. February 2000.
13. 'Crouching tigers, hidden dragons.' Barbara Ryan. *Perspectives on Life Sciences*. Cap Gemini Ernst & Young. Spring 2003, p. 2.
14. Charlish, 'Takeda takes top profit slot,' p. 35.
15. Charlish, 'Takeda takes top profit slot,' p. 35.
16. *The Influence of the Pharmaceutical Industry*. Report of the House of Commons Health Committee. 5 April 2005, para. 21.
17. Charlish, 'Takeda takes top profit slot,' p. 35.
18. Charlish, 'Takeda takes top profit slot,' p. 35.
19. *The Truth About the Drug Companies*. Marcia Angell. New York: Random House, 2004, p. 4.
20. 'Glaxo hit by $5 billion US tax demand.' Heather Stewart. *Guardian*. 8 January 2004.
21. 'Health, wealth and politics.' *Guardian* Business Notebook. 8 January 2004.
22. Telephone interview with Eric Topol, Summer 2005.
23. Telephone interview with Eric Topol, Summer 2005.
24. *The Influence of the Pharmaceutical Industry*, para. 21.

25. 'Science and profit.' *Economist*. 17 February 2001, p. 21.
26. 'Fighting the flab for future profit.' Susan Hughes. *Scrip Magazine*. July/August 1996, p. 47.
27. 'Wyeth offers $1.28 billion in fen-phen saga.' Christopher Bowe. *Financial Times*. 7 May 2004.
28. Hughes, 'Fighting the flab for future profit,' p. 47.
29. '34 deaths in sibutramine patients.' *Scrip World Pharmaceutical News*. 20 March 2002.
30. 'Abbot says calls to ban sibutramine are irresponsible.' *Scrip World Pharmaceutical News*. 10 September 2003.
31. 'Live off the fat of the land.' Clive Cookson. *Financial Times* Pharmaceuticals Supplement. 16 April 2003.
32. 'Scientists find fat cells live an active life.' Rob Stein. *Washington Post*. 13 July 2004.
33. Stein, 'Scientists find fat cells live an active life.'
34. Stein, 'Scientists find fat cells live an active life.'
35. 'Gut hormone replacement could treat obesity.' *Scrip World Pharmaceutical News*. 10 September 2003.
36. 'Fighting a growing problem.' Ailis Kane. *Scrip Magazine*. December 2004, p. 13.
37. 'The burger and fags jab.' Sam Lister. *The Times* Body & Soul. 13 August 2005.
38. 'Fast foods trick the body.' Andy Coghlan. *New Scientist*. 25 October 2003.
39. 'The fat controller: an interview with Andrew Prentice.' David Adams. *The Guardian* Life. 6 November 2003.
40. 'The perils of this obesity panic.' Susie Orbach. *Observer*. 30 May 2004.
41. Orbach, 'The perils of this obesity panic.'

3 *A question of trust*

1. 'The hookers.' David Rowan. *The Times* Body & Soul, 25 October 2004.
2. *MMR. Science and Fiction. Exploring the Vaccine Crisis*. Richard Horton. London: Granta, 2004, p. 81.
3. Horton, *MMR*, p. 82.
4. Rowan, 'The hookers.'
5. Rowan, 'The hookers.'
6. 'Defining disease.' Jenine Willis. *Scrip Magazine*. April 2001, p. 17.
7. 'US guidelines are reassessing blood pressure.' Denise Grady. *New York Times*. 15 May 2003.

8. *The Truth About the Drug Companies*. Marcia Angell. New York: Random House, 2004, p. 85.
9. Angell, *The Truth About the Drug Companies*, p. 85.
10. 'Bad cholesterol: the lower, the better.' Rob Winslow. *Wall Street Journal* European edition. 19 November 2003, p. A7
11. Winslow, 'Bad cholesterol.'
12. Winslow, 'Bad cholesterol.'
13. 'Treating to new targets: a new era in the treatment of established coronary heart disease.' See www.theheart.org.
14. 'In praise of good fat.' Alexandra Shimmings. *Scrip Magazine*. November 2004.
15. 'Selling sickness: the pharmaceutical industry and disease mongering.' Ray Moynihan, Iona Heath and David Henry. *British Medical Journal*. 13 April 2002. 2002;324:886.
16. Moynihan, Heath and Henry, 'Selling sickness,' p. 886.
17. Moynihan, Heath and Henry, 'Selling sickness,' p. 886.
18. Moynihan, Heath and Henry, 'Selling sickness,' p. 886.
19. *The Influence of the Pharmaceutical Industry*. Report of the House of Commons Health Committee. 5 April 2005, p. 4.
20. *The Influence of the Pharmaceutical Industry*, para. 142.
21. 'Strategies for survival selling.' Jacky Law. *Scrip Magazine*. May 2003, p. 41.
22. Law, 'Strategies for survival selling,' p. 41.
23. Law, 'Strategies for survival selling,' p. 41.
24. Law, 'Strategies for survival selling,' p. 41.
25. Law, 'Strategies for survival selling,' p. 41.
26. 'Doctors don't fall for the hard sell.' *New Scientist*. 28 June 2003.
27. 'Doctors accept $50 a time to listen to drug representatives.' David Spurgeon. *British Medical Journal*, News Section. 11 May 2002, p. 113.
28. Spurgeon, 'Doctors accept $50 a time,' p. 113.
29. *The Influence of the Pharmaceutical Industry*, para. 155.
30. Rowan, 'The hookers.'
31. 'Celebrity drug pushers.' Daniel B. Moskowitz. *Scrip Magazine*. May 2003, p. 7.
32. Rowan, 'The hookers.'
33. Moynihan, Heath and Henry, 'Selling sickness,' p. 886.
34. Moynihan, Heath and Henry, 'Selling sickness,' p. 886.
35. Moynihan, Heath and Henry, 'Selling sickness,' p. 886.
36. Moynihan, Heath and Henry, 'Selling sickness,' p. 886.
37. *The Influence of the Pharmaceutical Industry*, para. 165.

4 *Old pills in new bottles*

1. 'Drug ads hyping anxiety make some uneasy.' Shankar Vedantam. *Washington Post*. 16 July 2001, A1.
2. Vedantam, 'Drug ads hyping anxiety make some uneasy.'
3. *The Undiscovered Mind: How the Human Brain Defies Replication, Medication, and Explanation*. John Horgan. New York: Free Press, 1999, p. 79.
4. 'First, you market the disease ... then you push the pills to treat it.' Brendan I. Koerner. *Guardian*. 30 July 2002.
5. 'Lexapro still non-approvable for panic disorder.' *Scrip World Pharmaceutical News*. 4 March 2005.
6. Koerner, 'First, you market the disease ....'
7. *The Influence of the Pharmaceutical Industry*. Report of the House of Commons Health Committee. 5 April 2005, para. 197.
8. 'Antidepressant drugs used as placebos.' Press release from Alliance for Human Research Protection. 10 October 2003.
9. *Anatomy of an Illness as Perceived by a Patient*. Norman Cousins. New York: W.W. Norton, 1979, p. 65.
10. Cousins, *Anatomy of an Illness*, p. 65.
11. Cousins, *Anatomy of an Illness*, p. 63.
12. Cousins, *Anatomy of an Illness*, p. 63.
13. 'Spotting those who respond to placebos.' Leila Abboud. *Wall Street Journal*, European Edition. 21 June 2004, A7.
14. 'Cured by an imposter.' Jerome Burne. *The Times* Body & Soul. 10 April 2004.
15. Abboud, 'Spotting those who respond to placebos.'
16. Burne, 'Cured by an imposter.'
17. 'The problem pill for every ill.' Ailis Kane. *Scrip Magazine*. December 2002, p. 8.
18. Kane, 'The problem pill for every ill,' p. 8.
19. Abboud, 'Spotting those who respond to placebos.'
20. Abboud, 'Spotting those who respond to placebos.'
21. Abboud, 'Spotting those who respond to placebos.'
22. Kane, 'The problem pill for every ill,' p. 9.
23. Kane, 'The problem pill for every ill,' p. 9.
24. Cousins, *Anatomy of an Illness*, p. 65.
25. 'Drug makers offer patients two pills in one.' Scott Hensley. *Wall Street Journal*, Europe Edition. 29 January 2004.

26. 'Torcetrapib and atorvastatin – should marketing drive the research agenda?' Jerry Avron. *New England Journal of Medicine* 352.25. 23 June 2005.
27. *The Truth About the Drug Companies*. Marcia Angell. New York: Random House, 2004, pp. 184–5.
28. *The $800 Million Pill*. Merril Goozner. Berkeley: University of California Press, 2004, p. 222.
29. Angell, *The Truth About the Drug Companies*, p. 79.
30. Goozner, *The $800 Million Pill*, p. 222.
31. 'From deliverers to developers?' Peter Charlish. *Scrip Magazine*. January 2002, p. 6.
32. 'A matter of taste.' John Fraher. *Scrip Magazine*. January 2004, p. 28.
33. 'Here today, where tomorrow?' Lew Bender, *Scrip Magazine*. July/August 2003, p. 47. (Table, 'Changing trends in the drug delivery market, 1997–2003' with data supplied by Pharmaprojects).
34. 'Delivery firms fight for fair deals.' Nicole Yost. *Scrip Magazine*. June 2004, p. 11.
35. 'Breathing new life into the diabetics market.' Nicole Yost. *Scrip Magazine*. January 2004, p. 7.
36. Yost, 'Breathing new life into the diabetics market.'
37. Yost, 'Breathing new life into the diabetics market.'
38. Yost, 'Delivery firms fight for fair deals.'
39. Guy Furness, private conversation, summer 2005.
40. 'R&D revolution remains just around the corner.' Ian Lloyd. *Scrip Magazine* February 2002, p. 73.

5 *The story of Vioxx*

1. *The $800 Million Pill*. Merrill Goozner. Berkeley: University of California Press, 2004, p. 225.
2. 'Stress and peptic ulcer disease.' Susan Levenstein et al. *Journal of the American Medical Association*. 6 January 1999. 'Association of upper gastrointestinal toxicity of nonsteroidal anti-inflammatory drugs with continued exposure: cohort study.' T.M. Macdonald et al. *British Medical Journal*. 22 November 1997.
3. For examples of such articles, see the special supplement to the *American Journal of Medicine*, 30 March 1998.
4. Goozner, *The $800 Million Pill*, p. 226
5. 'Cured by an impostor.' Jerome Burne. *The Times* Body & Soul. 10 April 2004.

6. 'FDA approves pain reliever with fewer side effects.' *Washington Post*. 22 May 1999.
7. Jacky Law. *Scrip Magazine*.
8. 'The Coxibs, selective inhibitors of Cyclooxygenase-2.' Garret A. Fitzgerald and Carol Patrono. *New England Journal of Medicine*. 9 August 2001, pp. 433–42.
9. 'FDA should have required Vioxx safety study years ago, says Vanderbilt professor.' *Scrip World Pharmaceutical News*. 6 October 2004.
10. 'The lessons of Vioxx.' Henry A. Waxman. *New England Journal of Medicine*. 23 June 2005. p. 2576.
11. Waxman, 'The lessons of Vioxx.'
12. 'Risk of cardiovascular events associated with selective COX-2 inhibitors.' Debabrata Mukherjee, Steven E. Nissen and Eric J. Topol. *Journal of the American Medical Association* 286.22/29 August 2001, pp. 954–9.
13. Private interview, Summer 2005.
14. 'Demise of Vioxx leaves trail of confusion.' Ailis Kane. *Scrip Magazine*. February 2005, p. 52.
15. 'Failing the public health – Rofecoxib, Merck, and the FDA.' Eric J. Topol. *New England Journal of Medicine* 351. 21 October 2004, pp. 1707–9.
16. Private interview, Summer 2005.
17. Private interview, Summer 2005.
18. 'FDA is incapable of protecting FDA against another Vioxx.' Jeanne Lenzer. *British Medical Journal* 329 News Section. 27 November 2004. 2004;329:1253.
19. 'Vioxx withdrawal sets alarm bells ringing.' John Davis. *Scrip World Pharmaceutical News*. 6 October 2004, p. 2.
20. 'FDA should have required Vioxx safety study years ago, says Vanderbilt professor.' *Scrip World Pharmaceutical News*. 6 October 2004.
21. 'Vioxx withdrawn worldwide.' *Scrip World Pharmaceutical News*. 6 October 2004, p. 22.
22. *The Regulation of Medical Products*. Ed. J.P. Griffin and J. O'Grady. Oxford: BMJ Books, 2003, p. 6.
23. Private correspondence, May 2005.
24. *Don't Tell the Patient: Behind the Drug Safety Net*. Bill Inman. Bishops Waltham: Highland Park Productions, 1999, p. 22.
25. *Powerful Medicines: The Benefits, Risks and Costs of Prescription Drugs*. Jerry Avron. New York: Knopf, 2004, p. 44.
26. 'UK government takes non-critical view of pharma at parliamentary inquiry.' Elizabeth Sukkar. *Scrip World Pharmaceutical News*. 15 September 2004, p. 4.

27. 'The drugs industry and its watchdog: a relationship too close for comfort?' Rob Evans and Sarah Boseley. *Guardian*. 4 October 2004.
28. MMR: *Science and Fiction: Exploring the Vaccine Crisis*. Richard Horton. London: Granta, 2004, p. 151.
29. *The Influence of the Pharmaceutical Industry*. Report of the House of Commons Health Committee. April 5 2005, p. 3.
30. 'US government agency to investigate FDA over rofecoxib.' Jeanne Lenzer. *British Medical Journal* 2004;329:935.
31. Lenzer, 'FDA is incapable of protecting FDA against another Vioxx.'
32. 'FDA drug safety officer gagged over Vioxx.' *Scrip World Pharmaceutical News*. 15 October 2004.
33. 'FDA's Dr Graham says other drugs besides Vioxx also pose safety risks.' *Scrip World Pharmaceutical News*. 24 November 2004, p.14.
34. 'FDA to strengthen safety review procedures for marketed drugs.' *Scrip World Pharmaceutical News*. 12 November 2004, p. 12.
35. Memorandum submitted by Iain Chalmers to the Health Committee of the House of Commons, for its Inquiry into the Influence of the Pharmaceutical Industry.
36. 'Concerns raised over Cox-2 panellists' industry ties.' *Scrip World Pharmaceutical News*. 4 March 2005, p. 12

6 *The SSRI story*

1. Professor Joe Collier, private interview, Summer 2005.
2. Professor Joe Collier, private interview, Summer 2005.
3. 'Identification of off-label antidepressant use and costs in a network model HMO.' S.E. Streator and J.T. Moss Jr. *Drug Benefit Trends*. 1997;9:42, pp. 48–50, 55–6.
4. *Prozac and the New Antidepressants*. William S. Appleton. New York: Penguin, 2000, pp. 86–7.
5. *The Undiscovered Mind*. John Horgan. New York: Free Press, 1999, p. 37.
6. 'Are we "blaming" brain chemistry for mental illness?' Elliot Valenstein and Dennis Charney. *Cerebrum*. Winter 2000, p. 88.
7. Valenstein and Charney, 'Are we "blaming" brain chemistry for mental illness?' pp. 90–91.
8. *Mind Sculpture*. Ian Robertson. London: Bantam, 1999, p. 20.
9. 'Unhappy anniversary.' Simon Garfield. Observer Review section. 2 February 2003, p. 1.
10. Garfield, 'Unhappy anniversary.'

11. *The Power to Harm: Mind, Medicine and Murder on Trial.* John Cornwell. London: Viking, 1996, p. 99.
12. Cornwell, *The Power To Harm*, p. 105.
13. Cornwell, *The Power To Harm*, Preface p. 1.
14. Cornwell, *The Power To Harm*, Preface p. 2.
15. Cornwell, *The Power To Harm*, Preface p. 2.
16. Cornwell, *The Power To Harm*, Preface p. 2.
17. Cornwell, *The Power To Harm*, Preface p. 2.
18. 'Do these pills turn children into killers and drive mums to suicide?' Sally Eyden. *Daily Express*. 20 May 2002, p. 32.
19. Eyden, 'Do these pills turn children into killers and drive mums to suicide?'
20. Eyden, 'Do these pills turn children into killers and drive mums to suicide?'
21. Eyden, 'Do these pills turn children into killers and drive mums to suicide?'
22. BBC Panorama website. www.bbc.co.uk Go to Panorama; then to the programme: *The Secrets of Prozac*.
23. 'The chemistry of happiness.' Simon Garfield. *Observer Magazine*. 28 April 2002, p. 16
24. 'Bursting the happy bubble.' Simon Crompton. *The Times* Body & Soul. 18
25. Crompton, 'Bursting the happy bubble.'
26. 'Big pharma snared by net.' Cheryll Barron. *Observer* Business section. 26 September 2004, p. 11.
27. Barron, 'Big pharma snared by net.'
28. *The Influence of the Pharmaceutical Industry*. Report of the House of Commons Health Committee. 5 April 2005, para. 299.
29. 'New York attorney general accuses Glaxo of fraud.' Barbara Martinez. *Wall Street Journal* European edition. 3 June 2004, p. A1.
30. Martinez, 'New York attorney general accuses Glaxo of fraud.'
31. Martinez, 'New York attorney general accuses Glaxo of fraud.'
32. Martinez, 'New York attorney general accuses Glaxo of fraud.'
33. Martinez, 'New York attorney general accuses Glaxo of fraud.'
34. 'MHRA negligent over Seroxat, says MIND chief.' *Pharmaceutical Journal* 272. 20 March 2004, p. 339.
35. 'The drugs industry and its watchdog: a relationship too close for comfort?' Rob Evans and Sarah Boseley. *Guardian*. 4 October 2004.
36. Evans and Boseley. 'The drugs industry and its watchdog: a relationship too close for comfort?'
37. *The Influence of the Pharmaceutical Industry*, Summary, p. 4.

7 *A crisis in medicine*

1. 'Merck faces huge bill after widow wins $250 million Vioxx claim.' Caroline Merrell. *The Times*. 20 August 2005.
2. *The Influence of the Pharmaceutical Industry*. Report of the House of Commons Health Committee. 5 April 2005, para. 98.
3. *The Influence of the Pharmaceutical Industry*, para. 101.
4. 'All war is economic.' John Griffin. *Scrip Magazine*. September 2004, p. 3.
5. 'Legislative change – the answer to industry's ills?' Philip Brown. *Scrip Magazine*. July/August 2003, p. 4.
6. 'Torcetrapib and atorvastatin – should marketing drive the research agenda?' Jerry Avorn. *New England Journal of Medicine*, 352;25. 23 June 2005, p. 2575.
7. 'Was Viagra really so obvious?' Diana Sternfeld. *Scrip Magazine*. January 2001, p. 22.
8. 'Reforming the patent system', John H. Barton. *Science*. 17 March 2000, pp. 1933–4.
9. 'The politics of patenting human gene sequences.' Jacky Law. *Scrip Magazine*. September 2000. p. 41.
10. Law, 'The politics of patenting human gene sequences,' p. 41.
11. Law, 'The politics of patenting human gene sequences,' p. 42.
12. *Genome: The Autobiography of a Species in 23 Chapters*. Matt Ridley. London: HarperCollins, 2000, p. 17.
13. Ridley, *Genome*, p. 13.
14. Ridley, *Genome*, pp. 21–2.
15. 'The public and private approach to proteomics.' Jacky Law. *Scrip Magazine*. March 2001, p. 16.
16. '50 years of the double helix.' Lisa Davies. *Scrip World Pharmaceutical News*. 30 April 2003.
17. *Intellectual Property Rights and Research Tools in Molecular Biology*. A summary of a workshop held at the National Academy of Sciences, 15–16 February 1996. Washington DC: National Academy Press, 1997, p. 1.
18. *Science in the Private Interest: Has the Lure of Profits Corrupted Biomedical Research?* Sheldon Krimsky. Lanham, MD: Rowman and Littlefield, 2003, p. 179.
19. 'The biomedical sciences in context.' Philip A. Sharpe. In *The Fragile Contract: University Science and the Federal Government*. Ed. D.H. Guston and K. Keniston. Cambridge, MA: MIT Press, 1994, p. 148.

20. 'Universities as creators and retailers of intellectual property: life sciences research and commercial development.' Walter W. Powell and Jason Owen-Smith. In *To Profit or Not to Profit*. Ed. Burton A. Weibrod. Cambridge, UK: Cambridge University Press, 1991, p. 192.
21. *The Common Thread: A Story of Science, Politics, Ethics and the Human Genome*. John Sulston and Georgina Ferry. London: Bantam Press, 2002, p. viii.
22. Sulston and Ferry, *The Common Thread*, p. 154.
23. 'The people vs patents.' *New Scientist* editorial. 13 July 2002, p. 2.
24. Krimsky, Science in the *Private Interest*, p. 67.
25. 'Science and profit.' *Economist*. 17 February 2001, p. 21.
26. Sulston and Ferry, *The Common Thread*, p. 195.
27. Sulston and Ferry, *The Common Thread*, p. 213.
28. Private conversation, summer 2005.
29. Sulston and Ferry, *The Common Thread*, p. 223.
30. 'A bubble punctured by realism.' Geoff Dyer. *Financial Times* Inside Track. 11 November 2002.
31. Avorn, 'Torcetrapib and atorvastatin,' p. 2575.
32. Law, 'The public and private approach to proteomics,' p. 17.
33. Law, 'The public and private approach to proteomics,' p. 17.
34. 'Bioinformatics: where next?' Stephen Warde and Scott Khan. *Scrip Magazine*. November 2003, p. 8.
35. MMR*: Science and Fiction: Exploring the Vaccine Crisis*. Richard Horton. London: Granta, 2004, p. 79.
36. Krimsky, *Science in the Private Interest*, p. 43.
37. Horton, *MMR*, p. 86.

8 *A bit of a lottery*

1. 'Transformation in colon cancer.' Fil Maniguid. *Scrip Magazine*. June 2004, p. 15.
2. Maniguid, 'Transformation in colon cancer.'
3. 'End the cancer drugs lottery now.' *Observer* Leader column. 14 August 2005.
4. 'Why targeted drugs to battle cancer fall short of promise.' Sharon Begley. *Wall Street Journal*. 10–12 September 2004. Networking section. A10.
5. Maniguid, 'Transformation in colon cancer.'
6. Begley, 'Why targeted drugs to battle cancer fall short of promise.'
7. 'Folkman earns a place in medical folklore.' Geoff Dyer. *Financial Times* Companies International. 1 March 2004.

8. Begley, 'Why targeted drugs to battle cancer fall short of promise.'
9. 'Shares dive as drug giants halt key trials.' Richard Irving. *The Times*. 18 December 2004.
10. Dyer, 'Folkman earns a place in medical folklore.'
11. Dyer, 'Folkman earns a place in medical folklore.'
12. 'Glivec a once in a lifetime opportunity, says Dr Vasella.' *Scrip World Pharmaceutical News*. 18 July 2003.
13. 'A drugs deal for the world's poorest: now the fight over patents and cheap medicine is in middle-income countries.' Geoff Dyer. *Financial Times*. 2 September 2003.
14. Consumer Project on Technology, Brazilian Government, Novartis. Repr. in *Financial Times* on 2 September 2003.
15. Dyer, 'A drugs deal for the world's poorest.'
16. *Tackling Cancer in England: Saving More Lives*. National Audit Office, HC 364 Session 2003–2004. 19 March 2004.
17. *Tackling Cancer in England.*
18. 'New cancer drugs to cost NHS £50 million.' Jo Revill. *Observer*. 28 November 2004.
19. 'Variations in usage of cancer drugs approved by NICE.' Report of a review undertaken by the National Cancer Director. May 2004.
20. NICE press release, issued 28 March 2002.
21. 'Variations in usage of cancer drugs approved by NICE.'
22. 'NHS lottery rations new cancer drug.' Jo Revill. *Observer*. 14 August 2005.
23. 'End the cancer drugs lottery now.' *Observer* editorial. 14 August 2005.
24. 'End the cancer drugs lottery now.'
25. 'A combined effort in cancer.' Ailis Kane. Scrip Magazine. September 2004, p. 6.
26. Kane, 'A combined effort in cancer,' p. 6.
27. 'How Chiron convinced Medicare on Proleukin.' Rex Rhein. *Scrip World Pharmaceutical News*. 15 October 2003.
28. 'Ministers reprieve Alzheimer's treatment.' Jo Revill. *Observer*. 13 March 2005.
29. 'New studies on regimen for Alzheimer's patient.' Andrea Petersen. *Wall Street Journal*. 9 September 2004.
30. Petersen. 'New studies on regimen for Alzheimer's patient.'
31. 'NICE and companies clash on Alzheimer's drugs.' *Scrip World Pharmaceutical News*. 9 March 2005.
32. 'Alzheimer's drug has "minimal effect".' Clive Cookson. *Financial Times*. 25 June 2004.

33. The paper was published in the *Lancet*, 25 June 2004 by researchers at Birmingham University, and quoted in Cookson's article above.
34. Petersen. 'New studies on regimen for Alzheimer's patient.'
35. 'Getting the measure of QALYS.' Elizabeth Sukkar. *Scrip Magazine*. January 2002, p. 21.
36. 'Why Nice has to be nasty.' Mark Henderson. *The Times* Body & Soul 23 July 2005.
37. 'Too much medicine?' Richard Smith and Ray Moynihan. *British Medical Journal* 2002; 324: 859–60.
38. Professor Joe Collier, private conversation, summer 2005.
39. 'Breast cancer drug dilemma.' Sarah Boseley. *Guardian*. 12 December 2004.
40. Boseley, 'Breast cancer drug dilemma.'
41. 'Fears over breast cancer drug delay.' Jo Revill. *Observer*. 22 May 2005.
42. Genentech 2004 annual report. Letter to Stockholders, p. 4.
43. 'The stubborn approach that pays dividends.' Victoria Griffith. *Financial Times*. 18 December 2003.
44. Genentech 2004 annual report. Letter to Stockholders, p. 4.
45. 'A new deal for dealmakers.' Karen Beynon and Jacob Plieth. *Scrip Magazine*. February 2005, pp. 38–9.
46. Dr Philip Brown, private conversation, summer 2005.
47. *The Truth About the Drug Companies*. Marcia Angell. New York: Random House, 2004, pp. 40–41.
48. Angell, *The Truth About the Drug Companies*, p. 44.
49. Angell, *The Truth About the Drug Companies*, p. 44.
50. Dr Philip Brown, private conversation, summer 2005.
51. 'Rebuilding big pharma's business model.' Jim Gilbert, Preston Henske and Ashish Singh. Reprinted in *In Vivo*, November 2003.
52. Gilbert, Henske and Singh, 'Rebuilding big pharma's business model.'
53. *The Influence of the Pharmaceutical Industry*. Report of the House of Commons Health Committee. 5 April 2005, para. 165.
54. Professor Joe Collier, private conversation, summer 2005.
55. Dr John Griffin, private conversation, summer 2005.

9 *The people* vs *pharma*

1. 'Do US Seniors need help?' John Davis. *Scrip World Pharmaceutical News*. 18 July 2003.
2. 'America is high on drug delusion.' Amity Shlaes. *Financial Times*, Comment section, 4 August 2003.

3. 'US drug prices come under increasing pressure.' Jacky Law. *Scrip Magazine*. June 2001, p. 18.
4. 'DTC ads linked to rising drug costs in US.' *Scrip World Pharmaceutical News*. 21/26 December 2001.
5. 'DTC ads linked to rising drug costs in US.'
6. Law. 'US drug prices come under increasing pressure.'
7. Law. 'US drug prices come under increasing pressure.'
8. 'Pfizer: disease management did not fizzle in Florida Medicaid Ruckus.' John Carroll. *Managed Care*. September 2004.
9. 'Bayer and GlaxoSmithKline settle Medicaid fraud charges.' *Scrip World Pharmaceutical News*. 23/25 April 2003, p. 19.
10. *The Truth About the Drug Companies*. Marcia Angell. New York: Random House, 2004, p. 233.
11. Angell, *The Truth About the Drug Companies*, pp. 233–4.
12. IMS statistics used in annual review issues of *Scrip World Pharmaceutical News*.
13. IMS statistics used in annual review issues of *Scrip World Pharmaceutical News*.
14. 'Friends in high places.' Peter Rixon. *Scrip Magazine*. February 2005, p. 55.
15. 'Achieving the promise: transforming mental health care in America.' New Freedom Commission on Mental Health, press release. 22 July 2003.
16. 'Achieving the promise: transforming mental health care in America.'
17. 'Bush plans to screen whole US population for mental illness.' Jeanne Lenzer. *British Medical Journal*, 328. 19 June 2004. 2004;328:2458.
18. Lenzer, 'Bush plans to screen whole US population for mental illness.'
19. Lenzer, 'Bush plans to screen whole US population for mental illness.'
20. Lenzer, 'Bush plans to screen whole US population for mental illness.'
21. Lenzer, 'Bush plans to screen whole US population for mental illness.'
22. 'Where's the evidence for screening? Are systems in place for positive screens?' Laura Newman. *British Medical Journal* 328. 14 August 2004, letters page.
23. 'Bush's medical liability reform plan "protects drug manufacturers".' *Scrip World Pharmaceutical News*. 12 January 2005, p. 13.
24. 'Bush's medical liability reform plan "protects drug manufacturers".'
25. *The Corporation*. Joel Bakan. London: Constable, p. 107.
26. 'Friends in high places.' Peter Rixon. *Scrip Magazine*. February 2005, p. 55.
27. 'Relationships between the pharmaceutical industry and patients' organisations.' Andrew Herxheimer. *British Medical Journal* 326. 31 May 2003. 2003;326:1209.
28. Bakan, *The Corporation*, p. 106.

29. Bakan, *The Corporation*, p. 108.
30. 'A belated revolution.' Jacky Law. *Scrip Magazine*. April 2004, p. 41.
31. 'Batten down the hatches in 2005.' Viren Mehta. *Scrip Magazine*. February 2005, p. 57.
32. Mehta, 'Batten down the hatches in 2005,' p. 58.
33. *The Influence of the Pharmaceutical Industry*. Report of the House of Commons Health Committee. 5 April 2005, para. 28.
34. '"Non" means no for European prosperity.' Philip Brown. *Scrip Magazine*. July/August 2005, p. 7.
35. Reginald Rhein. *Scrip Magazine*. March 2005, p. 31.
36. Professor Joe Collier, private conversation, summer 2005.

10 *The European patient*

1. 'Relationships between the pharmaceutical industry and patients' organisations.' Andrew Herxheimer. *British Medical Journal* 326. 31 May 2003. 2003;326:1208–10.
2. 'The mark of Zorro.' Michael Jeffries. *Pharmaceutical Marketing*. May 2000, p. 24 (as quoted by Herxheimer).
3. Jeffries, 'The mark of Zorro.'
4. 'Selling you a cure on the telly.' Carol Lewis. *New Statesman*. 24 June 2002. p. 10.
5. 'DTC advertising is medicalising normal human experience.' Barbara Mintzes. *British Medical Journal* 324. 13 April 2002. 2002;324:908–11.
6. Jeffries, 'The mark of Zorro.'
7. Mintzes, 'DTC advertising is medicalising normal human experience.'
8. 'DTCA debate heats up.' Tove Gerhardsen. *Scrip World Pharmaceutical News*. 14 May 2003.
9. Consumer Association press release, 10 July 2001.
10. Peter Fletcher, private correspondence, summer 2005.
11. 'European Commission may reform drug advertising legislation.' Nigel Glass. *Lancet* 358, 28 July 2001.
12. 'University students told to get MMR jabs.' James Meikle. *Guardian*. 11 July 2005.
13. 'Vaccines fact sheet.' Richard Barr. 3 June 1997.
14. 'Study queries official line on MMR jabs.' Jamie Doward. *Observer*. 4 October 2004, p. 7.
15. Doward. 'Study queries official line on MMR jabs.'
16. 'Autism cases up; cause is unclear.' Erica Goode. *New York Times*. 26 January 2004.

17. *MMR: Science and Fiction: Exploring the Vaccine Crisis*. Richard Horton. London: Granta, 2004, p. 110.
18. 'The significance of ileo-colonic lymphoid nodular hyperplasia in children with autistic spectrum disorder.' A.J. Wakefield, P. Ashwood, K. Limb and A. Anthony. *European Journal of Gastroenterology and Hepatology* 17 August 2005. 2005;17(8):827–36.
19. Dr Peter Fletcher, private conversation, summer 2005.
20. 'Autistic disturbances of affective contact.' Leo Kanner. *Nervous Child* 2. 1943. 1943;2:217–50.
21. Horton, *MMR*, p. 91.
22. Horton, *MMR*, p. 115.
23. 'How the MMR row created a vaccine racket.' Jo Revill. *Observer*. 11 July 2004.
24. Revill, 'How the MMR row created a vaccine racket.'
25. Revill, 'How the MMR row created a vaccine racket.'
26. Medicines Partnership website. www.medicines-partnership.org.
27. Medicines Partnership website.
28. 'New UK service to boost patient compliance.' *Scrip World Pharmaceutical News*. 16 May 2003.
29. *Pharmacy in the Future – Implementing the NHS Plan*. London: Department of Health, 2000.
30. 'When medicines are wasted so much is lost: to society as well as patients.' *Pharmaceutical Journal* 272. 3–10 January 2004, p. 12.
31. 'Who will be the new voice of patients?' Jacky Law. *Scrip Magazine*. March 1999, p. 30.
32. 'Concordance – is it a synonym of compliance or a paradigm shift?' Christine Bond. *Pharmaceutical Journal* 271. 11 October, 2003, pp. 496–7.
33. Professor Joe Collier, private conversation, summer 2005.
34. Law, 'Who will be the new voice of patients?'
35. 'New UK service to boost patient compliance.' *Scrip World Pharmaceutical News*. 16 May 2003.
36. 'UK to benefit from the "expert patient".' *Scrip World Pharmaceutical News*. 21 September 2001.
37. *The Influence of the Pharmaceutical Industry*. Report of the House of Commons Health Committee. 5 April 2005, para. 158.
38. 'A wolf in sheep's clothing: a critical look at the ethics of drug taking.' Iona Heath. *British Medical Journal* 327. 11 October 2003. 2003;327:856–8.
39. Heath, 'A wolf in sheep's clothing.'
40. Heath, 'A wolf in sheep's clothing.'

41. 'Somtostatin fever mounts in Italy.' B. Simini. *Lancet* 351. 1998, p. 428.
42. 'The strange affair of the Italian "miracle" cure for cancer.' Ian Schofield. *Scrip Magazine*. July/August 1998, pp. 7–9.
43. Schofield, 'The strange affair of the Italian "miracle" cure for cancer.'
44. Schofield, 'The strange affair of the Italian "miracle" cure for cancer.'
45. 'We are the masters now.' Felicity Lawrence. *Guardian*. 10 August 2001.

11 *Genes, germs and general behaviour*

1. *The Role of Medicine: Dream, Mirage or Nemesis*. Thomas McKeown. Oxford: Blackwell, 1979, p. 5.
2. *The Rise and Fall of Modern Medicine*. James le Fanu. London: Abacus, 2000, p. 372.
3. Le Fanu, *The Rise and Fall of Modern Medicine*, p. 380.
4. Le Fanu, *The Rise and Fall of Modern Medicine*, p. 381.
5. Le Fanu, *The Rise and Fall of Modern Medicine*, p. 327.
6. Le Fanu, *The Rise and Fall of Modern Medicine*, p. 337.
7. 'Cholesterol: is lower really better?' Susan Hughes. *Scrip Magazine*. April 1993, p. 6.
8. Hughes, 'Cholesterol: is lower really better?'
9. Hughes, 'Cholesterol: is lower really better?'
10. *Plague Time: The New Germ Theory of Disease*. Paul W. Ewald. New York: Anchor, 2002, p. 82.
11. Ewald, *Plague Time*, p. 35.
12. Ewald, *Plague Time*, p. 80.
13. Quoted by Le Fanu, *The Rise and Fall of Modern Medicine*, p. 380.
14. 'High interest accounts.' Stefan Fritsch. *Scrip Magazine*. March 2005, pp. 18–19.
15. Fritsch, 'High interest accounts.'
16. Fritsch, 'High interest accounts.'
17. *The Whole Story: Alternative Medicine On Trial*. Toby Murcott. Basingstoke: Macmillan, 2005, p. 2.
18. 'Hype, hope and healing.' *New Scientist* editorial. 26 May 2001, p. 28.
19. Populus poll for *The Times* Body & Soul section. 10 January 2004.
20. 'Hype, hope and healing', p. 28.
21. 'The intelligent body.' Michael E. Hyland. *New Scientist* editorial. 26 May 2001, pp. 32–3.
22. Hyland, 'The intelligent body.'
23. Hyland, 'The intelligent body.'
24. Hyland, 'The intelligent body.'

25. Hyland, 'The intelligent body.'
26. 'Nil by mouth.' Rose Shepherd. *Observer* Magazine. 29 February 2004.
27. 'The eating cure.' Lucy Mayhew. *Guardian*. 4 May 2004.
28. Mayhew, 'The eating cure.'
29. Mayhew, 'The eating cure.'
30. Mayhew, 'The eating cure.'
31. 'Vitamin research: why is it so confusing?' Mark Peplow. *Medicine Today*. September 2003.
32. Quoted by Shepherd, 'Nil by mouth.'
33. 'Killer vitamins.' *Daily Mail*. 19 April 2005.
34. *Cancer and Vitamin* C. Linus Pauling and Ewan Cameron. Linus Pauling Institute of Science and Medicine, Menlo Park, CA 94025. 1979, p. 189. The editorial was in *Surgery, Gynaecology, and Obstetrics* 146. 1978, pp. 617–18.
35. Pauling and Cameron, *Cancer and Vitamin* C, p. 190.
36. Murcott, *The Whole Story*, p. 83.
37. 'Let's give it a fair trial.' Simon Crompton. *The Times* Body & Soul. 19 March 2005.
38. Crompton, 'Let's give it a fair trial.'
39. 'Complementary medicine and the patient.' Catherine Zollman and Andrew Vickers. *British Medical Journal* 319. 4 December 1999. 1999;319:1486–9.

12 *Patients take the lead*

1. 'Government's response to the health committee's report on the influence of the pharmaceutical industry.' September 2005. Crown Copyright 2005. HMSO Cm6655, p. 9.
2. *MMR: Science and Fiction: Exploring the Vaccine Crisis*. Richard Horton. London: Granta Books, 2004, p. 150.
3. Horton, *MMR*, p. 42.
4. Horton, *MMR*, p. 65.
5. 'The power of positive thinking.' Amy Dockser Marcus. *Wall Street Journal Europe* Networking Section. 29 October 2003, p. 1.
6. *The Truth About the Drug Companies*. Marcia Angell. New York: Random House, 2004, p. 239.
7. 'Government's response to the health committee's report on the influence of the pharmaceutical industry.' September 2005, para. 19.
8. 'Government's response to the health committee's report on the influence of the pharmaceutical industry.' September 2005, para. 20.

9. *The Influence of the Pharmaceutical Industry*. Report of the House of Commons Health Committee. 5 April 2005, recommendation 17.
10. *The Influence of the Pharmaceutical Industry*, paras 339–40.
11. 'The medicalisation of old age.' Shah Ebrahim. *British Medical Journal* 324. 13 April 2002. 2002;324:861–3.
12. Ebrahim, 'The medicalisation of old age.'
13. 'Too much medicine?' Richard Smith. *British Medical Journal* 324. 13 April 2002. 2002;324:859–960.
14. 'Power to the patient.' Jacky Law. *Scrip Magazine*. September 2000
15. Madeleine Bunting. *Guardian*. 2 May 2002.
16. 'Pharma denies inventing female sex disorder.' *Scrip World Pharmaceutical News* 2813. 8 January 2003.
17. 'Women resport P&G's patch boosts desire.' Alix M. Freedman and Sarah Ellison. *Wall Street Journal* Europe edition. 5 May 2004, p. A7.
18. 'The White Paper on public health.' Rosalind Raine. *British Medical Journal* 329. 27 November 2004. 2004;329:1247–8.
19. 'Government's response to the health committee's report on the influence of the pharmaceutical industry.' September 2005, para. 17.
20. 'Medicalisation, limits to medicine, or never enough money to go round?' Nick Freemantle. *British Medical Journal* 324. 13 April 2002. 2002:324:864–5.
21. *The Influence of the Pharmaceutical Industry*, recommendation 17.
22. 'Who pays for the pizza? Redefining the relationships between doctors and drug companies.' Ray Moynihan. *British Medical Journal* 326. 31 May 2003. 2003:326:1189–92.
23. 'Cultural revolution.' Patrick Pietroni, Fedelma Winkler and Lindsey Graham. *British Medical Journal* 326. 14 June 2003. 2003;326:1304–1306.
24. Michael Greenberg, private conversation, summer 2005.
25. *Anatomy of an Illness as Perceived by the Patient*. Norman Cousins. New York: W.W. Norton & Co., 1979, pp. 80–81.
26. Cousins, *Anatomy of an Illness*, p. 82.

Index